Education
Finance for
School Leaders

Education Finance for School Leaders

Strategic Planning and Administration

C. William Garner
Rutgers University

PEARSON

Merrill
Prentice Hall

Upper Saddle River, New Jersey
Columbus, Ohio

Library of Congress Cataloging-in-Publication Data

Garner, C. William.
  Education finance for school leaders : strategic planning and administration / by C. William Garner.
    p. cm.
Includes bibliographical references and index.
  ISBN 0-13-097862-0
  1. Education—United States—Finance. 2. Educational planning—United States. 3. School management and organization—United States. I. Title.
  LB2825.G36 2004
  371.2'06—dc22

                                                                                    2003022464

Vice President and Executive Publisher:
  Jeffery W. Johnston
Executive Editor: Debra A. Stollenwerk
Editorial Assistant: Mary Morrill
Production Coordination: Karen Ettinger,
  The GTS Companies/York, PA Campus
Production Editor: Linda Hillis Bayma

Design Coordinator: Diane C. Lorenzo
Cover Designer: Bryan Huber
Cover image: Corbis
Production Manager: Pamela D. Bennett
Director of Marketing: Ann Castel Davis
Marketing Manager: Darcy Betts Prybella
Marketing Coordinator: Tyra Poole

This book was set in Meridien by *The GTS Companies*/York, PA Campus. It was printed and bound by R.R. Donnelley & Sons Company. The cover was printed by Phoenix Color Corp.

Pearson Prentice Hall™ is a trademark of Pearson Education, Inc.
Pearson® is a registered trademark of Pearson plc
Prentice Hall® is a registered trademark of Pearson Education, Inc.
Merrill® is a registered trademark of Pearson Education, Inc.

Pearson Education Ltd.
Pearson Education Singapore Pte. Ltd.
Pearson Education Canada, Ltd.
Pearson Education—Japan

Pearson Education Australia Pty. Limited
Pearson Education North Asia Ltd.
Pearson Educación de Mexico, S.A. de C.V.
Pearson Education Malaysia Pte. Ltd.

10 9 8 7
ISBN: 0-13-097862-0

Dedicated with love to
my delightful grandchildren

Steven William Garner
Jessica Emily Garner
Rachel Karyl Garner
Kevin Adam Garner

Preface

In the latter part of the 20th century, the financial practices of school districts began to change. Specifically, some of these developments included:

- new accounting and budgeting rules along with stringent accountability demands,
- acknowledgment of the economic importance of education to people and society, which generated measures of effectiveness and efficiency from the national to the local level,
- legal directives from state legislatures and courts that placed new regulations on the distribution of educational money, and
- implementation of new standards for programs to prepare and license school administrators.

Indeed, these and other changes opened the 21st century to a new and shifting perspective on the financing of public schools and new financial skills for school leaders.

In response to these emerging rules, legal directives, standards, and other operating expectations, I developed a conceptual framework over a 12-year period while teaching a school finance course to aspiring school administrators. At the outset, I set a course parameter that future school administrators, as well as the professors who teach a school finance course, although needing a certain fluency with the process, could not be expected to become accountants. This book is a product of that work.

AUTHOR'S CONCEPTUAL AND THEORETICAL FRAMEWORK

Conceptual Framework. School finance, as presented in this book, is conceptually perceived and involves the following four interrelated components or features:

1. The management structure that is unique to education and varies from setting to setting, such as the differences between small rural and large urban school districts.
2. The programs, services, and activities of school districts that are both at the heart of education and assigned to school leaders located in the management structure.

3. The financial budget plan prepared for the programs, services, and activities.
4. The financial framework that houses the accounting and budgeting systems that, in turn, are used to administer the financial budget plan. To complete the circle, this financial framework must operate within the management structure and not outside of it.

Theoretical Framework.   With these interrelated components in mind, a basic premise for the book is that adequate financial resources for public education are tied to the economic vitality of the country and a community, and vice versa. To maximize the economic benefit gained from the scarce resources made available to a school district, school leaders must merge financial and strategic plans into one plan, which is referred to in this book as a *strategic financial plan*. School leaders must then administer the plan to achieve its intended ends.

To attain the full potential offered by a strategic financial plan, school districts must incorporate site-based units into the process. Once strategic financial plans are developed and administered by all schools, programs, services, and activities within a district, the district will be able to strive to meet the financial needs at the operational level. In other words, the needs of the unit define the budget and not vice versa.

Therefore, budget planning and management becomes the responsibility of site-based units and not the sole responsibility of a business office. To meet this expectation, school leaders must understand the accounting and budgeting systems and process, the financial framework mandated by the Generally Accepted Accounting Principles (GAAP), and the reports generated by the systems.

ALIGNMENT WITH ACCREDITATION AND LICENSURE STANDARDS

An important feature of this book is its alignment with accreditation standards set for programs in education administration by the National Council for the Accreditation of Teacher Education (NCATE) published in January 2002 by the National Policy Board for Educational Administration (NPBEA) and also the licensure standards of the Interstate School Leaders Licensure Consortium (ISLLC) in 1996. **ISLLC** appears in the margin each time there is a text reference to an ISLLC standard.

In 1995, guidelines for the preparation of education administrators were published by the Educational Leadership Constituent Council (ELCC) for approval by NCATE. Then, in 2000, NCATE called for a new direction for graduate programs in education administration with an orientation based on how well graduates would be prepared to perform administrative functions in the workplace. In response to a request from NCATE, the NPBEA appointed a working group to integrate the ELCC Guidelines and the ISLLC Standards, to include doctoral level reviews, and to add the performance assessment component called for by NCATE. The revised standards for school building and school district leadership programs were submitted to NCATE in 2001 by the NPBEA and published in January 2002 (http://www.ncate.org/ retrieved on 2/17/03).

The shift in the standards for collegiate programs is explained by the NPBEA (http://www.npbea.org/ retrieved 2/17/03) in their observation that "traditionally educational administration programs have focused on abstractions in an attempt to unify the field conceptually rather than examining the changing contexts and functions of educational leaders" (p. 3). The NPBEA continues, "Conditions require an outward looking, environmentally influenced vision of school leadership, moving away from the traditional inward looking, content dominated format. Defining the practice of leadership in contemporary school settings, identifying the knowledge and skills essential to effective practice, integrating theory and practice, and designing a quality accreditation process all reflect a useful direction for the field" (p. 3).

Where appropriate, standards are cited in the book to connect them to the content. This connection shows the realism and legitimacy of the responsibilities and duties set forth in this book for administrators.

TEXT OVERVIEW

General Overview.   This book is divided into three parts. The intent of the chapters in the first part is to explain *why* education and school finance are important and *why* current practices exist. The focus for the chapters in the second part is to describe *what* is contained in a strategic financial plan, the accounting and budgeting systems, and a financial framework. Finally, the third part examines *how* school leaders prepare and administer strategic financial plans.

Part 1: Financing Public Education.   These chapters provide a general foundation for the material presented in the following two sections. To accomplish this, these chapters include an introduction to major historical events associated with school finance; emerging developments, such as vouchers, charter schools, and open systems; special leadership considerations, such as policy making; the symbiotic and synergistic relationship between education and economics; and an overview and analysis of the major sources of revenue, including taxes. In addition, the evolution of educational equality in the United States is traced over time and through three primary focuses: access, treatment, and outcomes. The section concludes with an examination of the efforts of the courts and the federal and state governments to promote financial equity in public education.

Part 2: Constructing a Strategic Financial Plan.   First, the chapters in this section describe what is needed in a strategic plan: mission statements, goals, and objectives for the district with site-based goals, objectives, outcome, and output targets and benchmarks for programs, services, and activities. Then the strategic plan is broadened to become a strategic financial plan. Accounting funds are described and added to the organizational structure. The final two chapters in this section describe the accounting and budgeting systems that work within the financial framework.

These chapters also include a discussion on the use of computers as well as the national set of account numbers for use by accounting and budgeting systems.

Part 3: Preparing and Administering Site-Based and District Plans.   The first three chapters in this section explain how to plan and administer the financial operations in the accounting funds restricted for instructional programs, the construction of facilities, and noninstructional operations. This includes the identification of revenue and income sources for each accounting fund, how to calculate property tax assessments, how bonds are sold, how debt is added to a property assessment to pay off debt, how to read and administer budget reports, how to manage personnel salaries through the accounting and budgeting systems, how to prepare business plans for income generating operations (such as food services), and how fiduciary accounts should be managed. The last chapter then addresses the call for accountability and how to generate cost measures for effectiveness and efficiency evaluations.

SPECIAL FEATURES

- *Resources Section.*   The resource section at the end of the book presents the set of accounting and budget numbers prepared by the National Center for Education Statistics (NCES). These numbers, which are explained in the text, are to be used by all state departments of education. In addition, the tables provide a reference for students when they become practitioners.
- *Student Performance Exercises.*   Three types of exercises are offered to give students practical insights and experiences:
  - *Discussion Questions.*   At the end of each chapter, a set of questions is provided for stimulating thought-provoking discussions.
  - *Application Problems.*   At the end of selected chapters, problems are provided to allow students to apply the content of the chapter. These problems include the use of the resource tables for identifying budget categories (or vice versa), computing taxes, updating data from Web citations given in a chapter, vignettes, and so on.
  - *Clinical Field Practicum.*   From chapter 5 to chapter 12, a clinical field practicum for students is included at the end of each chapter. In this practicum, students collect information on the practices of a local school district and compare it to the content in the chapter. This set of exercises has been an extremely successful (and popular) part of my course as it offers numerous insights from practitioners for class discussions.
- *Final Thoughts.*   At the end of each chapter, final thoughts are provided to add related content, raise issues and concerns, and serve as a transition to the following chapter.
- *Glossary.*   Definitions for the finance, accounting, and budget terms used in the text are provided in a glossary at the end of the text.

- *Web Citations.* References to statistical data, professional standards, and other related material available on the Web are presented throughout the book with the Web addresses provided at the end of each chapter.
- *References.* At the end of each chapter, the cited references are provided. However, students are urged to go beyond these references and examine the broad literature base on school finance, as it is rich with theoretical and thought-provoking positions on the subject. Familiarity with the research and the views of leading educators in the field is career enhancing and will serve to make one a stronger administrator.
- *Accounting Standards.* Because the directives of the Governmental Accounting Standards Board (GASB) are followed by most states, they are used as the reference for presenting the Generally Accepted Accounting Principles (GAAP). Discussions of these principles and procedures do not require any prerequisite study in accounting.

ACKNOWLEDGMENTS

Finally, a word of gratitude to my students who over the years have read the handouts that led to this book. Their critiques, questions for clarification, delight in finding author errors, meaningful discussions of the content and exercises, and exceptional clinical field reports have been invaluable. I would like to thank the reviewers who provided invaluable comments and suggestions: Robert Buchanan, Southeast Missouri State University; E. E. Davis, Idaho State University; Billy Ray Dunn, Marietta College; Randy J. Dunn, Southern Illinois University; Gene Gallegas, California State University, Bakersfield; Virginia Garland, University of New Hampshire; Frank P. Merlo, Montclair State University; Glen C. Newman, California Baptist University; Catherine C. Sielke, University of Georgia; and Robert G. Stabile, Franciscan University of Steubenville.

Educator Learning Center

An Invaluable Online Resource

Merrill Education and the Association for Supervision and Curriculum Development (ASCD) invite you to take advantage of a new online resource, one that provides access to the top research and proven strategies associated with ASCD and Merrill—the Educator Learning Center. At **www.EducatorLearningCenter.com** you will find resources that will enhance your students' understanding of course topics and of current educational issues, in addition to being invaluable for further research.

HOW THE EDUCATOR LEARNING CENTER WILL HELP YOUR STUDENTS BECOME BETTER TEACHERS

With the combined resources of Merrill Education and ASCD, you and your students will find a wealth of tools and materials to better prepare them for the classroom.

Research

- More than 600 articles from the ASCD journal *Educational Leadership* discuss everyday issues faced by practicing teachers.
- A direct link on the site to Research Navigator™ gives students access to many of the leading education journals, as well as extensive content detailing the research process.
- Excerpts from Merrill Education texts give your students insights on important topics of instructional methods, diverse populations, assessment, classroom management, technology, and refining classroom practice.

Classroom Practice

- Hundreds of lesson plans and teaching strategies are categorized by content area and age range.
- Case studies and classroom video footage provide virtual field experience for student reflection.
- Computer simulations and other electronic tools keep your students abreast of today's classrooms and current technologies.

LOOK INTO THE VALUE OF EDUCATOR LEARNING CENTER YOURSELF

Preview the value of this educational environment by visiting **www.EducatorLearningCenter.com** and clicking on "Demo." For a free 4-month subscription to the Educator Learning Center in conjunction with this text, simply contact your Merrill/Prentice Hall sales representative.

Brief Contents

Contents

Note: Every effort has been made to provide accurate and current Internet information in this book. However, the Internet and information posted on it are constantly changing, and it is inevitable that some of the Internet addresses listed in this textbook will change.

Part 1

Financing Public Education

Chapter 1

Introduction to School Finance for School Leaders

School districts have become big business operations. The financing of public education and the administration of financial resources are increasingly complex assignments for school leaders, considering that school districts receive and spend millions of dollars of tax **revenue** annually. They are legal entities that may enter into contracts with private corporations, sell **bonds** to investors, manage investment of public money, make long-term lease arrangements (both as landlord and tenant), generate **income** from selling goods and services, manage income-producing **capital assets**, hold money in trust for another party, and so on.

In many communities the school district is the largest business enterprise in terms of expenditures, number of employees and clients, and value of capital assets. Likewise, school districts are often the largest governmental financial operation in a geographic region. Further, many metropolitan school districts have larger budgets, more teachers, and more students than most colleges and universities.

As a result, school leaders must be prepared to meet the challenges presented by these and the other assignments associated with running a big business operation. The author recognizes that staff advisors and consultants may provide necessary information and recommendations to school leaders when they are making decisions. School leaders, however, must possess the knowledge necessary to analyze the various recommendations and the effects of their decisions. As the author can testify from experiences as an administrator, staff advisor, and consultant: When leaders depend on the advice of others, their decisions may reflect the biases and competence of their advisors.

This chapter introduces selected topics that are intended to serve as a platform for the rest of the text. Specifically covered are (a) references to federal legislation calling for greater governmental accountability through the preparation of strategic plans with performance measures and related financial plans and reports and

(b) observations and proposals made by school leaders and others who recognize that economic and social changes are having an impact on the responsibilities of leadership.

In addition, to gain a full appreciation of current methods used to finance public education, the chapter reviews major activities and events that have led to current practices. Following this review, a brief discussion of developments influencing the financial operations of school districts, such as new accounting standards for education, vouchers, and charter schools, is offered. And finally, because education financing is directed by the creation and modification of public policy, the chapter examines the function of policy, the relationship of policy to administrative rules and regulations, and the tactics used to influence policy development and modification.

Throughout the book, two important sets of standards are referenced. One set is for practitioners and was adopted on November 2, 1996, by the Interstate School Leaders Licensure Consortium (ISLLC) and published in the *Standards for School Leaders*. These standards are the basis for national assessments for administrative certification. The other set is the accreditation standards for collegiate programs preparing school administrators by the National Council for Accreditation of Teacher Education (NCATE). In both cases, they document expectations proposed by leaders in education administration.

ISLLC

NATIONAL CALL FOR ACCOUNTABILITY

In 1990 Congress passed the Chief Financial Officers' Act (CFO Act), which further defined the **accounting** and reporting obligations of federal departments and agencies. Then, in 1993, Congress passed the Government Performance and Results Act (GPRA) that included requirements for government agencies to develop strategic plans, to set performance measurements (targets), and to link these targets to their budget reports (cost analyses). Next, in 1994 Congress amended the CFO Act by passing the Government Management Reform Act (GMRA). This act added more specificity to the CFO Act by directing federal agencies to develop performance and cost measures and to prepare results-oriented reports with budget, accounting, and program information (Dyer, 1996).

As a result of these and other acts, government agencies that provide money to school districts are required to prepare, to implement, and to analyze strategic plans. These agencies, therefore, must receive the information they need from school districts to comply with the legislative expectations. This includes cost measures with supporting accounting and **budgeting** information. Further, the actions taken by federal and state legislators promise to continue to evolve into the 21st century. In response, administrators must be able to relate to the current expectations if they are to react to future modifications.

Finally, the legislative actions of the federal government correspond to the strategic financial planning process described in this book. That is, according to federal directives, school districts should prepare strategic financial plans with performance targets that are tied to the accounting and budgeting systems that, in turn, are referenced when preparing valid financial reports, follow-up analyses of performances, and cost assessments.

SCHOOL LEADERS AND THE STRATEGIC FINANCIAL PLAN

ISLLC   As explained by the ISLLC (1996) in their preface, "significant changes have been reshaping our nation" and "new viewpoints have redefined the struggle to restructure education for the 21st century." It continues with the "social fabric of society is changing" and the "economic foundations of society are being recast" (p. 5).

In the introduction to the NCATE standards, the National Policy Board for Educational Administration (NPBEA) note how "changing school and community contexts create unusual demands as well as exceptional opportunities for school leaders" (NPBEA, 2002a, p. 2). Further, the NPBEA declares that public schools must meet challenges to the traditional notion of public school governance. Two of those challenges that are relevant to this book are fiscal efficiency and accountability for learning processes and results.

Because of the challenges for greater **efficiency** and accountability, school leaders must ensure that they and their financial operations keep pace with the changes taking place in society and the economy. To accomplish this task, school leaders must learn to prepare a visionary strategic plan that supports the school district's mission that, in turn, must be responsive to the changes taking place in society. Therefore, the current and future financial needs of the school district must be incorporated into the strategic plan. When this occurs, the strategic plan evolves into a strategic financial plan.

The preparation, implementation, and analysis of a strategic financial plan correspond to the expectations of the ISLLC (1996) standards. Specifically, in **ISLLC**   Standard 1 the ISLLC states that administrators should attain a "knowledge and understanding of the principles of developing and implementing strategic plans," of "systems theory," and of "information sources, data collection, and data analysis strategies" (p. 10).

Likewise, NCATE Standard 3.2 requires education leadership programs to provide their students with a "knowledge of strategic, long range, and operational planning (including applications of technology) in the effective, legal, and equitable use of fiscal, human, and material resource allocation and alignment that focuses on teaching and learning" (NPBEA, 2002b, p. 8). One of the purposes of this book is to describe the components and process of constructing a strategic financial plan.

First, however, school leaders must recognize that due to changing expectations and challenges, new agendas will continue to affect their strategic financial plans. In response, school leaders must adopt a philosophy of acceptance of new rules and new technology. A basis for a philosophy held by the author is in the quotation by Thomas Jefferson that appears on the fourth panel in the Jefferson Memorial. On this panel Jefferson is quoted as saying:

> I am not an advocate for frequent changes in laws and constitutions, but laws and institutions must go hand in hand with the progress of the human mind. As that becomes more developed, more enlightened, as new discoveries are made, new truths discovered and manners and opinions change, with the change of circumstances, institutions must advance also to keep pace with the times. We might as well require a man to wear still the coat which fitted him when a boy as civilized society to remain ever under the regimen of their barbarous ancestors.

Of course, institutions cannot advance unless their leaders are capable and willing to move them forward. As the following review of the development of public school finance over the past 200 years testifies, the changes in the financial practices of public schools have been revolutionary. This did not occur without the conviction and dedication of many leaders who were willing to take on the burden of keeping public education in pace with the changing times. From all appearances the administration of schools and school districts has moved into an important era of continuing advances in practice. As history attests, this calls for leadership that is willing to take risks and make efforts to continue the reformation.

THE DEVELOPMENT OF PUBLIC SCHOOL FINANCE IN THE UNITED STATES

A historical review of education financing must begin with the practices of the colonies that had a major impact on educational conduct in the early years of the new federated states. For example, in most colonies the church had complete oversight of the content, attendance, and financing of educational programs.

The first legislation on education was passed by the General Court of the colony of Massachusetts in 1647. This legislation was known as the "Old Deluder Satan Act," and it required every town of 50 or more households to offer instruction in reading and writing so that men could acquire the knowledge of the scriptures. Towns with 100 or more households were to offer instruction in Latin Grammar to prepare young men for the university. The teacher's wages were paid by the students' parents or inhabitants of the town. Although some communities made arrangements for young girls, schooling was typically limited to the male population (Meyer, 1967).

After the Old Deluder Satan Act, other New England colonies passed similar laws. The educational practices, however, varied greatly across the New England, middle, and southern colonies primarily because of differences in religious doctrines and the need to find an acceptable method to finance the schools. In view of the dissimilar educational practices and the directive in the First Amendment of the Constitution that "Congress shall make no law respecting an establishment of religion, or prohibiting the free exercise thereof," the absence of a national educational policy in the Constitution is not surprising. Actually the ability to create a federated agreement is surprising!

After the Revolution

In the early years of our country, education was offered primarily through private sectarian schools with some receiving financial support from the state or locally via methods carried over from the colonial period. For example, some communities continued the rate bill method, which assessed parents for the education of their children. Unfortunately, many parents either refused to send their children to school, or, since the tuition was based on attendance, limited the days of schooling to an amount they could afford. Nevertheless, this method was actually continued in a few states until the beginning of the 20th century (Meyer, 1967; Pulliam, 1976; Rippa, 1980).

In some states the pauper approach was used. With this method parents declared themselves paupers, and then the public paid their child's tuition to a private school. Several of the new states set up schools in each county and the 1776 Constitution of Pennsylvania provided for the state to pay the salaries of public school teachers. In 1795, Connecticut, and later a few other states, set up education funds that were expected to provide money to schools for an indefinite period. For a number of reasons, the money in these funds did not last as expected (Meyer, 1967; Pulliam, 1976; Rippa, 1980).

The first collection of local tax money was in 1805 for private, and usually sectarian, schools. Free public schools were finally possible in 1834 in Pennsylvania under The Free School Act. This legislation eliminated the pauper method by permitting (not requiring) districts to collect tax money for local schools. A short time later, in 1842, New York legislators gave the New York City Board of Education the authority to set up a system of nonsectarian free schools (Meyer, 1967; Pulliam, 1976; Rippa, 1980).

The initial tax collections were limited to the support of elementary schools. The inclusion of high schools did not become a popular idea until after 1872, when Michigan, in the Kalamazoo Case, declared them legal. This obviously contributed to the increase in high school enrollments from 10% of the eligible students in 1900 to 85% by mid-20th century. By 1915 all states, except Georgia and Mississippi, had compulsory attendance laws (Meyer, 1967; Pulliam, 1976; Rippa, 1980).

The 20th Century

At the turn of the 20th century the most popular method of raising local revenue was by taxing property. The need to finance two world wars and to deal with the Great Depression are likely the reasons there were no innovative efforts or startling changes in public school financing during the first half of the 20th century. At the same time, the attendance required by the states (or state laws) was for less than 12 years of education. This varied from state to state; whereas some required only minimal attendance, others required the completion of middle school.

After World War II, public school enrollments and **costs** increased dramatically because of the baby boom and changes in attendance requirements. For example, in the author's school district in Pennsylvania, after World War II, students were expected to attend nine years of public school and frequently reminded that education was a privilege and not a right. High school attendance in this district was optional until the mid-1950s.

Significant changes in the financing of public schools began in the 1960s when federal and state governments began providing a larger share of dollars to local schools. For instance, the break down of funds provided to public schools by percentage was as follows: in 1919–1920, federal government .3%, state governments 16.5%, and local governments 83.2%; and in 1996–1997, federal government 6.6%, state governments 48.0%, and local governments 45.4% (National Center for Education Statistics, 2002).

In the 1960s, the increases in aid to public schools by some states occurred after a number of state and federal legislative and court actions (discussed in chapter 4) aimed at reducing the unequal availability of local tax dollars to school districts and supporting programs for students with special educational needs. *Robinson v. Cahill* was a landmark ruling in 1973 by the New Jersey Supreme Court. In their ruling, the Supreme Court declared the distribution of New Jersey state education dollars a violation of the state constitution's guarantee of a thorough and efficient education. This case was followed by similar constitutional challenges in other states, although the decisions of the other state courts were mixed (Valente & Valente, 2001).

In the legal challenges to a state's system of financing education, is the failure of the local property tax to adequately support public education commonly referenced, especially in poorer communities and rural areas. This position has also been taken by Guthrie, Garms, and Pierce (1988), as well as by several court decisions, who point out that local property taxes cannot meet the costs of the public school systems. This failure has also been validated by the successful property tax revolts in a number of states including California in 1978, Massachusetts in 1980, Oregon in 1990, and Michigan in 1994 (Gold, 1995). Efforts to lower the costs of running school districts through private contractors, vouchers, and **charter schools** are further evidence of dissatisfaction with the property tax burden. Another consequence of the agitation prompted by the failure to find an acceptable means of paying for public schools is the call for greater accountability for the dollars collected and spent by school districts.

EMERGING DEVELOPMENTS FOR SCHOOL FINANCE AND THE 21ST CENTURY

In recent years, a number of emerging developments have promised to have either a direct or an indirect impact on school finance. Several of these developments, discussed in this section, are the new accounting practices established for school districts, charter schools, **magnet schools**, the **privatization** of school districts or school operations (such as food services), vouchers, open systems, and site-based management.

Accounting

The changes in accounting practices have had the most direct influence on the management of school resources. Because the Constitution of the United States did not require any specific accounting and budgeting procedures for the states to follow, each state set up their own practices. As a result, there has been considerable variance in the methods used for counting and reporting the expenditure of public money.

In 1984 the **Governmental Accounting Standards Board (GASB)**—which is a nonprofit, nongovernmental board that reports to the Financial Accounting Foundation (FAF)—was established to set forth **Generally Accepted Accounting Principles (GAAP)** for state and local governments. To date, while all states have agreed to implement an accounting system based on the GAAP, not all have put them into practice. Of those states that have instituted the GAAP, most have selected the principles set forth by the GASB, although a few have chosen to establish their own principles. The guide referenced in this book is the one presented by the GASB for state and local governments, including school districts.

The implementation of the GAAP, whether those of the GASB or of a state-designed system, has caused considerable anxiety. The primary reason is that GAAP and the related standards are quite different from the old practices of many, if not most, school districts. This, in turn, has required a major paradigm shift for many school administrators and professors of education.

For example, the GAAP require a business framework and **double entry accounting**, a budgeting system integrated into the accounting system, and public disclosure of all financial activities and resources. The old method was referred to as **single entry accounting**, or the checkbook method, and it relied on one annual budget, limited to the revenue received and expended over the fiscal year, for allocating and recording all of the business transactions for a school district and a checkbook to maintain the cash balance. In many cases unspent revenues from previous years as well as money received as donations and from the sale of goods and services (such as tickets to sports events) were not reported.

Charter Schools

A charter school may offer regular or specialized educational programs that go through some form of approval process. Upon approval, they may receive public tax money, such as a specified number of dollars per child from the state or local school district. The effect on the financial operations of a school district, therefore, is a loss in revenue, which can place limitations on a strategic financial plan.

Many states have approved the use of charter schools. These schools are typically created and managed by private citizens or by an existing private school.

The arrangements under which they may operate vary from state to state. In some states these schools are exempt from many state and local regulations.

Magnet or Choice Schools

A magnet or choice school is typically a specialized school created by a school district; for example, a school that focuses on art or science. These schools may attract students from within the district as well as those from other districts, depending on the specialization. Because the district provides the money for the magnet or choice school, fiscal stress may be felt on facilities and transportation as well as on the instructional budget.

Privatization

The privatization of a school district simply means that a district hires a private company to run it. Another arrangement is for a school district to hire a private or nonprofit company to run an operation in the district, such as the cafeteria.

When a school district hires such a company, tax revenues collected for the district or for an operation, money received from the sale of goods and services, and facilities of the district or operation are likely to be turned over to the company. The privatization of operations within a school district is discussed further in chapter 11 on noninstructional operations.

Vouchers

The use of school vouchers has been a controversial topic in many states. Typically in these cases, the district provides a **voucher** that represents an amount of money to students. A student may then take the voucher to another school district, or in some cases to a private school, and apply it toward the tuition.

If a student transfers to another school district or private school, the student's home school district that issued the voucher must pay the receiving district the amount of money guaranteed by the voucher. One problem with the voucher system is that the amount of the voucher may not completely cover the cost of the tuition charged by the other district or school. Thus, low-income students may not be afforded the opportunity to transfer to some school districts or private schools.

Open Systems

Open systems theory proposes that successful organizations interact with their environment and, therefore, are able to shift their focus from structure to process in terms of both their internal operations and their form as a business or service entity. The idea is that for an organization to survive, it must adapt, and to accomplish this, it must be open to its environment. As adaptation and change comes from feedback, an organization may need to redefine itself (Hage & Aiken, 1967; Katz & Kahn, 1966; Klees, 1986; Morgan, 1986; Scott, 1981).

An open systems structure can be established in a school district by creating administrative units throughout the district where the daily activities and services are conducted. These activity units, which are commonly referred to as site-based units by school districts, may use teams to prepare strategic financial plans for the units. This requires school leaders at all levels to possess knowledge and skills that are quite different from those needed in a "top down" centralized system.

Site-Based Units

ISLLC

ISLLC

Ideally, site-based units permit the practice of the performance directive in Standard 6 of the ISLLC (1996). This standard proposes that administrators should "facilitate processes and engage in activities ensuring that communication occurs among the school community concerning trends, issues, and potential changes in the environment in which the school operates" (p. 21). Further, according to Standard 1 of the ISLLC, administrators are expected to work with and among all stakeholders—meaning the staff, parents, students, and community members. In addition, the standards require these stakeholders to participate in the development of a school's vision, which is then used to develop the educational programs and plans and actions of a school.

In other words, stakeholders should be on site-based teams that prepare strategic financial plans for the units in the district. These plans should guarantee that changes in the activities at the site-based level drive the budget and not vice versa! To ensure the plan is current, it must be reviewed and updated annually.

The knowledge and skills needed by school leaders in a site-based structure are recognized by NCATE in Standard 3.2. Specifically, this standard states that candidates in school-building leadership programs must be able to "involve staff in conducting operations and setting priorities" and "to develop communication plans for staff," including opportunities "to develop family and community collaboration skills." In addition, they require candidates in the school district leadership programs to "demonstrate the ability to involve stakeholders in aligning resources and priorities to maximize ownership and accountability" (NPBEA, 2002b, p. 8).

After completion by site-based teams, the strategic financial plans are processed through the organizational structure of the school district for administrative review and approval. As a result, the plan for the school district is a consolidation of the plans prepared by the site-based units. When this happens, the plan, which defines the way a school district will work, will help the district "to keep pace with the time" as suggested by Jefferson. Thus, adaptation to a changing environment occurs.

PUBLIC POLICY

The study of the history of school finance shows that many changes in public education financing have been driven through the development of public policy. This is still the case today. As a result, the direct and indirect influence of policy on practice is recognized throughout this book. Examples include changes brought about through court decisions and legislation, administrative directives at the state and federal level, and changes in accounting standards. Because of these influences, education leaders must have a clear picture of the definition and function of policy as well as of the tactics of those attempting to influence policy development.

With respect to the definition of policy, Houle (1989, p. 125) sees policies as "principles that define the way [a school district] prefers to work." Adding to this definition, Caldwell and Spinks (1988) suggest that a policy is a statement of purpose with guidelines describing how it is to be achieved.

The highest form of policy comes from or within a law: constitutional, legislative, case, and administrative. School districts adopt by default any state and federal policies that are relevant to them, such as any education directives set forth in the federal and state constitutions, legislative acts, and administrative codes. While these legal directives often place unfunded mandates upon school districts, they cannot be ignored owing to Dillon's Rule. Dillon, who was a judge in Iowa, held in 1868 that a state could legally impose mandates on local governments. This decision was challenged in 1923 in the case, *City of Trenton v. New Jersey*. The U.S. Supreme Court, however, upheld Dillon's decision. Thus, although numerous complaints continue to be voiced about the use of mandates, school districts must abide by them.

At the same time, school boards, like other elected and appointed boards that represent the people, make policies. When a school board passes a policy, it has legal authority. Thus, when a board passes a school district budget, it becomes a policy that has law behind it. For this reason, administrators do not have the legal privilege to disregard or modify policies without board approval.

The function of policy, according to Bagin and Gallagher (2001), is to outline "realistic and valid goals with objectives and strategies to reach them" and to "provide a framework to properly evaluate the total program after given periods of time, such as a year or five years" (p. 38). According to Kille, Martin, and Scott (1991), the function of school board policy is to "chart the district's course of action." Policies, they continue, indicate "what is wanted and may also include why and how much" and are to "establish the responsibility of the appropriate administrator . . . but . . . leave enough leeway for the administration to develop detailed directions on how to put policies into practice" (p. 4). This corresponds to the position held by Rebore (2001) whereby policies "should not be confused with administrative rules and regulation, which constitute the detailed manner by which policies are implemented" (p. 5).

Because policies lead to rules and regulations, the effect of a policy may not be as predictable as some might suppose. This is because assumptions made by administrators and others who implement the rules may actually add to or modify a policy's intention. In some cases the actual purpose of a policy may be shifted to suit those who make up the rules. This may not become readily evident when a policy is evaluated if the review is limited to the rules and procedures as opposed to the reason the policy was established.

A further concern is that policies may outlive their usefulness. For this reason, periodic evaluations should determine if there is a declining commitment to a policy's original intent, if it has been maintained in spite of its inefficacy, if it has a high social cost, if the undesirable effects of the policy outweigh desirable ones, if there is no connection to the purposes for which it was established, if it has become irrational or unduly complex, and if its purpose has been altered (Haller & Strike, 1979).

Tactics of Policy Making

Educational leaders need to provide expert input into any policy-making meetings that may have an impact on education. The relevance of this input is affirmed in Standard 6 of the ISLLC (1996), which proposes that the "administrator facilitates processes and engages in activities ensuring that public policy is shaped to provide quality education for students" (p. 21). The NPBEA (2002a) also recognizes a shift in the knowledge and skills required of educational leaders "from policy recipient to policy participant" (p. 4). With respect to school finance, Coombs and Hallak (1987) believe that policy input is needed to ensure the policymakers "understand the main factors that influence educational costs and revenues, how these behave under changing conditions, and to what extent educational decision makers and managers can or cannot control them" (p. 19).

When administrators participate in the discussions regarding the way a policy should be stated and implemented, however, they must be aware that arguments may be biased in favor of the particular interests and beliefs of a specific program or group. In fact, often the purpose of such an attempt is to direct or redirect the use of resources. For example, a policy or policy change may be proposed giving financial priority to a specific program or group while setting expenditure limits for others.

Administrators, including those at the site-based level, must comprehend the tactics used by groups to influence policy development. For example, Swanson and King (1997) make the point that in policy making "the focus of the power play is on means (policy), not ends (**objectives**)" (p. 13). They explain that one technique is an advocacy process that uses an incremental rather than a revolutionary approach. When tactical efforts require an incremental approach, the means take on a purpose of their own; however, the tacticians always keep the objective in focus.

There are several popular tactical theories related to policy making. One of these is group theory (Dye, 1987; Truman, 1951), which is a direct approach simply proposing that people get together and make up formal and informal groups to influence policy. Basically, these groups interact with each other to their mutual benefit, influencing the action of policymakers. As the need to influence policy shifts, the groups and their interactions change.

Another approach to policy change is the elite theory (Dye & Zeigler, 1981). In this strategy, a group of people, who are considered the elites, takes an active interest in the development of a policy. To influence a policy, the elites appeal to people who are not actively interested in the event taking place. If the elites can gain a majority of voters to increase public pressure to support them, their policy can be passed.

An alternative approach discussed by Swanson and King (1997) is the rational approach. This strategy strives to ensure that policy making results in maximum social gain based on economic, not political, principles through a mathematical methodology. The rational approach should be the preferred means employed when school boards make policy, especially budget policies.

FINAL THOUGHTS

Because the federal government did not make any arrangements for education in the Constitution, it became the responsibility of the individual states by default and not by choice. However, the refusal of the federal government to assume any responsibility for public education did not occur without considerable debate and perhaps regret by some. As a result of the federal inability to act on education, many states initially followed the educational practices of the colonies in their early years; however, the country was on a dramatic path leading to the separation of church and state (and education) as per the 1st Amendment to the Constitution, the equal rights of all people, and the homogenization of society.

The move toward a new and unknown form of government was perplexing to the efforts of providing a free public education to all children in the 19th century. The road to creating a free and public system of education regardless of sex, race, religion, national origin, or cost in the 20th century proved to be long and arduous. In the 21st century, while this admirable endeavor still needs work, our system of education is considered radical by many countries in the world.

By leaving the responsibility for public education to the states, Meyer (1967) as well as Guthrie et al. (1988) point out that our country really has 51 systems of education, counting Washington DC. Their perception is further intriguing in view of an observation made by the historian Shelby Foote in the video series on the Civil War produced by Burns & Burns. In the video, Foote commented that prior to the Civil War the name "United States" was a plural noun (for example, "the United States are . . ."), but, after, the use of the name was changed to a singular noun ("the United States is . . ."). Thus, the point for school leaders to recognize is that public education in the United States is still plural (systems) and not singular (system). Still, all 51 systems provide a free and public education for all children!

At the same time, some of the emerging developments noted in this chapter are attempts to generate market competition for school districts under the theory that competition can improve performance and reduce costs. A concern held by many is that although the theory suggests that competition for students may be beneficial to cost, effort, and achievement, creating a competing educational system may cause financial harm to the idealistic free and public system providing an education for everyone regardless of sex, race, religion, national origin, or cost. Another worry is that the financial stress will cause the public system to become a substandard alternative for students unable to afford, to be transported to and from, or to be admitted to a competing alternative.

DISCUSSION QUESTIONS

1. How would the administrative responsibilities differ for a principal, department chair, and supervisor in a centralized versus a site-based management structure?
2. How might a superintendent influence public policy at the state, regional, and local level?
   a. What actions might this person take to initiate interest in public education?
3. If a school principal had to influence policy at the local level, what actions might the principal take?
4. When working with policy-making bodies, how could a school administrator guard against the influence of tacticians utilizing the group and elite methods?
5. When an administrator reviews policy rules and procedures, what should be considered?
   a. How might such a review be conducted?
6. School finance has been influenced by numerous major events in the 19th and 20th century. In each of these time periods, identify the major social, economic, labor, industrial, and warfare events that had an impact on school finance?
   a. How did each event help shape or retard the public education movement in the United States?

APPLICATION PROBLEMS

In this chapter, several ISLLC and NCATE standards were cited. In essence, the standards propose that administrators should prepare communication plans that maximize feelings of ownership and accountability among teachers, staff, parents, students, and community members. With this in mind, answer the following questions.

1. You are the principal of a school with grades kindergarten through 8th. You are expected to conduct a needs assessment and recommend a set of priorities for your school. You must have this assessment completed in 30 days.
   a. How would you include input from teachers, staff, parents, students, and community leaders?
   b. Outline a plan you would follow to obtain input from members of each group for a recommendation in 30 days.
2. Assume you are the superintendent and have received the needs assessments from all site-based units in the district. You must appoint a committee to review the assessments to set priorities and make a recommendation.
   a. Who would you select for your committee, and how would you conduct the reviews?
   b. How would you consolidate the reports?
   c. How would your plan prevent possible tactical strategies from influencing a policy recommendation?

WEB ADDRESSES

National Council for Accreditation of Teacher Education
http://www.ncate.org

National Center for Education Statistics
http://nces.ed.gov

National Policy Board for Educational Administration
http://www.hpbea.org

REFERENCES

Bagin, D., & Gallagher, D. R. (2001). *School community relations* (7th ed.). Boston: Allyn & Bacon.

Burns, K., & Burns, R. (Producers). (1989). Episode nine: 1865—the better angles of our nature. *The Civil War.* [Television series episode] Washington, DC: Florentine Films.

Caldwell, B. J., & Spinks, J. M. (1988). *The self-managing school.* London: Falmer Press.

City of Trenton v. New Jersey, 262 U.S. 182 (1923).

Coombs, P. H., & Hallak, J. (1987). *Cost analysis in education.* Baltimore: The Johns Hopkins University Press.

Dye, T. R. (1987). *Understanding public policy* (6th ed.). Upper Saddle River, NJ: Merrill/Prentice Hall.

Dye, T. R., & Zeigler, H. (1981). *The irony of democracy.* Monterey, CA: Brooks/Cole.

Dyer, J. L. (1996). Financial management in the Bowsher years—Progress made. *The Government Accountants Journal, 45*(3), 18–23.

Gold, S. D. (1995). *The outlook for school revenue in the next five years.* New Brunswick, NJ: Consortium for Policy Research, Rutgers University.

Guthrie, J. W., Garms, W. I., & Pierce, L. C. (1988). *School finance and educational policy: Enhancing educational efficiency, equality and choice* (2nd ed.). Upper Saddle River, NJ: Merrill/Prentice Hall.

Hage, J., & Aiken, M. (1967). Relationship of centralization to other structural properties. *Administrative Science Quarterly, 12,* 72–92.

Haller, E., & Strike, K. A. (1979). Problem finding in education administration. In G. Immegart & W. Boyd (Eds.) *A methodology of policy research.* Lexington, MA: Lexington Books.

Houle, C. O. (1989). *Governing boards.* San Francisco: Jossey-Bass.

Interstate School Leaders Licensure Consortium (1996). *Standards for school leaders.* Washington, DC: Council of Chief State School Officers.

Katz, D., & Kahn, R. (1966). *The social psychology of organizations.* New York: Wiley.

Kille, E. A., Martin, M. M., & Scott, C. A. (1991). *Policy.* Trenton, NJ: New Jersey School Boards Association.

Klees, S. J. (1986). Planning and policy analysis in education: What can economics tell us. *Comparative Education Review, 30,* 574–607.

Meyer, A. E. (1967). *An educational history of the American people* (2nd ed.). New York: McGraw-Hill.

Morgan, G. (1986). *Images of organization.* London: Sage.

National Center for Education Statistics (2002). *Digest of Educational Statistics 2002* [Online]. Retrieved November 15, 2002, from http://nces.ed.gov

National Policy Board for Educational Administration (2002a). *Standards for advanced programs in educational leadership* [Online]. Retrieved February 17, 2003, from http://www.npbea.org

National Policy Board for Educational Administration (2002b). *Standards for advanced programs in educational leadership for principals, superintendents, curriculum directors, and supervisors* [Online]. Retrieved February 17, 2003, from http://www.ncate.org

Pulliam, J. D. (1976). *History of education in America* (2nd ed.). Upper Saddle River, NJ: Merrill/Prentice Hall.

Rippa, S. A. (1980). *Education in a free society* (4th ed.). New York: Longman.

Rebore, R. W. (2001). *Human resources administration in education: A management approach* (6th ed.). Boston: Allyn & Bacon.

Robinson v. Cahill, 62 N.J., 473, 303 A.2d 273 (1973).

Scott, W. R. (1981). *Organizations: Rational, natural, and open systems.* Upper Saddle River, NJ: Merrill/Prentice Hall.

Swanson, A. D., & King, R. A. (1997). *School finance: Its economics and politics* (2nd ed.). New York: Longman.

Truman, D. B. (1951). *The government process.* New York: Knopf.

Valente, W. D., & Valente, C. M. (2001). *Law in the schools* (5th ed.). Upper Saddle River, NJ: Merrill/Prentice Hall.

Chapter 2

Economics and Education: A Synergistic Relationship

The value of education to a society is most often perceived as self-evident—it is the obvious benefit derived from acquiring knowledge that is appropriate and relevant to both society and the person being educated, such as the ability to read and write. At the same time, education is noted for providing a variety of other benefits to a society; for instance, allowing self-governing people to read and thus to participate in government.

The major point in this chapter, however, is regarding the important relationship between education and the economy. The National Commission on Excellence in Education stressed this connection in their landmark report, *A Nation at Risk*, in 1983. More so today than ever before, the economic health of a country, state, county, city, town, and therefore citizen, depends on the quality of the education delivered to the people. NCATE Standard 6.1 (NPBEA, 2002b) encourages the study of this relationship.

THE RELATIONSHIP BETWEEN EDUCATION AND ECONOMICS

According to Toffler and Toffler (1995), a new civilization is emerging. In their opinion, civilization has gone through two great waves of change: an agricultural revolution and an industrial revolution. Then beginning around 1955 a new wave began to collide with the second wave. The third wave, symbolized by the computer, contains a brain-based economy that thrives on mind-work as opposed to muscle-work.

Mind-work, the Tofflers (1995) explain, depends on knowledge, and more financially successful people occupy mind-work positions. Of course, mind-workers must be better educated, and the geographic areas where mind-work people live will have more financial resources. Another viewpoint is proposed by Thurow (1996), who claims quite bluntly that people with "third world skills will earn third world wages, even if they live in the first world" (p. 75). To add another dimension to these thoughts, the NPBEA (2002a) points out that "unskilled labor in a system of international free trade will ordinarily be performed where it can be most cheaply obtained" (p. 1).

Reich (1992) also recognizes that a person's financial potential is related to the amount and quality of knowledge acquired. He proposes that civilization is moving from high-volume to high-value businesses. Within the high-value enterprises he suggests there are three major job categories ranging from routine production jobs to symbolic-analytic jobs. The higher job category requires more education, and, correspondingly, these workers earn more money. To back up his claim, Reich presents data to show the widening income gap that has evolved between workers in the lower and higher job categories.

Because of the relevance of education to personal income, many educational leaders realize that teaching reading, writing, and arithmetic skills is not adequate for a person or community facing the demands of the third wave or high-value enterprises. Rather, a quality education requires numerous other exposures, such as the development of analytical and thinking skills. Put another way, the NPBEA (2002a) explains that our graduates must compete in a worldwide work skills market. As a result, their "levels of content knowledge and cognition and applied skills must meet international standards" (p. 1).

The delivery of a quality educational program that will keep pace with the advances in society is not as simple as some may suggest. To keep up, educational leaders must constantly review their curriculums, student performances, and the observations of educational researchers. For example, Anyon (1980) observed in her research of curriculums that students living in a working-class environment were given instruction focused on discipline and obedience while the programs in schools in upper socioeconomic areas encouraged students to become leaders and problem solvers. In addition, numerous research studies over the past 50 years have shown that lower achieving students living in a poor socioeconomic environment have problems with their perceptions about success and failure, self-worth, and maturity as well as their developmental ability to cognitively process information (Coleman et al., 1966; Garner & Cole, 1986, 1996; Miller, 1978; Rotter, 1954, 1966; Weiner, 1972, 1974, 1979; Wigfield & Asher, 1984).

Thus, the difficulty and cost of refining a curriculum that prepares students to meet the expectations of a symbolic-analytic job, especially for children with personal limitations, is considerably greater than popularly assumed. Such efforts are complicated because the cost of education in a wealthy school district is proportionally less in relation to the income and property values of the taxpayers in that district as compared to those in a poor school district. For this reason state and federal educational subsidies have been provided to school districts; however, the amount of money awarded to many of the low-wealth regions has not been adequate.

The Interactions

As evidenced in many government reports, newspaper articles, and magazine reviews, both the educational system and the economic vitality of many cities and rural regions in the United States are in decline. When geographic regions deteriorate economically and the quality of education weakens, the living standards of people also degenerate; for example, more children live in poverty, infant mortality rates rise, crimes go unchecked, and health care is unavailable. Under these conditions the focus is naturally on meeting the more basic needs, such as shelter and food as proposed by Maslow's (1954) theory on the hierarchy of needs. In such cases the needs of the school system do not receive a high priority.

The economic future for citizens in a low-income community is not promising and, in some cases, is quite grim. Likewise the collateral damages, such as social instability and health problems, are an inherent reality. As Labaree (1997) explains, schools "occupy an awkward position at the intersection between what we hope society will become and what we think it really is, between political ideals and economic realities" (p. 41).

The hope is that with strong leadership and some form of financial assistance, poor school districts will prepare graduates who will take their community into the third wave. The foundation for this proposal is based on an observation noted by Thurow (1996) that "man-made brainpower industries don't have predetermined homes" because these industries are "geographically free" (p. 9). As Thurow recognizes, the brainpower industries, which are the fastest growing in the world, may be located wherever someone "organizes the brainpower to capture them" (p. 67).

Due to the mobility of brainpower industries, the theory behind the push for educational investment in poor regions has been that if a community produces graduates with the knowledge needed by the symbolic-analytic brainpower industries, those industries can be attracted to the community. Unemployment will decrease, and personal incomes will increase.

However, the competition among communities to attract mind-work industries is intense. In fact, school districts that enjoy the benefits offered by the existence of third wave enterprises within their region must not only maintain their currency but they must keep up with the changes in these enterprises.

Symbiosis and Synergism

Therefore, education and economics are bound together in an inescapable symbiotic clinch since their interdependence offers mutual advantages to each other. For example, the earning potential for graduates who will be employed by a brainpower industry is an economic benefit to a community, providing more revenues to both the community and the school district.

If the expanded wealth of the school district is then used to help the educational curriculum to continue to evolve, new and even higher paying brainpower industries will be attracted to the community. These higher paying industries will have a greater economic impact, which will increase the benefit to the school district, and so on. For this reason, economics and education have a synergistic relationship; that is, the effect of their symbiotic relationship is greater than the sum of the two effects taken independently.

ISLLC   The importance of the relationship between education and economics is recognized by the ISLLC (1996), who take a stance that society is failing many children.

In their standards for school leaders, they propose that among the many challenges facing educational leaders are the recasting of the economy, shifts to a postindustrial society and a global marketplace, and a greater reliance on technology.

ECONOMICS

Economics is the study of how people use scarce resources to satisfy unlimited wants for goods and services. Resources may be natural resources, human resources, or capital goods. The economic problem, therefore, is that the "wants" for goods and services are virtually unlimited while the resources available to satisfy the wants are limited. As a result, some economic problems are budget problems, and there is a need to develop a plan for allocating scarce resources to meet un- limited *wants*. Of course, if adequate resources are not available to buy essential wants, such as the basic needs proposed in Maslow's (1954) hierarchy of needs theory, the economic problem takes on a different dimension.

Monitoring the economy, therefore, is a serious prerequisite for the prepara- tion of a financial plan for a school district. For example, how available are the state and local resources needed by a school district to meet its basic needs? Are economic resources available to take on a new initiative?

One measure of the economic vitality of the country is the **Gross Domestic Product (GDP)**, which is the market value of goods and services produced for consumption by workers and capital in the United States, regardless of national- ity. The GDP does not include income generated by U.S. citizens from foreign in- vestments and possessions but is limited to the goods and services produced in the country. The **Gross National Product (GNP)** is an economic measure that includes income earned by U.S. citizens from foreign investments and excludes domestic earnings by foreign investors (Bannock, Baxter, & Davis, 1998).

Because the GDP focuses on production within the country, it has become an important economic reference. For example, when the GDP indicates the economy is growing, from increases in the production of goods and delivery of services, busi- nesses and people earn money (resources) to purchase goods and services. If the GDP declines, business and personal earnings decline, unemployment may in- crease, and money may become scarce and lead to a rise in interest rates.

Another measure of economic activity that may be more relevant to school leaders is the **Gross State Product (GSP)**. The GSP is a state's counterpart to the GDP, whereby the GSP measures the market value of goods and services produced by labor and property located in a specific state. The major difference between the GSP and the GDP is that the GDP includes "the compensation of federal civilian and military personnel stationed abroad and government consumption of fixed capital for military structures located abroad and for military equipment, except office equipment" (Bureau of Economic Analysis, n.d., p. 6).

Using 1997 as a base year for exhibiting a range of comparisons in this and later chapters from a variety of sources, Table 2.1 presents the GSP for each state plus Washington, DC (Bureau of Economic Analysis, n.d.). In addition, this table includes

TABLE 2.1

Gross State Product and Education Revenues by State: 1997

State	Gross State Product for 1997 ($ millions)	Total Revenues for Education 1997–1998 ($ millions)	Revenue % of GSP
AL	104,213	4,147	4.0
AK	26,575	1,218	4.6
AZ	122,273	4,732	3.9
AR	59,141	2,601	4.4
CA	1,045,254	38,143	3.6
CO	129,575	4,327	3.3
CT	134,968	5,161	3.8
DE	31,263	914	2.9
DC	50,546	707	1.4
FL	389,473	14,988	3.8
GA	235,733	9,041	3.8
HI	38,537	1,283	3.3
ID	29,388	1,321	4.5
IL	400,327	14,195	3.5
IN	162,953	7,513	4.6
IA	81,695	3,346	4.1
KS	72,998	3,122	4.3
KY	101,535	3,932	3.9
LA	123,549	4,494	3.6
ME	30,409	1,601	5.3
MD	154,646	6,455	4.2
MA	223,571	7,894	3.5
MI	279,503	14,330	5.1
MN	152,334	6,529	4.3
MS	58,743	2,408	4.1
MO	155,811	6,005	3.9
MT	18,907	1,030	5.4
NE	49,275	1,964	4.0
NV	59,248	1,911	3.2
NH	37,470	1,365	3.6
NJ	299,986	13,190	4.4
NM	47,829	1,952	4.1
NY	663,337	27,782	4.2
NC	221,629	7,189	3.2
ND	15,910	682	4.3
OH	326,451	13,458	4.1
OK	79,423	3,416	4.3
OR	97,510	3,884	4.0
PA	347,306	14,838	4.3
RI	29,409	1,264	4.3
SC	95,447	4,055	4.2
SD	19,767	794	4.0
TN	151,738	4,816	3.2
TX	608,622	24,179	4.0
UT	55,070	2,305	4.2
VT	15,510	862	5.6
VA	212,105	7,758	3.7
WA	175,242	6,896	3.9
WV	38,281	2,217	5.8
WI	148,194	7,060	4.8
WY	16,244	702	4.3
Average	161,273	6,392	4.1

Note: Data are from the Bureau of Economic Analysis [Online]. Retrieved November 15, 2002 from http://www.bea.doc.gov/bea/regional/gsp/ and the National Center for Education Statistics [Online]. Retrieved November 15, 2002, from http://nces.ed.gov/

the total local, state, and federal money provided to each state for public education for 1997–1998 reported by the National Center for Education Statistics (NCES, 2002). The third column in the table presents the percentage of revenue provided for public education in reference to the state's GSP. As shown, the percentages range from a low of ~3% to nearly 6%, with the exception of Washington DC.

The 1997–1998 GSP for each state is presented again in Table 2.2 but in descending order along with the related amount of revenue provided for public education plus the expenditures made by public education (NCES, 2002). The correlation coefficient, which is a calculation of the relationship between the two columns of numbers, was calculated for the GSP and education revenues, GSP and the expenditures for education, and education revenues and expenditures. A correlation of 1.00 represents a perfect relationship between the two columns of numbers. In other words, as the numbers in one column increase, the numbers in the other column increase correspondingly. As shown in Table 2.3, the correlation coefficients for the three comparisons are .99. Note that the correlation between revenues and expenditures is greater than .999, or almost perfect. More important, the correlations indicate that as a state's GSP increases, so do the revenues provided by the federal, state, and local governments as well as the money expended for public education.

If revenues and expenditures for public education increase as the GSP increases, as shown in the correlations in Table 2.3, it may be logically concluded that a school district in a city or region with high economic productivity will receive more revenue than a school district located in a city or region with low economic productivity. If this is the case, the goods produced and the level of production that generates resources for people are critical to a school district. Luke, Ventriss, Reed, and Reed (1988) explain that the "traditional strategy of recruiting manufacturing plants by promoting the advantages of low-cost labor, cheap land and governmental subsidies no longer works as well as it once may have" (p. 6). Low-paying jobs reap limited resources for a community.

In addition, according to the calculations shown at the bottom of Table 2.1, the average GSP for 1997 was $161,273 million with an average of $6,392 million made available for public education, or an average of 4.1%. Further, according to the NCES, $326 billion was made available nationally for public elementary and secondary education in 1997–1998. As per the Economic Report of the President (1999), the 1997 GDP was $8,110.9 billion (U.S. Government Printing Office, 2002). As a result, the percentage of money allocated nationally to public education in relation to the amount of the country's GDP for 1997–1998 was 4%. The difference between the GSP's average amount made available for education (4.1%) and the percentage calculated in relation to the GDP (4%) is due to the difference noted previously between the two economic measures.

The important point here, however, is that the two percentages are essentially the same. The question is whether the allocation of 4% of a state's or nation's income to public education is adequate. Is this sufficient to provide future workers with the knowledge called for by the brainpower industries and symbolic-analytic jobs in a third-wave society?

TABLE 2.2

1997–1998 Gross State Product, Education Revenues, and Expenditures by State in Descending Order

State	Gross State Product for 1997 ($ millions)	Total Revenues for Education 1997–1998 ($ millions)	Total Expenditures ($ millions)
CA	1,045,254	38,143	32,759
NY	663,337	27,782	25,333
TX	608,622	24,179	21,189
IL	400,327	14,195	12,473
FL	389,473	14,988	12,737
PA	347,306	14,838	13,085
OH	326,451	13,458	11,449
NJ	299,986	13,190	12,057
MI	279,503	14,330	12,004
GA	235,733	9,041	7,770
MA	223,571	7,894	7,382
NC	221,629	7,189	6,498
VA	212,105	7,758	6,739
WA	175,242	6,896	5,987
IN	162,953	7,513	6,235
MO	155,811	6,005	5,068
MD	154,646	6,455	5,844
MN	152,334	6,529	5,453
TN	151,738	4,816	4,409
WI	148,194	7,060	6,281
CT	134,968	5,161	4,765
CO	129,575	4,327	3,887
LA	123,549	4,494	4,030
AZ	122,273	4,732	3,741
AL	104,213	4,147	3,633
KY	101,535	3,932	3,489
OR	97,510	3,884	3,475
SC	95,447	4,055	3,507
IA	81,695	3,346	3,005
OK	79,423	3,416	3,139
KS	72,998	3,122	2,684
NV	59,248	1,911	1,571
AR	59,141	2,601	2,149
MS	58,743	2,408	2,165
UT	55,070	2,305	1,917
DC	50,546	707	647
NE	49,275	1,964	1,744
NM	47,829	1,952	1,660
HI	38,537	1,283	1,112
WV	38,281	2,217	1,906
NH	37,470	1,365	1,241
DE	31,263	914	831
ME	30,409	1,601	1,433
RI	29,409	1,264	1,216
ID	29,388	1,321	1,154
AK	26,575	1,218	1,092
SD	19,767	794	665
MT	18,907	1,030	929
WY	16,244	702	604
ND	15,910	682	599
VT	15,510	862	750

Note: Data are from the National Center for Education Statistics [Online]. Retrieved November 15, 2002, from http://nces.ed.gov/

TABLE 2.3
Correlations between 1997–1998 Gross State Product, Education Revenues, and Expenditures

	State GSP	Total Revenues	Total Expenditures
State GSP	1		
Total revenues	0.9926	1	
Total expenditures	0.9914	0.9992	1

Note: Calculations were made by the author from data in Table 2.2.

PRODUCTIVITY AND EDUCATION

Another measure of the relationship between education and economics is seen in productivity and personal income. The initial discussion of this concern began in 1776 with the work of Adam Smith (1991), who recognized the importance of an educated workforce to business as well as to society. Later, empirical research conducted by Schultz (1963), Denison (1962), Benson (1978), and others provided the important foundation for **human capital theory**. This theory, initially developed by Schultz, proposes that the return on the investment of time and resources in education is related to production and individual earnings.

Two methods used to examine the relationship between the time and resources invested in education and human capital production are either: (a) the average annual earnings of workers in reference to their years of education or (b) a person's lifetime earnings in relation to the level of education attained by that person. As an example, Table 2.4 presents the median annual income by level of education for 1998 as reported by the U.S. Census Bureau, 2002.

TABLE 2.4
Median Earnings: Full-Time, Year-Round Workers by Sex: 1998

	Median Earnings ($)	
Education	Females	Males
Less than 9th grade	14,132	18,553
9th to 12th (no diploma)	15,847	23,438
High school graduate (includes GED)	21,963	30,868
Some college, no degree	26,024	35,949
Associate degree	28,337	38,483
Bachelor's degree	35,408	49,982
Master's degree	42,002	60,168
Professional degree	55,460	90,653
Doctorate degree	52,167	69,188
Total	26,711	36,679

Note: Data are from the U.S. Census Bureau [Online]. Retrieved November 15, 2002, from http://www.census.gov

As shown in Table 2.4, the increase in earnings per level of education acquired and the differential between the male and female earnings are dramatic. After reviewing these statistics, a personal question that each individual might ask is whether the investment of time and resources to attend college or graduate school justifies the potential increase in earnings. Likewise, a community can easily gauge its human capital potential by examining the educational level of its residents. In other words, the economic potential for a town with 90% of the workforce at an education level at or below a high school diploma will likely be less than a community where 60% of the workforce has a college degree or higher.

Another measure of human capital production is called the **internal rate of return**. In this measure the expected lifetime earnings of people at different levels of education are related to the actual cost of providing that education up to and including the level of education being measured. The higher the earnings and the lower the cost, the greater the return of the investment.

Research on measures of the returns on educational investments over the past 40 years by Becker (1964), Psacharopoulos (1981, 1985), Woodhall (1987), and others have shown that an elementary provides the best return, and this is followed by the return for a secondary education. Because of their findings, as well as a number of pedagogical concerns, some researchers argue that there is a serious underinvestment at the early childhood and elementary level. Their conclusions are important in underdeveloped regions where leadership must decide how to allocate the scarce resources available for education.

MONITORING ECONOMIC INDICATORS

While education contributes to the health of an economy, it also uses up economic resources in the delivery of its services. Education money that comes from taxes, donations, and tuition is also sought by other government agencies. In addition, individuals who are providing the tax money to a school district might prefer to spend it on other "wants."

Because money is a scarce resource, educators must pay close attention to the amount available to them. If the economy is healthy and the supply of money is increasing so that essential needs are being met, educators may have an opportunity to increase services, to improve programs, or to enlarge facilities. If, on the other hand, the economy is in a decline and money is scarce, educators must be careful not to exacerbate the economic plight of a community by putting forth costly initiatives.

To plan appropriately, administrators should prepare a 3-year financial plan with budget options related to different economic scenarios. Administrators must then monitor one or more economic indicators on a regular basis to modify their budget options accordingly. Luke et al. (1988) propose that state and local governments need to use strategic planning techniques that "help them adapt to technological change, fiscal stress and . . . economic shifts" (p. 35).

The actions taken by the seven member Federal Reserve Board are important economic indicators for school leaders to monitor. Created in 1913 by the Federal Reserve Act and modified by the Banking Act of 1935, the Federal Reserve Board, called "the Fed," directs the changes in the way the 12 Federal Reserve Banks loan money.

The U.S. president with Senate approval appoints the members of the board for terms of 14 years and the chair for a term of 4 years. Through the 12 regional banks, 25 branches, and 11 offices, the Fed acts like a central bank for the country and helps manage the nation's monetary policies, keeping the country's economy healthy (Bannock et al., 1998). Understanding the actions of the Fed can help school administrators gain insight into the Fed's view of economic shifts taking place at the national level.

The Fed's purpose is to control both the money supply and the cost of borrowing money. For example, if there is a fear of inflation, the Fed may wish to cool the economy down by reducing the supply of money and/or making it more expensive to borrow. On the other hand, if there is a concern about a recession, the Fed may wish to stimulate the economy by increasing the money supply and/or reducing the cost of borrowing money. Following are three methods the Fed has to influence the money supply or the cost of money.

Discount Rate

One of these methods is to raise or lower the **Federal Reserve Board discount rate**, which is the interest rate banks pay on loans from one of the 12 Federal Reserve Banks. A bank will then make loans to customers at rates scaled up from the discount rate. As a result, if the discount rate is lowered, the borrowing rates for the customers of the bank are lowered, and vice versa. All seven members of the Federal Reserve Board must approve changes in the discount rate. In practice, the 12 district banks change their discount rates at the same time.

Reserve Requirement

A second method the Fed may use to influence the money supply is to increase or decrease the **Federal Reserve Board reserve requirement**, which is the amount of money a bank must set aside as cash either in its vault or in a reserve account with its district Federal Reserve Bank. Thus, if the Fed wishes to take money out of circulation, it can simply increase the reserve required of the banks. Likewise, if the Fed wishes to encourage spending, it can reduce the reserve and banks can loan more money to customers.

Open Market

Open market operations is a term used to identify the third method the Fed may call on to influence the money market. Through open market operations the Fed may purchase or sell U.S. Treasury securities via the marketplace. When the

Fed sells Treasury securities, it takes money out of the banking system. When the Fed wishes to put money into the system, it buys the securities for cash so that investors will place their money in some other account. The types of U.S. securities are Treasury bills, Treasury notes, and Treasury bonds.

Treasury bills, or "T-bills" as they are popularly called, are discount securities, which means people make bids to buy them from the federal government at a price below their face value and receive the face value in 13, 26, or 52 weeks. Treasury notes and Treasury bonds are purchased through an auction process. Treasury notes may mature in less than a year or up to 10 years, and Treasury bonds mature in 10 or more years. In addition, Treasury securities can be sold on the secondary market, which means the holder can sell them to someone else before maturity (Zipf, 1997).

Changes in the discount rate and reserve requirement take place only occasionally. Open market operations are conducted every business day and have the greatest impact on the nation's money supply. Other economic indicators for educational leaders to track are changes in the GDP/GSP, changes in the money supply or M (reported by the federal government on a regular basis), the trade deficit, the unemployment rate, the rate of inflation, retail sales, the consumer price index, and factory inventory levels. Information on these indicators should be followed at the national as well as the state and local level on a continuing basis.

MONEY AND EDUCATION

A country, state, or geographic region, such as a city or township, can be perceived economically as a family. Businesses and people who live in a region, like family members, must have a predictable income. If money in an area becomes scarce, the volume of business, personal incomes, and tax revenues will begin to decline. Unless something occurs to turn the economy around, the decline may continue, unemployment will rise, and businesses may leave the area. Historically, such a set of events unfortunately has taken place too often, especially in many large cities.

The Multiplier Effect

Understanding the impact of additional money on the economy is important to school leaders. When money is available, an economic phenomenon referred to as the *multiplier effect* takes place. The multiplier effect represents the relationships between income, investment, and spending. Although the multiplier effect and related opinions are quite complex, the proposal is simply that additional money in an economy leads to the eventual spending and investment of an amount that is greater than the initial infusion. The **multiplier** is calculated by economists who divide an increase in income by an increase in spending generated by the additional income (Bannock et al., 1998).

The multiplier process begins when additional money enters an economy. Some of the new money will be invested, and some of it will be spent on goods and services. From the extra money spent on goods and services, a portion will be placed in savings and some of it will be spent again. In the next round, some of the money spent will be spent again and some of it will be invested. This cycle continues until new economic activity is no longer generated. The total economic impact on the region, therefore, is greater than the initial infusion of money.

The proportion of the extra income spent is called the **Marginal Propensity to Consume (MPC)**, and the proportion saved is the **Marginal Propensity to Save (MPS)**. If the multiplier is 4, then $1,000 of extra income will generate a total increase of $4,000 in income. If the MPC is 75%, then $3,000 (three fourths of the additional income) will be the increase in extra consumption and $1,000 will be the increase in savings (one fourth of the extra income and equal to the initial increase).

The recognition of several features associated with the multiplier effect is important. The first is whether the additional income is permanent or temporary. If the money is a one-time infusion, then the effects must be recognized accordingly. For example, a small city on a river experienced a quick spring thaw that caused a severe flood. The federal and state relief plus insurance money was a large but temporary infusion of money. The economic reports for the city for the remainder of the year were very positive. The economic potential for the city appeared to be exceedingly strong. The next year, however, the picture changed dramatically with economic measures that mirrored those of the years before the flood.

Second, while a small increase in income can cause a greater increase in spending, the multiplier also can work the other way. A decrease in the amount of money in an economy may cause the reverse effect. If money is removed from investment and spending, the net effect can also be magnified. More specifically, in a period when a region was experiencing a sharp economic decline, a large property tax increase was imposed on the local residents. The combination of the economic decline and the tax increase caused a much harsher effect than anticipated from the negative multiplier.

Third, the ideal would be to gain additional income on a continuing basis from new industries attracted to the region as opposed to a one-time infusion of new money. If new businesses are not attracted to a region, the only possible way to have a positive impact on the local economy is for existing companies to produce more. Such dependencies can be dangerous, especially if the existing companies are no longer competitive.

A good example of a situation where a city was too dependent on one major industry is exhibited in the movie *Roger and Me* (1989) directed by Michael Moore. In the beginning of the film, Moore, the narrator, explains how several generations of his family worked at the local GM plant. He explains how he lived in a model city and that life was good. Later in the movie when the factory closes, the film gives a tour through the town to the sounds of the Beach Boys singing in the background "Wouldn't It Be Nice." The tour shows abandoned houses, empty stores, and vacant streets; all of which indicate a city in an economic decline with falling income and property values.

An education system in such a setting would surely have major financial problems due to reduced property tax revenue. The possibility of offering programs to a student body that would attract new third-wave industries would have limited financial support. According to the people interviewed in the movie and the narrator, the advice given to the people was to move to other states where there were jobs. The movie clearly shows that many people took that advice. The symbiotic relationship between education and economics was obviously in a downward synergistic spiral.

Therefore, in terms of financial planning, school district administrators must be careful in making their revenue projections. The infusion of new income into a community must be regarded carefully in terms of its origin and flow plus the timing for an increase in taxes must be sensitive to the larger economic picture.

FINAL THOUGHTS

The public education industry in the United States is a huge enterprise. According to the NCES, in 1998–1999 there were 90,874 public schools and in 1999–2000 the public school attendance was 46.9 million students who were taught by 2.9 million teachers (NCES, 2002). Trying to influence changes in anything so large is almost beyond comprehension. At the same time, the efforts to change something so complex and important to individuals and society must be done with very careful forethought.

While the connections between education and economics, especially in relation to personal earnings, is accepted by the experts in the field, the related issues are numerous. For example, as discussed earlier, how much money should society invest in education? This question becomes more complex when asked in reference to an observation by the NPBEA (2002a) whereby educational leaders must "identify and accomplish the mission of the changing and globally driven school" (p. 2).

A further issue is raised by Levin (1998) who questions the proposition that new and higher educational performance standards will lead to greater economic productivity. He points to the weak relationships between test scores and productivity, adult earnings (although they have been improving), and supervisory ratings. Because of these weak associations, he has reservations about the arbitrary performance standards set for students. The concerns expressed by Levin are some of the hot topics to be addressed by educational researchers and policymakers over the next decade.

Another related matter is the proposal that educators must take proactive measures and address economic problems. This assignment may seem extreme to some educational leaders who believe their responsibilities should be limited to

ISLLC

the operation of the schools in the district. However, Standard 4, set for school leaders by the ISLLC (1996), proposes that school administrators mobilize community resources. Then, under Standard 6, the council directs that school administrators are to respond to and influence "the larger political, social, economic, legal, and cultural context." They continue by stating that an "administrator believes in, values, and is committed to actively participating in the political and policy-making context in the service of education" (p. 20). In their participation, school leaders may have to assume the role of a teacher to help the policymakers in their community understand and appreciate the synergistic relationship between education and the local economy.

DISCUSSION QUESTIONS

1. As an educator, what major economic indexes would you monitor for the administration of a school district? Why?

2. Assume there are the following three communities. One is a low-socioeconomic area with high unemployment and unskilled workers employed primarily in mass production factories. A second has a workforce of highly skilled technicians with cyclical work and, therefore, a cyclical economy with a high turnover of people in the community. The third is a more affluent area with corporate offices employing communication/computer technicians and operators, middle and upper level managers, and maintenance/support service personnel.

    a. How would the workers in each community relate to the descriptions given in this chapter for a nation at risk, the third wave, symbolic-analytic jobs, and brainpower industries?

    b. What data could be collected (financial, curriculum, student, socioeconomic, and so on) to assess the economic effectiveness of the school districts in each community?

    c. What would be your expectation with respect to a human capital analysis of the schools in the three communities? Why?

    d. Describe the educational strategy a school administrator might develop in each community.

3. The symbiotic and synergistic relationships between education and economics were discussed throughout the chapter. Explain how these relationships may be impacted positively or negatively by the multiplier effect.

APPLICATION PROBLEMS

1. Tables 2.1 and 2.2 present the Internet citations for 1997–1998 Gross State Product for the different states and Washington, DC, plus their education revenues and expenditures.

    a. How does your state compare to the other states and the nation in these tables?

  b. Using the Internet citations, what are the most recent GSP data, education revenues, and expenditures for your state?

  c. How does your state compare to the other states and the nation with respect to the most recent report on the Internet?

  d. Have the amounts and ranking changed for your state? Why or why not?

  e. Has the percentage of education revenue compared to the GSP changed for your state? Why or why not?

2. Select two economic indices and report their changes over the past 6 months and 1 year. Based on these changes, what is your view of the economic climate for public education:

  a. For the nation?

  b. For the state?

  c. For the community in which you live?

WEB ADDRESSES

U.S. Government Printing Office
http://www.access.gpo.gov

Bureau of Economic Analysis
http://www.bea.doc.gov/bea/regional/gsp/

U.S. Census Bureau
http://www.census.gov

National Council for Accreditation of Teacher Education
http://www.ncate.org

National Council for Education Statistics
http://nces.ed.gov

REFERENCES

Anyon, J. (1980). Social class and the hidden curriculum of work. *Journal of Education, 162,* 67–92.

Bannock, G., Baxter, R. E., & Davis, E. (1998). *Dictionary of economics* (6th ed.). London: Penguin Group.

Becker, G. S. (1964). *Human capital: A theoretical and empirical analysis, with special reference to education.* New York: National Bureau of Economic Research.

Benson, C. S. (1978). *The economics of public education* (3rd ed.). Boston: Houghton Mifflin.

Bureau of Economic Analysis (2002). *Gross state product: New estimates for 2000 and revised estimates for 1998–1999* [Online]. Retrieved June 10, 2002, from http://www.bea.doc.gov/bea/regional/gsp/

Coleman, J. S., Campbell, E. Q., Hobson, C. J., McPartland, J., Mood, A. M., Weinfield, F. D., et al., (1966). *Equality of educational opportunity* (Catalogue No. FS 5.238–38001). Washington, DC: U.S. Government Printing Office.

Denison, E. F. (1962). *The sources of economic growth in the United States.* New York: Committee on Economic Development.

Economic Report of the President (1999). [Online]. Retrieved November 15, 2002, from http://www.access.gpo.gov

Garner, C. W., & Cole, E. G. (1986). Motivation and the non-achieving students in a low SES environment: A taxonomy for achievement. *Reading Improvement, 23*(2), 114–123.

Garner, C. W., & Cole, E. G. (1996). The achievement of students in low SES settings: An investigation of the relationship between locus of control and field dependence, in *Teaching students to be responsible*, Hot Topics Series, *Phi Delta Kappan,* 97–114. (Reprinted from *Urban Education, 21*(2), 189–206, published 1986.)

Interstate School Leaders Licensure Consortium (1996). *Standards for school leaders.* Washington, DC: Council of Chief State School Officers.

Labaree, D. G. (1997). Public goods, private goods: The American struggle over educational goals. *American Educational Research Journal, 34*(1), 39–81.

Levin, H. M. (1998). Educational performance standards and the economy. *Educational Researcher, 27*(4), 4–10.

Luke, J. S., Ventriss, C., Reed, B. J., & Reed, C. M. (1988). *Managing economic development.* San Francisco: Jossey-Bass.

Maslow, A. H. (1954). *Motivation and personality.* New York: Harper & Row.

Miller, H. L. (1978). *Social foundations of education: An urban focus* (3rd ed.). New York: Holt, Reinhart & Winston.

Moore, M. (Writer/Director)(1989). *Roger and me.* [Motion picture]. United States: Warner Studios.

National Center for Education Statistics (2002). *Digest of Educational Statistics 2002* [Online]. Retrieved November 15, 2002, from http://nces.ed.gov

National Commission on Excellence in Education (1983). *A nation at risk: The imperative of educational reform.* Washington, DC: U.S. Government Printing Office.

National Policy Board for Educational Administration (2002a). *Standards for advanced programs in educational leadership* [Online]. Retrieved February 17, 2003, from http://www.npbea.org

National Policy Board for Educational Administration (2002b). *Standards for advanced programs in educational leadership for principals, superintendents, curriculum directors, and supervisors* [Online]. Retrieved February 17, 2003, from http://www.ncate.org

Psacharopoulos, G. (1981). Returns to education: An updated international comparison. *Comparative Education, 17,* 321–341.

Psacharopoulos, G. (1985). Returns to education: A further international update and implications. *The Journal of Human Resources, 20,* 583–604.

Reich, R. B. (1992). *The work of nations.* New York: Vintage Books.

Rotter, J. B. (1954). *Social learning and clinical psychology.* New York: Prentice Hall.

Rotter, J. B. (1966). Generalized expectancies for internal versus external control of reinforcement. *Psychological Monographs: General and Applied, 80,* 1–26.

Schultz, T. W. (1963). *The economic value of education.* New York: Columbia University Press.

Smith, A. (1991). *Wealth of nations.* Amherst, NY: Prometheus Books. (Reprinted from *An inquiry into the nature and cause of the wealth of nations,* published 1776.)

Thurow, L. C. (1996). *The future of capitalism: How today's economic forces shape tomorrow's world.* New York: Morrow.

Toffler, A., & Toffler, H. (1995). *Creating a new civilization.* Atlanta: Turner.

U.S. Census Bureau [Online]. Retrieved November 15, 2002 (created October 28, 1999, and revised August 22, 2002) from http://www.census.gov

Weiner, B. (1972). *Theories of motivation.* Chicago: Markham.

Weiner, B. (1974). *Achievement motivation and attribution theory.* Morristown, NJ: General Learning Press.

Weiner, B. (1979). A theory of motivation for some classroom experiences. *Journal of Educational Psychology, 71,* 3–25.

Wigfield, A., & Asher, S. R. (1984). Social and motivational influences on reading. In D. Pearson (Ed.), *Handbook of reading research.* New York: Longman.

Woodhall, M. (1987). Human capital concepts. In G. Psacharopoulos (Ed.), *Economics of education: Research and studies* (pp. 21–24). Oxford: Pergamon Press.

Zipf, R. (1997). *How the bond market works* (2nd ed.). Paramus, NJ: New York Institute of Finance.

Chapter 3

Revenue, Income, and Fiduciary Money: The Base for Financial Planning

A prerequisite for the study of school finance, especially financial planning, is familiarity with the sources of money received to operate school districts. This is a prerequisite to one of the expectations in NCATE Standard 6.1 (NPBEA, 2002) that future district leaders should be able to "explain the system for financing public schools" (p. 14). To introduce the sources of money received by a school district, this chapter places the money streams into one of three categories. These categories—revenue, income, and **fiduciary** money—correspond to the way the accounting system sorts school money for deposit into financial records; this is explained in chapters 6 to 8.

Revenue, the first category discussed in this chapter, comes from tax collections. This money is received prior to the offering of any services; thus, it is unearned at the time of its receipt. Further, these receipts provide the majority of the money received and spent for the instructional and instructionally related operations of a school district (the topic for chapter 9). As a consequence, this chapter takes a special look at the different types of tax money and criteria used for their economic evaluation.

Another type of revenue, which is introduced in this chapter and elaborated on in chapter 10, comes from the sale of bonds. Bond money is used for large capital expenditures, such as the construction of a new school building. It is included in the revenue category because it is repaid from public tax collections.

The income category represents money obtained from the sale of goods and services to individuals and other entities. Therefore, income money is received at or after the time a service or good is delivered; for example, money received in exchange for food in a cafeteria. Because income depends on business transactions, administrators must project receipts, anticipate expenditures in a proposed budget, and continually monitor both of them.

A fiduciary is a person or organization that holds money in trust for another person or organization. As a result, money received as a donation or to be held in trust is considered fiduciary money. Fiduciary receipts are typically neither large sums of money nor critical to the instructional operations of a school district. These receipts, however, must be handled with special care for legal as well as public relations reasons. Income and fiduciary money are the focus in chapter 11.

REVENUE RECEIPTS: LOCAL, STATE, AND FEDERAL GOVERNMENTS

Revenue receipts are generated through some form of tax assessment paid by the public or by for-profit companies. Because a government collects tax money for school districts, the accounting system labels this as government money and the GAAP expects it to be kept in accounts that are formally separated from income and fiduciary money.

School districts receive nearly all of their revenue for instruction, either directly or indirectly, from federal, state, intermediate, and local governments; although the majority comes from local and state tax collections. Receipts from intermediate governments, which are county or regional governments, are quite small or nonexistent in most states.

The percentages of education revenue received in 1997–1998 by individual states and Washington, DC, plus the national average from the four levels of government were obtained by NCES and are shown in Table 3.1. Although the states depend, and often place great importance on the amount of federal aid received, the percentages for federal support shown in Table 3.1 range from 3.6% for New Jersey to 14.1% for Mississippi and 16.5% for Washington, DC. Thus, the federal contributions are small in relation to local and state revenue received.

Also noted in Table 3.1 are the percentages of revenues provided to education by state and local governments. Some states provide well over 50% of the revenue for education, whereas in other states the revenues between the state and local level are almost equal, while in still others the majority comes from local tax revenue.

Recognizing the proportion of revenue provided to their state from state and local tax levies is important for school leaders. This is because the sources of the state and local tax receipts are not likely the same. For example, the source of money for one tax may come from the sale of goods, another may come from income earned by individuals, another from corporate profits, and another from property owners. As suggested in the previous chapter, school leaders must monitor economic indices related to the tax sources for insights into changes that will have an impact on them, such as changes in retail sales on a sales tax. However, to accomplish this task, school leaders must be aware of the source of money for each tax group and the criteria for evaluating their stability.

TABLE 3.1
Within State Percentage of Revenues for Education: 1997–1998

	Local Revenue	Intermediate Revenue	State Revenue	Federal Revenue
U.S.	44.50	0.40	48.40	6.80
AL	27.70	0.50	62.50	9.40
AK	25.60	0.00	62.20	12.30
AZ	41.80	3.70	44.30	10.20
AR	31.40	0.10	57.70	10.80
CA	31.60	0.00	60.20	8.20
CO	51.30	0.20	43.40	5.10
CT	58.80	0.00	37.30	3.90
DE	28.00	0.00	64.40	7.60
DC	83.50	0.00	0.00	16.50
FL	43.60	0.00	48.80	7.60
GA	42.00	0.00	51.20	6.80
HI	2.40	0.00	89.00	8.60
ID	30.30	0.00	62.70	7.00
IL	64.80	0.00	28.40	6.70
IN	43.10	0.70	51.40	4.80
IA	43.20	0.20	51.30	5.30
KS	32.60	3.60	57.90	5.90
KY	28.70	0.00	61.70	9.60
LA	38.30	0.00	50.40	11.30
ME	47.50	0.00	45.50	7.00
MD	55.80	0.00	39.00	5.20
MA	54.30	0.00	40.70	5.00
MI	27.30	0.10	66.00	6.60
MN	39.50	3.20	52.30	4.90
MS	30.50	0.00	55.40	14.10
MO	53.60	0.50	39.70	6.20
MT	33.90	9.00	46.90	10.20
NE	59.50	0.70	33.10	6.70
NV	63.60	0.00	31.80	4.60
NH	86.80	0.00	9.30	3.80
NJ	56.60	0.00	39.80	3.60
NM	14.60	0.00	72.20	13.20
NY	54.40	0.40	39.70	5.40
NC	25.50	0.00	67.30	7.20
ND	45.50	1.10	41.10	12.40
OH	52.80	0.20	41.20	5.80
OK	27.90	1.90	61.60	8.60
OR	35.30	1.50	56.80	6.40
PA	55.40	0.10	38.70	5.90
RI	54.40	0.00	40.10	5.40
SC	40.00	0.00	51.50	8.50
SD	53.20	1.20	35.60	10.00
TN	43.40	0.00	47.70	8.80
TX	47.90	0.30	44.20	7.60
UT	32.10	0.00	61.00	6.90
VT	65.40	0.00	29.40	5.20
VA	63.40	0.00	31.40	5.20
WA	27.60	0.00	66.00	6.40
WV	28.10	0.00	62.70	9.20
WI	41.80	0.00	53.70	4.50
WY	38.40	7.80	47.00	6.70

Note: The totals for the rows may not equal 100% due to rounding. Some values contain imputation for missing data. An imputed value is less than 2% of total revenues in any one state. Data are from the National Center for Education Statistics [Online]. Retrieved June 10, 2002, from http://nces.ed.gov

THE FOUR TAX GROUPS

Taxes and their analyses have been major topics of discussion in numerous economic and school finance books (Alexander & Salmon, 1995; Birrup, Brimley, & Garfield, 1999; Guthrie, Garms, & Pierce, 1988; Hack, Candoli, & Ray, 1998; Odden & Picus, 2000; Swanson & King, 1997). Over the years, the discussions as well as the studies of taxes by many authors and researchers have placed the various taxes into one of the following four groups: (a) **income taxes** (both personal and business); (b) **wealth taxes** (such as property taxes); (c) sales and **excise taxes** (sometimes called consumption taxes); and (d) **privilege taxes**, fees, and other charges. Selected criteria have been used to examine their strengths and weaknesses.

This section briefly describes the four groups of taxes. The next section presents the basic criteria used to examine them. Using the criteria, the following section offers a limited analysis of each tax group.

Income Tax

This is the most common tax. In addition, it may be the easiest to understand because its base is the amount of income a person or business receives. In some cases this tax assessment makes a distinction between earned and unearned income. A community, for example, may have a 1% personal income tax on earned income only, meaning money received in exchange for work. In these cases, incomes from retirement, social security benefits, investments, capital gains, unemployment, and disability insurance would not be taxed because they are unearned.

In addition to the tax receipts from personal income, another large source of tax revenue collected by federal, state, and local governments comes from taxes on profits generated by corporations. One criticism of the tax system, however, is regarding the income tax on dividends paid from corporate profits to stockholders. The complaint is that corporate profits are double taxed, meaning the two taxes (one on the corporate profits and another on the shareholder's earnings) are on the same money.

Taxes on the business profits of proprietorships and partnerships are typically not on the business earnings, although some state and local governments may assess a form of business or privilege tax. The profits earned by proprietors or partners who own a business are declared as personal income on their tax returns. A tax on the business income is then levied at the personal income tax rate.

Wealth Tax

The common wealth tax is the personal residential property tax. This is because for centuries the ownership of land has been considered evidence of personal wealth. Due to dramatic changes in recent years in lifestyles, this evidence is being questioned. For example, some states place a wealth tax on other property, such as automobiles. Regardless of the definition of property, the base for the wealth tax is the value assigned by the government to the property owned by a person or business.

One of the problems with the property tax is that the public has difficulty comprehending the process used to arrive at the amount they must pay to a school district. To begin the calculations of the property tax, the assigned value of the property must be determined. The value assigned to property may come either from the most recent sales price of the property and building or from an estimate on the value of the property and building provided by an assessor. Estimates are usually based on the sales price of similar properties and buildings in the area.

Once a value of the property and buildings is established, an assessed value for each parcel of property is determined. This value is calculated by taking a percentage of the market value. The benefit of using an assessed value is that the differences in market value may be somewhat minimized. For example, a 20% assessment on a property and house with a value of $100,000 would be $20,000 and a similar house with a value of $110,000 would be $22,000.

The tax levied on property is on its assessed value. If the tax levy on the property in a district is 100 mills (a mill is equal to $.001 or one-tenth of a cent), then the tax is .10 per dollar of assessed value (100 mills × .001 = .10). Thus, a 100-mill tax on a property assessed at $20,000 would be $2,000 ($.10 × $20,000) and $2,200 on the $22,000 house and property.

Nearly all school districts depend heavily on the revenue generated by property taxes. In some cases school districts assess property and collect the tax money from the owners. In others the districts receive the tax money from a municipal, county, or state government, who make the assessments.

Examples of two different approaches to property tax collections occur in Pennsylvania and New Jersey, two of the original 13 colonies. In Pennsylvania the board of a school district assesses property owners by passing a property tax levy and then collecting the money. In New Jersey the school district determines the amount needed from property owners; however, the public votes to approve the levy. If passed, a municipal government collects the money for the district. If the public does not pass the school budget, the school district must negotiate with the local municipalities and then state officials if a compromise is needed.

Sales and Excise Taxes

The sales and excise, or consumption, tax is popular in many states as well as some communities. The sales tax is a tax assessed on the price of a good or service when purchased. The seller of the merchandise or service collects the tax money at the time of the purchase. The owner of the business then sends the sales tax money to a state revenue office.

An excise tax is also a sales tax except that it is a federal tax on selected goods, such as cigarettes, alcohol (known as the sin taxes), gasoline, jewelry, and furs. A sales tax on a product should not have an effect on the demand for the product, except possibly the "sin taxes." If individuals or businesses sell an asset, such as stock, mutual funds, or other investments, they do not collect a sales tax. Rather, the seller may pay a tax based on the capital gains, or profit, made on the sale.

Privilege Tax

Receipts from privilege taxes are from fees charged by a government for a variety of reasons, such as license fees (payment by teachers for state instructional certificates), fines levied when someone does not obey the rules (library fines), inspections, copies of records, estate and gift taxes, and inheritance taxes.

Usually privilege fees received by a school district are minimal relative to other receipts. In their research on the direct fees levied by school districts, Bouman and Brown (1996) divided them into five categories as follows: (a) curricular fees that students pay for special supplies, (b) extracurricular charges required for trips and equipment, (c) incidental costs for such items as yearbooks, (d) supplemental fees for special courses and correspondence, and (e) nonuser fees such as tuition from nonresident students.

CRITERIA FOR EVALUATING TAXES

To examine the strengths and weaknesses of a tax, school leaders may consider a number of criteria. A criterion may have an influence on the amount of revenue received by the school district and/or on the financial welfare of the people in their community.

Yield

The first factor to consider in an evaluation of a tax is the yield the tax generates. Is the tax yield adequate to cover the expenditures of the government body that depends on it? Is the yield flexible so that, when needed, an increase in revenue is possible? For example, property taxes collected by some school districts may not provide enough money to meet their needs. If additional revenue is needed during the year, an increase in the property tax rate will not generate more money immediately. An increase in the sales tax, however, is quite different.

Elasticity

Another criterion measures the relationship between tax revenues and economic change. Ideally, a tax should have a neutral affect on the economy; that is, it should not change personal spending or investment habits or the demand for a product or service (except possibly "sin taxes"). At the same time, ideally, an economic decline should not cause a greater decline in the amount of tax revenues generated. The examination of the effect of economic change on tax receipts is through a measure of **elasticity**.

Elasticity represents the proportional change in tax yield in relation to changes in economic growth. In this definition, attention to two parts is necessary. The first is that it denotes a *proportional change* and is not a direct measure. The second is that it is a measure of *changes in economic growth,* which is determined by a percentage change and not a dollar amount (Bannock, Baxter, & Davis, 1998). The researcher or administrator has to select the economic measure to use in the formula, such as a change in GDP, GSP, personal income, or property values.

The formula for calculating the elasticity, or *e,* of the proportional change between a tax yield and a measure of economic growth is as follows:

$$e = \frac{\% \text{ change in tax yield}}{\% \text{ change in economic growth}}$$

If the elasticity is 1.0, it is at equilibrium or unity, meaning the percentage change (i.e., 10%) in economic growth is equal to the percentage change in the yield (i.e., 10%). If the elasticity is greater than unity, or 1.0, the percentage change in tax yield is greater (i.e., 10%) than the percentage change in economic growth (i.e., 5%). The tax is, therefore, elastic. If the elasticity is less than unity, or less than 1.0, the percentage change in tax yield (i.e., 5%) is less than the change in economic growth (i.e., 10%). The tax, therefore, is inelastic and may not be stable.

Equity

Another tax criterion considers the fairness, or equity, of a tax on people. Specifically, does a tax treat equal equally? Do people who earn the same amount of money pay the same amount of taxes? That is the question related to the principle of horizontal tax equity.

On the other hand, vertical tax equity considers the treatment of unequals. Does a tax treat unequals unequally? For instance, do people with higher incomes or more expensive homes pay more tax than people with lower incomes or less expensive homes? If so, the tax is considered to be vertically equitable.

Incidence/Impact

A further set of criteria concerns who actually pays the tax and who bears the financial burden. In the examination of a tax for fairness, the identification of the person who actually bears the financial burden is important. For example, when property taxes are increased, the owner of an apartment building pays the tax (impact) but may pass the increase on to the tenant. The tenant then bears the burden (incidence).

Progressive, Proportional, Regressive

A set of criteria compares the amount of income earned by people to the amount of taxes paid to determine if the tax is progressive, proportional, or regressive. Specifically, a **progressive tax** collects more money from people as their income increases. An example of such a tax is the federal graduated income tax, in which the tax assessed increases as the amount of income increases. A progressive tax, therefore, is horizontally and vertically equitable.

In a **proportional tax** the same tax percentage is assessed on everyone regardless of income. A proportional tax is a state tax where people pay a 2% tax on their income. Such a tax treats everyone equally, and so it meets the principal of horizontal, but not vertical, equity.

A **regressive tax** is the opposite of a progressive tax whereby the tax takes a decreasing amount of money as a person's income increases. While a regressive tax may treat equals equally, a greater burden is placed on people with low incomes. Thus, it is not vertically equitable.

Cost

The cost to collect and manage a tax is a burden on taxpayers. The costs to tax the people are paid from the tax collected. As a consequence, another consideration when evaluating a tax concerns the cost required to administer it.

ANALYSIS OF THE FOUR TAX GROUPS

An evaluation of the strengths and weaknesses of the different taxes should be conducted through the use of the previous criteria. The following discussion is a general overview of an analysis; however, such an evaluation must take into consideration the state and local legal parameters associated with each tax source.

Income Tax

With respect to the income tax, the revenue yield is typically considered to be stable and elastic in reference to national and personal income. When the government needs additional tax revenue, the imposition of a larger tax assessment can result in an immediate increase.

If the income tax table is graduated, it should be horizontally and vertically equitable whereby equals are treated equally, and unequals, unequally. Also, if a tax table is indexed to inflation, which is the case with the federal tax table, any effects from inflation should be minimized. Tax deductions help make an income tax more equitable, although the types of deductions permitted can skew the tax to favor the higher income brackets.

In some states where the income tax is a set percentage for all people, and there are no deductions, the tax is not vertically equitable but is proportional. Some people, however, argue that because unequals are not treated unequally, the use of the same percentage for all income earners is regressive. A 2% tax on people earning $10,000 is likely to have a greater personal impact on their quality of life than a 2% tax on people earning $100,000.

Since the levy of an income tax is on the money received by an individual, incidence and impact fall on the same person. Thus, an increase in the income tax rate results in an increase in the taxes paid by the person who earned the money.

Finally, the administration of an income tax is expensive, which puts a considerable burden on the taxpayers. Even though employers collect and remit the income tax, the filing of returns, collection of money owed to the government, remissions of overpayments, audits, and enforcement require considerable effort and expense.

Wealth Tax

The wealth, or property tax, has several advantages. First, it provides a relatively consistent yield that is stable. Second, property offers a collateral, or security guarantee, ensuring that the owner of the property will pay the tax. In other words, people may leave town and not pay their property tax, but they cannot take their land and house with them. If taxes are not paid, the government may claim the property.

With respect to elasticity, the proportion depends on the denominator selected to represent economic growth. If the denominator is the percentage of growth in the market value of property, the elasticity will likely be at equilibrium. In other words, as the value of property increases, the tax will also increase proportionally. If the denominator is the percentage of growth in income, and the increase in income leads to a greater increase in the cost of housing, the property tax will be elastic; otherwise, it will be inelastic and unstable.

Therefore, one of the greatest problems with the property tax occurs when the assessed value of properties in a school district is not current. When the market value assigned to a piece of property is only updated at the time the property is sold and reassessments are not made, then the market values of many or most properties will be out of date. For example, a person may be an original owner of a property with an assessed value of $70,000 while an identical house and property in the neighborhood may have recently sold for $150,000. The failure to maintain currency on the value of all properties causes the measures of elasticity to be irrelevant. On the other hand, because the reassessment of properties is costly and this administrative expense increases the burden on the taxpayers, communities are reluctant to conduct them.

Another problem occurs because communities usually have different assessment rates for different classes of property, such as residential, business, and industrial properties. Further, because people vote and businesses do not, the temptation is to shift the property tax burden to business and industrial properties. Of course, if this occurs, there is a risk that businesses will relocate to other communities, states, or even countries. New businesses may choose to locate in a community with a more favorable rate. On the other hand, in an effort to attract jobs to their area, some communities create industrial parks with low or no tax assessments for a given period of years. At the same time, some states have declared low-wealth communities, especially cities, to be enterprise zones with special low, or no, property tax for businesses and industrial plants along with a lower sales tax rate.

Because of the inherent problems caused by the competition for businesses and industrial plants among communities, Brent (2000) suggests that school districts should not levy a property tax on nonresidential property. Rather, he recommends that the tax on these properties should be at the state or regional level. Then the distribution of the tax proceeds would be allocated to the local communities and school districts by the state or regional taxing authority.

Probably the major problem associated with the property wealth tax, however, concerns the vertical equity of the tax. Is property ownership an appropriate gauge of a person's wealth? Is it an appropriate gauge of the wealth of a community? In nearly every community a significant number of property owners are retired and live on a fixed income. Others may depend on some form of public assistance. Owing to their fixed and unearned incomes, many are not able to meet escalating property tax expectations.

This dilemma occurs because the property tax is based on the value of the property in relation to other property in the taxing area and not on income. As a result, a property tax may be proportionally greater for low-income people, especially in a low-wealth district, as opposed to those with larger incomes, especially in a high-wealth district. For this reason, some argue that the property tax lacks vertical equity and is regressive, especially when applied to upper and lower income recipients.

In response to the problems with vertical equity, some state governments provide an annual homeowner's tax rebate. The rebate gives money to property owners based on the amount of property tax paid. In other states, such as California and Illinois, laws were passed to limit the increases in property tax levies. Research by Hylbert (2002) compared the Illinois school districts that were required to comply with the law to a select number of districts that were not. He found the limitation law significantly restricted the revenue growth of the school districts required to limit their increase in taxes as compared to districts that were not.

In addition, when most money provided for education depends on local property taxes, a high-wealth school district, meaning a district with very expensive homes, will have more money to spend than a district with low-cost housing. This variation is most markedly seen in two of the school districts included in a study by the author. District A is in a large low-wealth city with an enrollment of over 47,000 students whereas district B is a high-wealth suburban district in the same county with a student enrollment of less than 4,000. The local tax levy in district A for 1999 provided $80,000,000 ($1702 per student) to the school district. District B's 1999 local tax levy provided over $31,000,000 ($7720 per student) to the district. Although chapter 4 provides further discussion of this data, the point to recognize is that the property tax may cause vertical inequity for school districts as well as for individuals.

Finally, as noted previously, a concern with the property tax relates to impact and incidence where the impact is on the owner but the incidence is on the tenant. There is no direct relationship between the tenant's property wealth or income and the tax that is added to the rent. In response, some cities have enacted laws restricting the rent increases levied by landlords. On the other hand, however, rent control can create hardships for property owners because, ideally, a tax should not have an influence on the potential of the owner's ability to stay in business. Again, when rent control is enforced, measures of elasticity are irrelevant.

Sales Tax

The sales tax is somewhat different than the income and property tax because it is based on retail sales. The tax base may differ among states and cities because the sales of some products, such as clothing, may be taxable in one and not the other. Due to the dependency on sales, the tax yield is quite elastic. As income and inflation rates increase or decrease, so does sales tax revenue. Thus, it is only as stable as the economy.

Retailers collect the sales tax and so the costs to administer it are quite low. Of course, the government has to rely on the compliance of the business owner to turn in the tax collected.

The implementation of a sales tax increase can be immediate with a corresponding instantaneous increase in revenue. However, an increase in the sales tax risks having a negative effect on the sale of a product and on the economy. For example, a large increase in the gas tax may discourage people from taking vacations. Further, if a tax rate in one state is greater or on more goods than in another, people may travel to the neighboring state to make their purchases.

A weakness in the sales tax is that it is vertically inequitable and regressive. For example, everyone, regardless of how much money they earn, must purchase goods, such as soap. If there is a sales tax on soap, then the tax takes a greater portion of income from someone earning a low wage to buy a bar of soap as opposed to a person with a much higher salary. In addition, in some states, there is a sales tax on goods and services, such as automobile repair parts and labor charges. A lower income person may be more inclined to own older cars and when repairs are required, they are subject to a sales tax. Higher income people may own new cars covered by warranties that are not taxed.

Privilege Tax

Privilege taxes and other fees and charges refer to a variety of assessments made by school districts to cover the costs of services enjoyed by the person participating or receiving a benefit from an activity. Examples of these costs include supplies for a vocational class, uniforms, instruments for music or labs, gym uniforms, costs associated with field trips, student insurance, club memberships, social events, yearbooks, and graduation gowns.

The yield from student fees and charges, as well as the cost to offer the activity, usually depends on the participation of students. As a result, the stability of the revenue is a problem when too few students participate; for example, a class trip may require a minimum number of students. Of course, the wealth of the community and the economic climate can have a direct effect on the yield and elasticity of the income.

With respect to student fees, vertical student equity may be a major issue. Are some students excluded from some school-sponsored programs, activities, events, and services because of the fee? Arguments in favor of fees are powerful. One is that fees are necessary because a school budget cannot cover all of the costs. Without the revenue provided by the participants, some activities, such as class trips, proms, or yearbooks, could not be made available through the school. Another argument in favor of the fee notes the impact and incidence whereby those who benefit or attain advantages from the activity should be the ones to pay for it.

An approach to alleviate the potential inequitable and regressive affects caused by student assessments is to differentiate between elective and compulsory activities. For example, a student participating in an elective activity or a project taken home (a table made in a shop) should pay for the materials. On the other hand, when a fee is associated with a required course or activity and a student cannot pay or has financial limitations, the student should not be excluded. Likewise, financial limitations should not require a student to undertake a less challenging project. In these cases, to ensure vertical equity, a school district should apply an ability-to-pay principle in which a fee waiver is given to students under financial hardship (Monk, 1988). The gray area concerns those activities that are not compulsory and require a fee or special equipment. Many of these are important to students for understandable reasons, such as participation on athletic teams as a means to keep students engaged in school.

BOND REVENUE

Receipts associated with bond revenue must be noted due to their economic influence, although the bond process is covered in considerable detail in chapter 10. Money received from a bond sale creates a debt necessary for the financing of expensive projects that extend beyond a fiscal year. Typically this money is used to construct, remodel, and furnish school buildings. If possible, undertaking a major construction project requiring the sale of bonds should be sensitive to national and local economic conditions, such as a period when the interest rates are low.

At the same time, the money collected for the retirement of a bond issue, along with the payment of the interest on the bonds, comes primarily from an addition to the local tax levy. Consequently, the same strengths and weaknesses discussed for the property tax apply to this assessment. The only difference in the impact on the local economy is that local construction may create new jobs and lead to additional spending. Understanding the multiplier effect, the additional money could be an advantage in a community needing stimulation; however, the property owners must pay off the bonds over an extended period of time.

INCOME

Income, as explained earlier, is money received from a business transaction in which goods or services are provided in exchange for money. Income may come from a variety of sources such as food services, tickets to sports and artistic events, transportation, rental of a building, rental of classrooms and other facilities, goods and services provided via vocational shops, consultation services, school stores, and tuition from other school districts.

Like any business, the economy can influence the amount of income earned by a school. As a result, school leaders need to be sensitive to changes in economic indexes and the elasticity of the income. For example, if cafeteria sales decline in response to an economic decline, the school district may have to subsidize the cafeteria operations as opposed to increasing prices or reducing the staff. The amount of the subsidization must be considered in relation to the stability of the school district's tax revenue sources. If the revenue source is not stable, and the school provides a basic meal program plus optional meal selections—such as a salad bar, pizza, and desserts—the optional offerings may have to be reduced.

In addition, not unlike a private business, the salaries of some employees may depend on income from the operations. This requires school districts to prepare a strategic business plan that estimates their income receipts at the beginning of the year and the corresponding expenses of the operation in reference to economic projections (explained in chapter 11). If a business operation does not meet or exceed its projected receipts or exceeds their operational costs, business adjustments or revenue supplements will be required.

Lottery

Another source of government income may be money received from a lottery or assessment on legalized gambling. Some people believe the proceeds from these sources can provide large sums of money for education. The problem, of course, is that the amount of money received in relation to the cost is quite limited. Second, research has shown that the individuals most susceptible to the promises of a lottery are in the low-income bracket, which makes the proceeds regressive and vertically inequitable.

FIDUCIARY RECEIPTS

Money awarded by donors, foundations, and individuals for a specific purpose is another source of revenue for a school district. In addition, every school district is a fiduciary for money collected for student clubs, different classrooms, and graduating classes. When a school district receives money as a fiduciary, it agrees to hold the money in a trust to ensure it is used as intended by the depositor. Because the placement of this money must be in special accounts with other money from the school district as per the GAAP, school administrators must carefully monitor its use.

Some school districts, especially large districts in wealthy areas, receive donations and gifts from a number of sources. For example, school districts may receive money from auctions, parents who purchase special services for their child's school, money from fund-raisers by people in the community, and so on. One booster club, for example, raised $240,000 for their school.

Some states and cities, however, are having problems with the inequities created through the donations. For instance, in one case parents hired an additional teacher for the grade in which their children were assigned. Because inequities may be created within schools, school districts, cities, and states, some have been referred to school boards and judicial bodies for resolution. Regardless of the legal rulings (which vary), the school district must act as a fiduciary if the money is accepted.

FINAL THOUGHTS

As reviewed in chapter 2, the relationship between education and economics is important to a community, state, and country. This chapter adds a dimension to the discussion by pointing out that if the economy is not strong, education may suffer the consequences from weakening tax bases. This points to the possibility that an overreliance on one particular type of tax is not suitable. Another tax may be more appropriate or perhaps more than one type of tax is needed to provide a stable supply of revenue.

The analyses of strengths and weaknesses of the various taxes must be ongoing. Obviously, research and history shows the property tax has inherent disadvantages and is falling from favor. The most obvious benefit to this tax is the direct link to home rule; that is, the residents of a school district have the right to determine how much to tax themselves for public education.

The problem the property tax creates for society, however, is that low-wealth districts cannot maintain educational programs and services at the level needed by their students to compete for college admission and high-paying jobs. Without this level of education, the community suffers as well. This scenario is not simply an abstract concern but has become a legal issue addressed by state courts and legislatures. School administrators must be aware of actions taken by the courts and legislative bodies in their attempts to prevent and overcome the effects of tax inequities on public education. This topic has a direct bearing on the resources of many school districts and is discussed in chapter 4.

DISCUSSION QUESTIONS

1. Why must school administrators be sensitive to horizontal and vertical tax equity?
   a. When is a tax horizontally inequitable?
   b. When is a tax vertically inequitable?
   c. Explain why the examples you have given are inequitable.
2. Why should school administrators recognize the difference between incidence and impact with respect to taxes?
3. Explain how high-density residential projects might be reviewed by a school district with respect to their impact on tax receipts?
4. Describe the difference between progressive, proportional, and regressive taxes. Give an example of each.

5. What are the strengths and weaknesses of the property tax? If you were conducting a measure of its elasticity, what denominator would you use and why?

6. How can a sales tax reduce its regressive affects?

7. With respect to student fees, how would you implement an ability-to-pay policy?

APPLICATION PROBLEMS

The answers to Problems 1 and 2 are provided after the chapter references.

1. If the elasticity for a state income tax is 1.1 and the average income has increased 5%, what is the percentage increase in tax revenue?
   a. If the school budget of $8 million receives 45% of its budget from the state income tax, what would be the most you could expect with respect to an increase in revenue? Do you think such an expectation is realistic? Why or why not?

2. If a residential property has a value of $250,000 and the assessed value is $50,000, what is the percentage rate used to arrive at the assessed value?
   a. If the tax levy is 80 mills, what is the tax amount to be paid by the property owner?
   b. If the district has issued bonds to construct a new building and the tax levy to cover that sale requires an increase of 10 mills on the property tax, what is the amount of the additional property tax?

3. Compare the current revenue receipts for your state (National Center for Education Statistics, 2002) to those in Table 3.1. Have there been any significant changes? If so, why? If not, should there be any modifications in the distributions? Why or why not?

WEB ADDRESSES

National Council for Accreditation of Teacher Education
http://www.ncate.org

National Center for Education Statistics
http://nces.ed.gov

REFERENCES

Alexander, K., & Salmon, R. (1995). *Public school finance*. Boston: Allyn & Bacon.

Bannock, G., Baxter, R. E., & Davis, E. (1998*). Dictionary of economics* (6th ed.). London: Penguin Group.

Birrup, P. E., Brimley, V., Jr., & Garfield, R. R. (1999). *Financing education: In a climate of change* (7th ed.). Boston: Allyn & Bacon.

Bouman, C. E., & Brown, D. J. (1996). Public school fees as hidden taxation. *Education Administration Quarterly, 32*(Suppl.), 665–685.

Brent, B. O. (2000). The influence of regional nonresidential expanded tax base approaches to school finance on measures of student and taxpayer equity. *Illinois Association of School Business Officials, 12*(2), 37–48.

Guthrie, J. W., Garms, W. I., & Pierce, L. C. (1988). *School finance and educational policy: Enhancing educational efficiency, equality and choice* (2nd ed.). Upper Saddle River, NJ: Merrill/Prentice Hall.

Hack, W. G., Candoli, I. C., Ray, J. R. (1998). *School business administration: A planning approach* (6th ed.). Boston: Allyn & Bacon.

Hylbert, A. (2002). The effects of the property tax extension limitation law upon revenue growth, bonded debt, and school business leader perceptions within selected Illinois school districts. *The Journal of School Business Management, 14*(2), 9–14.

Monk, D. H. (1988). *Educational finance: An economic approach.* New York: McGraw-Hill.

National Center for Education Statistics [Online]. Retrieved June 10, 2002, from http://nces.ed.gov

National Policy Board for Educational Administration (2002). *Standards for advanced programs in educational leadership for principals, superintendents, curriculum directors, and supervisors* [Online]. Retrieved February 17, 2003, from http://www.ncate.org

Odden, A., & Picus, L. O. (2000). *School finance: A policy perspective* (2nd ed.). New York: McGraw-Hill.

Swanson, A. D., & King, R. A. (1997). *School finance: Its economics and politics* (2nd ed.). New York: Longman.

ANSWERS TO APPLICATION PROBLEMS

1. 5.5% increase in tax revenue
   a. $198,000
2. 20%
   a. $4,000
   b. $500

Chapter 4

Financing Educational Equality: Access, Treatment, and Outcomes

Administrators need to have a comprehensive awareness of both the successes in providing an equal public education to children over the past 225 years and the efforts currently being made for enhancing public education opportunities for all children. The purpose of such an awareness is expressed clearly by the National Council for Accreditation of Teacher Education (NCATE) in Standards 3.1 and 3.2 (NPBEA, 2002). These standards propose that school-building and district leaders should consider equity indicators in the decision-making process and apply the legal principles that promote educational equity. Their efforts both influence and are influenced by financial operations.

This chapter presents three stages in the evolution of educational equality. The first stage concerns providing equal access to education for all children. This progresses to the second and third stages: attempts to ensure equal educational treatment and the call for equal educational outcomes, respectively. The first section of this chapter describes each of these stages and how they merged into the current blend of practices that vary from state to state.

Next, a brief overview of the legal actions that caused the evolution of equalization practices and created the mix of practices among the states is presented. The chapter then concludes with a review of three hallmark legal decisions critical to funding equal access, treatment, and outcomes; several considerations related to the assessment of financial equity; and categories of financial support for the equalization of public education.

It is critical for school leaders to recognize the subtle differences in understanding among leaders of the concept that all children receive an equal education. That is, the meaning of *equal education* to one person or state may be different from that of another person or state; however, in some cases the expectation is that all of the definitions apply.

As the definitions and arguments for advancing educational equality are presented in this chapter, the introductory wording of Interstate School Leaders Licensure Consortium (ISLLC, 1996) and NCATE (NPBEA, 2002) standards must be kept in mind. Each ISLLC standard begins with: "A school administrator is an educational leader who promotes the success of all students by. . . ." The NCATE standards, with the exception of 7.0 on internships, state that "Candidates who complete the program are educational leaders who have the knowledge and ability to promote the success of all students by. . . ."

ISLLC

INTRODUCTION TO EDUCATIONAL ACCESS, TREATMENT, AND OUTCOMES

At the time of the founding of the country, education still had strong ties to religious groups and, although most people valued an education, the financing of it was not seen by most as a public responsibility. Thus, a national plan for the education of all children was not included in the U.S. Constitution or in its Bill of Rights.

In the 19th century the popular attitude toward the offering of a public education softened. The principle that children should have equal access to a public education in every community became a more acceptable proposition. Under the access principle, children were offered a basic education, which at that time was the teaching of the three R's; reading, writing, and arithmetic. Because of the shift of education to a local governmental responsibility, the quality of the learning experience was left up to local school officials (Meyer, 1967).

To support equal access to a public education, states provided minimum aid to local school districts for an elementary level of education. This aid was typically determined by the number of children in attendance or by the salaries of the teachers. Today, some form of minimum aid for general financial assistance is still provided by many states.

With the emergence of the public high school in 1821 in Boston, school districts began to extend public education beyond the teaching of the three R's. Then in 1874 the Michigan Supreme Court handed down the famous Kalamazoo decision. Their decision held that taxes could be collected for the support of public high schools. As the movement to offer a free public secondary education gained momentum, the Kalamazoo case was cited by other states. Likewise the public began to realize that access alone was not sufficient and that all children must receive equal educational treatment. For example, some students had access to a high school with science labs, other high school science classes did not have labs, and some communities did not even have a high school. The amount of money required to provide equal treatment caused the financial equity threshold to increase considerably.

Because equal treatment did not generate the expected educational results, eventually the call for educational equality shifted to equal **outcomes**. While equal access and treatment were still important, legal challenges to the financing of public education called for school districts to exhibit that students were achieving a specified level of competence, especially in the basic skills. In other words, changes in school finance policy were tied to educational equality, which was defined in terms of improvements in educational outcomes.

As a consequence of the shift in focus to equal outcomes, school districts became accountable for generating predetermined levels of student accomplishments in the latter part of the 20th century. Of course, the money required for attaining a specified level of student achievement was considerably greater than that needed to ensure equal access or treatment. As a result of the increase in dollars provided to public education, greater financial accountability was demanded.

Currently, the popular expectations are that children will have access to a public education, receive equal treatment, and be provided with an educational experience that will meet the learning needs of each child and ensure the attainment of a specified level of achievement. Although this evolution from access to outcomes has been slow and dependent on a willingness to finance the changing expectations, it is likely that those who argued for a simple federal policy on public education in the 18th century would be amazed at the current practices.

THE STRUGGLE FOR A NATIONAL PUBLIC EDUCATION POLICY

Written in 1787, the Constitution of the United States established a new government in 1789. The Bill of Rights (the first 10 amendments to the Constitution) was passed by the House and Senate in 1789 and ratified by the states in 1791. Neither of these documents provided for a national educational system nor did they provide any authority to the federal government over a public educational system.

The absence of a reference to public education by the new federal government was not because of a lack of interest. Washington, Jefferson, and others argued for a national education system but to no avail. Evidence of strong support for a free public education by some of the early leaders was seen in the Land Ordinance of 1785 passed by the Continental Congress. This act, which was passed before the adoption of the Constitution and the creation of the U.S. Congress, included a requirement that land in the Northwest Territory be set aside for education. If sold, the money from the sale of the land would be used for education, although it was soon evident that more financial support was needed to provide a free education for all of the children in the territory (Rippa, 1988).

The passage of the Northwest Ordinance of 1787 by the Continental Congress continued to encourage support for education. Written by Jefferson, the main thrust of the Northwest Ordinance was to guarantee settlers in the territories the same rights and privileges of the residents in the 13 colonies. The first draft in 1784, written by Jefferson, was not put into effect because Article 6, which prohibited slavery, was rejected by one vote. The second draft, which included Article 6, passed on July 13, 1787 (Wilson, 1987).

Another effort to stimulate political support for public education came in 1795 when the American Philosophical Society ran a contest with a prize for the person with the best proposal for a national education system. Numerous plans by well-known political and educational leaders, such as Benjamin Rush, Noah Webster, Samuel Smith, Samuel Knox, and Du Pont de Nemours (Knox and Rush shared the prize), were prepared that advocated a system of education supported and controlled by the public. Even President Washington called for supporting education for the welfare of the nation in his farewell address in 1796. To the surprise of many political and educational leaders, Congress rejected all of the proposals. Whereas vested religious interests were behind some of the opposition to a free public education, the strongest came from the wealthy, whereby they did not wish to be taxed to educate the children of the poor (Pulliam, 1976; Rippa, 1988).

After Congress rejected proposals for a national policy supporting public education, the subject never surfaced again. Because the Tenth Amendment provides that "The powers not delegated to the United States by the Constitution, nor prohibited by it to the States, are reserved to the States respectively, or to the people," the responsibility for providing the public with educational services was passed on to state governments. In response, at the end of the 18th century, seven of the 16 states mentioned education in their constitutions (Meyer, 1967; Pulliam, 1976).

The state directives, however, were typically vague and the responsibility for providing a public education was passed on to local governments. The local rule, popularly referred to as *home rule,* of education was born by default and not out of ideology. Eventually all states provided a form of public education, although access was limited.

ESTABLISHING A LEGAL FOUNDATION FOR EQUAL ACCESS

As a study of American history shows, the 19th century was tumultuous. With slavery permitted in the original 13 colonies, a free public education could not exist for all children. At the time of Lincoln's first inaugural address, one public complaint was that Article 6 of the Northwest Ordinance of 1787 prohibited slavery in the new territories. On September 22, 1862, Lincoln issued a preliminary Emancipation Proclamation that would become effective on January 1, 1863. Once he signed the Proclamation on January 1st, he declared that slaves in all states would be forever free. This proclamation became the Thirteenth Amendment to the Constitution, was passed by Congress on February 1, 1865, and was ratified December 18, 1866. The elimination of slavery, of course, was an important prerequisite for equal access to a public education for all children.

Although not directly related to equal educational access, two additional amendments to the Constitution after the Civil War were important to the shift in attitudes toward public education. The first was the Fourteenth Amendment, passed by Congress on June 16, 1866, and ratified on July 28, 1868. This amendment provides that "All persons born or naturalized in the United States, and subject to the jurisdiction thereof, are citizens of the United States and of the State wherein they reside." It also prohibits a state from making or enforcing a law that may "deprive any person of life, liberty, or property, without due process of law; nor deny to any person within its jurisdiction the equal protection of the laws." The second amendment added after the Civil War was the Fifteenth Amendment, passed by Congress on February 26, 1869, and ratified on March 30, 1870. This amendment provides that citizens of the United States "shall not be denied or abridged by the United States or by any State" the right to vote "on account of race, color, or previous condition of servitude."

Essentially, these amendments provided for the equal treatment of all people, including the equal educational treatment of children. The Supreme Court decision in *Plessey v. Ferguson* (163 U.S. 537, 16 S.Ct. 1138, 41 L.Ed. 256) in 1896, however, limited this effect for over 50 years. Specifically, this decision permitted schools to be set up for White and non-White children under an *equal-but-separate* rule. Under this directive, the form of educational equality was based on the *equal-access* principle as opposed to equal treatment. As shown in some communities, those who enjoyed political and social power also enjoyed unequal privileges with respect to the availability of public money for education.

Another important amendment, which passed on June 5, 1919, was the Nineteenth Amendment. Ratified on August 26, 1920, it provides that "The right of citizens of the United States to vote shall not be denied or abridged by the United States or by any State on account of sex." Although not addressing education, it did signal that women had equal rights in society, thus broadening the apparent legal right to educational access.

LEGAL ACTIONS TO PROMOTE ACCESS

After a depression and two overwhelming world wars, the country again addressed equal rights via a court decision that dramatically changed public education. In what is known as the 1954 and 1955 Brown cases I and II, the Supreme Court overturned *Plessey v. Ferguson* (*Brown v. Board of Education I*, 347 U.S. 483; *Brown v. Board of Education II*, 349 U.S. 294).

A key point for public education in the Brown decisions was the fundamental, or constitutional, right under the Fourteenth Amendment that prohibits states and their agencies, including school districts, from denying people the equal protection of the law because of their race. The court decision declared that race, like religion and national origin, created a suspect classification. This means that a legal action taken by a government cannot treat a suspect group of people differently unless there is a compelling state interest, which is almost impossible to meet (Valente & Valente, 2001). Therefore, the equal-but-separate rule per *Plessey v. Ferguson* was out, but the ensuing change was slow and distressing (Meyer, 1967).

As a result, in the absence of a compelling state interest to deny equal protection to people of the same race, racial segregation of students and staff became unconstitutional. The *Brown v. Board of Education* decisions opened schoolhouse doors to the integration of students and equal educational access for all people. Further, it set up the legal calls for equal educational treatment in the next decade.

LEGAL ARGUMENTS FOR EQUAL TREATMENT

The legal issue in the 1960s was that equal access was not effective if students did not receive equal treatment. Further, the availability of sufficient financial resources was a prerequisite to equal educational treatment. The legal challenges and court decisions involved complicated legal arguments and the corresponding rationales behind the court decisions were quite complex. The following discussion focuses on the actions connected to education financing. Birrup, Brimley, and Garfield (1999); Coons, Clune, and Sugarman (1970); Guthrie, Garms, and Pierce (1988); Odden and Picus (2000); Swanson and King (1997); and Valente and Valente (2001) offer more detailed information on the legal arguments and rationales for the court decisions.

With respect to financial equity, legal claims were made that some school districts were unable to provide equal educational treatment because of the low property values in the district. Arguments proposed that the low property wealth per pupil, as with religion, national origin, and race, created a suspect classification of students because the government treated them differently. The proposal was that these students had the right to equal protection under the Fourteenth Amendment, as in the Brown decision, and that education was a fundamental right under the federal Constitution.

Consequently, the complaints challenged the use of local property taxes to finance education. The recommendation was that school financing should be fiscally neutral, meaning the quality of a child's education should be based on the wealth of the state and not on the wealth of the child's school district.

Illustration

As an example of the relationship between property wealth and the revenue made available per student, Table 4.1 presents a comparison of three pairs of school districts for the years 2000–2001. Each pair of school districts is located in the same county in New Jersey. An urban district was selected along with a second district adjacent to or in close proximity to the urban district.

The first column in Table 4.1 presents the number of students in each district while the second column represents an estimated market value, referred to as *Equalized Property Value* (EPV). State governments calculate the EPV through the use of the property assessment rates of the school districts. The EPV is then used for the allocation of state aid for equalization.

As shown in Table 4.1, a greater number of students attended the urban districts than the adjacent districts. The third column exhibits the striking difference between the property wealth (EPV) available per child in the urban and the adjacent district (EPV divided by the number of students). The fourth column presents the local tax levy, while the fifth shows the dramatic differences (from $382 to $9,251 per student) in the amount of local tax money made available for each pupil.

TABLE 4.1
Comparison of Property Values and School District Taxes in Select Districts in New Jersey: 2000–2001

	Number of Students	Equalized Property Value (EPV) (millions $)	EPV per Pupil (thousands $)	Local Tax Levy (millions $)	Local Tax Received per Pupil ($)
County #1					
Urban District	47,758	5,922	124	80	1,675
Suburban District	3,459	4,732	1,368	32	9,251
County #2					
Urban District	3,356	349	104	4.9	1,460
Suburban District	1,020	989	970	6.6	6,470
County #3					
Urban District	19,377	872	45	7.4	382
Suburban District	10,720	4,792	447	83.1	7,752

The difference in the educational treatment of students because of property wealth is obvious. Without substantial state aid, equal treatment for students in the low-wealth districts would not be possible.

THREE HALLMARK LEGAL DECISIONS

The initial legal challenges based on the above legal reasonings were not successful. Even so, the court decisions provided invaluable reactions by the judiciary; for example, the courts indicated that it was necessary to establish standards to measure educational need and would not accept equal treatment and outcomes as definitions for educational equality (Guthrie et al., 1988). The following three legal cases resulted in hallmark decisions with respect to school financing.

The first hallmark case filed in California in 1969 was *Serrano v. Priest* [96 Cal. Rptr. 601, 487 P.2d 1241, 5 Cal. 3d. 584 (1971)]. This case eventually went to the California Supreme Court where the justices refused to overturn a lower court decision. The upheld ruling had decided that education was a fundamental interest and, therefore, that the equal protection provisions of the California Constitution and the Fourteenth Amendment were violated through the disparities in property wealth. In the court's opinion, low property wealth per pupil created a suspect classification.

The California court, however, did not disallow using the property tax or require that the same amount of money be spent on each child. At the same time, the court supported the **fiscal neutrality** standard whereby educational expenditures could not be based on the wealth of the child's school district but were to be based instead on the wealth of the state. Although the *Serrano* case was appealed many times, it was upheld and the financing of public education in California was changed.

The second hallmark case, and most important to the nation, was *San Antonio Independent School District v. Rodriquez* [411 U.S. 1 (1973)]. A Texas federal district court first heard this case, which levied the same basic charges as those set forth in the *Serrano* case. The district court held for the plaintiff, and the case was appealed to the U.S. Supreme Court. The Supreme Court's 5–4 decision in March 1973 supported the Texas method of school financing, although it was not complimentary toward the use of the local property tax.

In this precedent-setting case, the justices held that education was not a fundamental right guaranteed by the federal Constitution and that the children in property-poor districts did not create a suspect classification making them eligible for equal protection. The justices held, instead, that the state's system of education funding was reasonable and that protection of the right to home rule was a compelling interest of the state.

The *San Antonio v. Rodriquez* decision, as in the early decisions by those who prepared the Constitution and the Bill of Rights, rejected the suggestion that public education should be a federal responsibility. If the Supreme Court had acted otherwise, all state constitutions would have been affected, and public education would have been changed significantly. However, a larger question to address is whether such a change should be made by the justice system rather than by an amendment to the federal Constitution.

At the time when the *San Antonio v. Rodriquez* case was being handed down, the New Jersey Supreme Court was hearing the *Robinson v. Cahill* [303 A.2d 273 (NJ, 1973)] case. In this case the plaintiffs were also charging that education was a fundamental right and that property wealth created a suspect class. In addition, the plaintiffs charged that the education system violated the state constitution, which required the state to create a "thorough and efficient" system for education.

Because this legal challenge followed the *Rodriquez* case, the New Jersey Supreme Court did not find in favor of the first two charges that education was a fundamental right and that property wealth created a suspect class. The Court, however, held that the school financing system violated the state constitution by not providing a "thorough and efficient" public education.

The New Jersey Court was not complimentary toward the use of the property tax and referred the problem to the state legislature. In response, after considerable pressure, the state legislature passed a state income tax to relieve the property tax burden and restricted the use of the tax revenue to supporting education. The challenge to the state constitution and the corresponding decision rendered by the New Jersey Supreme Court were important actions repeated in other states as well.

FOLLOW-UPS ON THE HALLMARK DECISIONS

Brimley and Garfield (2002) reported that, as of July 2000, the state Supreme Court decisions in response to challenges to state finance systems were as follows: 17 cases won and 10 cases lost by the plaintiffs, 11 cases lost but with further complaints pending or a waiting settlement, and 10 cases not yet decided. With respect to the states involved in the above hallmark decisions, the legal challenges continued.

In 1977 in California the *Serrano v. Priest II* [557 P.2d 929 (Cal. 1977)] case was heard as a result of the *Rodriquez* decision. The California Supreme Court again upheld the state constitution's equal protection guarantee and fiscal neutrality. In 1989 in Texas in *Edgewood Independent School District v. Kirby* [777 S. W.2d 391 (Texas 1989)], the Texas State Supreme Court ruled that the state's system of financing education violated the state constitution and had to be changed.

The Legal Call for Equal Outcomes in New Jersey

From 1985 to 1998 the *Robinson v. Cahill* decision by the New Jersey Supreme Court was challenged via a series of six *Abbott v. Burke* court cases. These challenges were filed on behalf of the children living in 28 (later expanded to 30) low-wealth districts. The cases focused on the inability of these districts (known as the Abbott districts) to offer a thorough and efficient education as a result of the legislature's failure to respond appropriately to the *Robinson v. Cahill* decision.

The major complaint in the *Abbott v. Burke* cases was that the efforts to provide equal financial treatment did not ensure a thorough education as promised by the state constitution. The eventual response came on May 1, 1996, when the New Jersey State Board of Education defined a *thorough* education by setting forth 56 Core Curriculum Content Standards in seven subject areas and five Cross-Content Workplace Readiness Standards. In addition, achievement outcomes for the standards were set for students at the end of their 4th, 8th, and 11th grades. To finance this curriculum and prepare the students in the Abbott districts for the achievement tests, the vast majority of the state income tax was allotted to those districts. (Note that the three urban districts presented in Table 4.1 are Abbott districts.) Considerable financial aid is provided to these districts, whereas two of the adjacent districts did not receive any support and one was provided minimal aide.

Of course, the non-Abbott school districts in New Jersey had to offer a thorough and efficient education as ordered by the judiciary and defined by the State Board of Education. As a result, they also had to meet the curriculum and achievement expectations set forth for the 30 property-poor districts. These changes to the curriculums have caused the non-Abbott districts to incur ongoing, additional financial costs with limited or no assistance from the state.

Thus, in a short period of time, property taxes in New Jersey became the highest in the nation, and calls for tax reform have been made. Most important, the New Jersey case has attempted to achieve the idealist aspiration of equalizing educational outcomes for all children. The success of the efforts in New Jersey and in other states attempting to overcome the effects of generations of educational neglect will not be known for some time.

HORIZONTAL AND VERTICAL EQUITY

To support the evolution of educational equalization from access to treatment to outcomes, federal and state governments in more recent years have provided financial assistance to school districts. In many cases, these financial awards have aimed to maintain horizontal and vertical equity. Similar to horizontal tax equalization, horizontal educational equity regards the treatment of equals, equally, while vertical equity represents the treatment of unequals, unequally.

With horizontal equity, efforts are made to present students with the same abilities the same educational treatment. Likewise, vertical equity attempts to equalize treatment; however, the focus is on students with unequal needs—for example, students with physical, intellectual, and emotional disabilities require unequal treatment. Obviously, efforts to establish a method of financing vertical equity for children are more difficult than those needed for horizontal equity.

To examine the unequal needs of students as well as the **effectiveness** of the programs intended to provide equitable treatment, numerous statistical measures have been developed and applied. These measures, which are usually conducted by federal and state officials as well as by independent researchers, vary from a simple comparison of the range of support (highest to the lowest expenditure per pupil) to correlations, regressions, and multivariate analyses. While the more complex assessments may not be relevant to local school administrators, horizontal and vertical comparisons within a district as well as with neighboring school districts should be conducted. For example, the average mean and median expenditures of programs in a district along with the range of expenditures for all similar programs can quickly reveal unusual differences. These findings can then be compared to the expenditures of other districts.

DEVELOPMENT OF FEDERAL FINANCIAL SUPPORT FOR EDUCATION

Federal money supporting educational programs in public schools was first made available through the Smith-Hughes Act of 1917. This act offered financial support to public school districts if they added vocational programs in agriculture, home economics, and trade and industrial education. Because public education was solely controlled by state governments, this act was extremely controversial but successful beyond the expectations of many political and educational leaders. The Smith-Hughes Act was continued and broadened through amendments and supplemental acts, but, more important, it demonstrated how the federal government could influence public education through the infusion of federal dollars.

In the first half of the 20th century, in spite of the success of the Smith-Hughes Act, the federal government limited its financial assistance to educational support programs such as school lunches, youth unemployment, and school construction. In the 1950s and early 1960s the federal government expanded its support programs through a variety of acts, including providing educational assistance to unemployed adults, to economically underdeveloped areas, for science and math development (the National Defense Education Act passed upon the successful launching of the Soviet Union's satellite, Sputnik), and so on.

In 1963 Congress again took direct action to influence local education by passing the Vocational Education Act. This act expanded vocational programs and provided money for the construction of vocational schools. Its purpose was to answer the need for additional educational opportunities in job preparation for the large number of children born after World War II and entering high school in the 1960s (referred to as "baby boomers"). The Vocational Education Act also extended the Smith-Hughes Act and continued into the 21st century through new legislation.

On the heels of the Vocational Education Act, Congress passed the Elementary and Secondary Education Act of 1965, and public schools entered a new era with respect to their relationship with the federal government. This legislation, which has also continued into the 21st century, provided money to states for horizontal and vertical equity through programs targeting financially disadvantaged children, compensatory education, technology for children, bilingual education, and many others.

Another major education act that came 10 years later was for special education. Passed in 1975, the Handicapped Children Act P.L. 94–142 addressed vertical equity by providing money so that appropriate educational programs would be made available to all children regardless of their disability. This support was continued through the Individuals with Disabilities Education Act (IDEA).

In sum, in 1963 the federal government changed its position on providing support for public education at the local level. Since then a number of legislative actions have provided money to states for local schools. While federal money supplied to local school districts represents a small percentage of their total revenue, as discussed in chapter 3, an award may represent the greater share of the money spent by a program; for instance, for a specific disability or educational need.

CATEGORIES OF STATE AND FEDERAL FINANCIAL AID

With the call for educational outcomes and financial equity, state aid packages became more and more sophisticated. Coupled with federal financial assistance, the multiple sources of revenues to school districts evolved into a complex array of programs with different, constantly changing rules and expectations. Thus, administrators must maintain currency by monitoring the federal and state aid programs. Changes in federal support for a program may be signaled by a shift in national priority and policy. For example, the promotion/demotion of program leadership or program assignment in the organizational hierarchy as well as changes in legislative directives often suggest a shift in spending.

One method of tracking and evaluating changes in the programs offering financial assistance is to separate them into unrestricted and restricted grant categories. Because each has a set of advantages and disadvantages, the potential assistance offered by a program must be related to the needs and programs in the school district.

Taking a "shotgun" approach and applying for anything that is available is discouraged. A grant that does not correspond to the needs of the district will likely create problems if it requires the use of district personnel and assets, such as physical space, and does not support the district's mission and goals. For example, the financial needs of a school district where 65% of the graduates attend college is likely different from a district where 25% of the students do not graduate.

Unrestricted Grants

Unrestricted grants allow the school district discretion on how to spend the money. Flat grants, which may be referred to as minimum aid grants, and some foundation awards are an example of unrestricted grants that are intended to support horizontal equity. Flat grants, or minimum aid grants, are basic financial awards intended to support equal access. These awards are usually based on the number of children or schools in a district. Foundation aid is used to promote equal treatment and outcomes. The amounts of these awards, therefore, are more likely based on district wealth.

The intent of addressing horizontal equity through the use of unrestricted grants is hindered when wealthy school districts spend more than low-wealth districts after receiving the state grant. Thus, hypothetically, the low-wealth districts can never attain equal treatment. The argument, however, is that under the home rule, a local board of education has the right to spend as much as the taxpayers permit.

Another problem with home rule rights occurs because school districts likely have the authority to use unrestricted aid as they wish. Thus, they may use the money to supplant, not supplement, local revenue receipts to reduce the local tax levy. Although a number of formulas have been developed by leaders of education finance to prohibit this practice, the cooperation of the school board is needed for them to work successfully (for a presentation of these formulas, see Brimley & Garfield, 2002; Guthrie et al., 1988; Odden & Picus, 2000; Swanson & King, 1997).

Restricted Grants

Financial awards that specify how the money must be spent are considered restricted grants. The Generally Accepted Accounting Principles (GAAP) requires that restricted financial awards be maintained in separate accounts by the accounting system to ensure that compliance can be verified by an audit.

Restricted grants are often awarded for the support of vertical equity; for example, for special education, bilingual education, or compensatory education. In these cases the students or programs are identified, and then a formula is applied to determine the amount of revenue awarded. Other restricted money may be received for special programs being promoted by the state or federal government (such as for vocational and adult education). In all cases, the money received by a district is restricted to the conditions of the award and compliance must be demonstrated by the school districts.

SEAs AND LEAs

When federal money, on its way to being spent at the local level, is first provided to a state education agency (SEA), the state office may retain a percentage to cover their administrative costs. The balance of the award is then passed on to the local education agency (LEA), which may be a school district, university, or other public agency not under the direct governance of the state. In turn, an LEA may be permitted to contract with either nonprofit organizations or companies for goods and services (such as food services or building maintenance contracts).

Therefore, federal support may be referred to as "pass through money," meaning a state office applies for the money and the financial award passes through the state to the LEAs. Further, the state office reports how the money was spent to the federal agency. In some states, the federal money may first go from a state office to a municipal, county, or regional office before it passes on to a school district. Since the money from these financial awards is typically received in incremental amounts, a school district administrator must monitor the receipts and expenditures to ensure the account maintains a positive cash balance.

FINAL THOUGHTS

Educational and financial equity have changed significantly over the years. The window of opportunity to continue improving educational opportunities and performances for the success of all children is likely more open now than ever before. A concern, however, is that some of the research efforts, which are discussed in chapter 12, are finding that the infusion of money is not resulting in equal outcomes. The challenge for school leaders, therefore, is to analyze the results of the research and provide a vision for the continuing improvement of public education along with plans to move it forward. Such plans must take into account past experiences with the variety of federal and state programs available to gain further improvements in performances.

Further, because financial support offered through federal and state programs changes from time to time, the long-range planning process must also prepare for change. To accomplish this, strategic financial plans should include contingency plans; for example, plans for decreases in restricted and unrestricted grant allocations, the passing or increased use of school vouchers, the creation of new charter schools, the privatization of public school services, increased or decreased costs for support services and activities, and so on. The next chapter describes the development of strategic financial plans.

DISCUSSION QUESTIONS

1. This chapter notes the political and legal actions that were important to the evolution of educational equality and financial equity. What do you consider to be the most significant changes in the 18th, 19th, and 20th centuries? Why?
   a. How might the advancement of education been hastened in these centuries?

2. What changes could be made in the 21st century to continue the advancement of public education?

   a. Is the call for equal educational outcomes realistic? Why or why not?

   b. What should be the objectives of the prespecified achievement levels (for example, to exhibit a basic understanding of the subject, gaining a job, college admission)?

3. This chapter presents two categories for evaluating the different types of financial aid provided by the federal and state governments.

   a. How would you explain to a taxpayer the purpose of these categories and the reason for your failure to apply for a grant?

   b. Do you believe school districts should or should not be permitted to use foundation awards to supplant the revenues collected from the local property tax? Why?

   c. To ensure horizontal equity, should wealthy school districts be limited in the amount of money they may spend on education? Why or why not?

4. Some public officials are calling for the privatization of public school services, for school vouchers, and for the creation of charter schools.

   a. Do you believe these changes will affect educational and financial equity? Why or why not?

APPLICATION PROBLEMS

1. You are a special assistant to the superintendent and have been asked to examine the district's standing with respect to horizontal and vertical equity. What information would you collect to make the horizontal and vertical assessments and how would you use this data in a report?

WEB ADDRESSES

National Council for Accreditation of Teacher Education
http://www.ncate.org

REFERENCES

Birrup, P. E., Brimley, V., Jr., & Garfield, R. R. (1999). *Financing education: In a climate of change* (7th ed.). Boston: Allyn & Bacon.

Brimley, V., Jr., & Garfield, R. R. (2002). *Financing education: In a climate of change.* (8th ed.). Boston: Allyn & Bacon.

Brown v. Board of Education I, 347 U.S. 483 (1954).

Brown v. Board of Education II, 349 U.S. 294 (1955).

Coons, J., Clune, W., & Sugarman, S. (1970). *Private wealth and public education*. Cambridge, MA: Belknap Press of Harvard University.

Edgewood Independent School District v. Kirby, 777 S. W.2d 391 (Texas 1989).

Guthrie, J. W., Garms, W. I., & Pierce, L. C. (1988). *School finance and educational policy: Enhancing educational efficiency, equality and choice* (2nd ed.). Upper Saddle River, NJ: Merrill/Prentice Hall.

Interstate School Leaders Licensure Consortium (1996). *Standards for school leaders*. Washington, DC: Council of Chief State School Officers.

Meyer, A. E. (1967). *An educational history of the American people* (2nd ed.). New York: McGraw-Hill.

National Policy Board for Educational Administration (2002). *Standards for advanced programs in educational leadership for principals, superintendents, curriculum directors, and supervisors* [Online]. Retrieved February 17, 2003, http://www.ncate.org

Odden, A., & Picus, L. O. (2000). *School finance: A policy perspective* (2nd ed.). New York: McGraw-Hill.

Plessey v. Ferguson, 163 U.S. 537 (1896).

Pulliam, J. D. (1976). *History of education in America* (2nd ed.). Upper Saddle River, NJ: Merrill/Prentice Hall.

Rippa, S. A. (1988). *Education in a free society* (4th ed.). New York: Longman.

Robinson v. Cahill, 303 A.2d 273 NJ (1973).

San Antonio Independent School District v. Rodriquez, 411 U.S. 1 (1973).

Serrano v. Priest I, 96 Cal. Rptr. 601, 487 P.2d 1241, 5 Cal. 3d. 584 (1971).

Serrano v. Priest II, 557 P.2d 929 (California 1977).

Swanson, A. D., & King, R. A. (1997). *School finance: Its economics and politics* (2nd ed.). New York: Longman.

Valente, W. D., & Valente, C. M. (2001). *Law in the schools* (5th ed.). Upper Saddle River, NJ: Merrill/Prentice Hall.

Wilson, V., Jr. (Ed.). (1987). *The book of great American documents*. Brookeville, MD: American History Research Associates.

Part 2

Constructing a Strategic Financial Plan

Chapter 5

The Components of a Strategic Financial Plan

This chapter describes a strategic financial plan and how it is prepared. When considering constructing a strategic financial plan, several basic principles should be understood. The first, as Woodard (2001) explains, is that "the strategy of an organization provides key information about why it exists, what it does and will continue to do, and the image it intends to have in the future" (p. 37). In public school districts, this information is found in their **mission statements** (why it exists), **goals** (vision for the future), and objectives (what it will do).

Using these sources, school administrators must be able to assemble a strategic financial plan for meeting the expectations of the Interstate School Leaders Licensure Consortium (ISLLC, 1996) and the National Council for Accreditation of Teacher Education (NCATE; NPBEA, 2002b). Specifically, the first standard of ISLLC calls for administrators to be able to develop plans "in which objectives and strategies to achieve the vision and goals are clearly defined" (p. 11). At the same time, Standard 3.2 of NCATE proposes that future building and district administrators must acquire a "knowledge of strategic, long-range and operational planning" (p. 8).

ISLLC

A second principle is that the strategic financial plan must include a budget. This is also expected by NCATE (NPBEA, 2002b), which suggests that candidates be able to "identify how specific budget allocations support the school improvement plan/district strategic plan" (p. 9). This requires comprehension of the budgeting process imbedded within a strategic financial plan.

In addition, school leaders must be aware of the political significance of budgets and past budgeting practices. For example, as explained in this chapter, the use of budgets by a government has a distinguished history. The initial rationale for the creation of the first public budget in 1215 was to establish a process in which the taxpayers authorize tax assessments. Currently, as per this tradition, when an elected board or the public approves a school district's budget, they authorize the levy of a tax. As a consequence, deviations from an approved budget require the action of either the individuals who voted for it or their representatives.

The third principle is that strategic financial plans must be prepared for all site-based programs and services, preferably with stakeholders at the operational level. Their plans should present what the unit will accomplish in measurable outcomes and outputs and include a schedule for periodic benchmark reviews. As a consequence, the determination of the success or failure of a plan should not wait until after the school year has ended but administrators and stakeholders should check them periodically throughout the fiscal year.

A strategic financial plan can be compared to preparing for a long automobile trip from New York to Florida. In planning such a trip, travelers must know where they wish to go in Florida and then look up the routes they must take to get there. They should break the trip down into the number of days they have to travel, how many miles they can realistically cover in a day, alternative routes, and the estimated cost for each alternative. If a travel plan is not prepared or if one is not monitored during the trip, the traveler could end up in Iowa instead of Florida. Some school districts metaphorically end up in "Iowa instead of Florida" at the end of the fiscal year and do not know why!

PREPARATION OF A SCHOOL DISTRICT'S STRATEGIC FINANCIAL PLAN

The preparation of a strategic financial plan for a school district requires the development of a series of policies, statements, and plans that are linked together as shown in Figure 5.1. The basis for the district plan begins with the district's mission, continues with the goals that support the mission, and follows with objectives that are aligned with the goals.

As exhibited in Figure 5.1, the district's mission, goals, and objectives build to define the programs, services, and activities it will offer. These programs, services, and activities are the site-based units that, in turn, must prepare their own goals and objectives. Each unit objective should have performance targets, which are stated in terms of outcomes and outputs.

As a result, site-based units develop a strategic plan to explain how the targets will be met. By including a budget that presents the anticipated costs of achieving the outcomes and outputs, the strategic plan is expanded into a strategic financial plan, as shown in Figure 5.1. After a team prepares and approves a plan, it is forwarded to the appropriate administrators who must approve it. The site-based plans are then consolidated for the school board.

The process for preparing a strategic financial plan for a school district is presented in Figure 5.2. By referring to the school district's mission, goals, and objectives, the site-based units in the district prepare their own goals, objectives, and targets. When this occurs, the goals and objectives for the site-based units become subordinate to the district policies and an organizational strategic theme is created.

In turn, as shown in Figure 5.2, the goals, objectives, and targets of a site-based unit lead to the development of a strategic financial plan for the unit. The units' plans are then consolidated to create a strategic financial plan for the whole

FIGURE 5.1
**Sequence of Statements
for a Strategic Financial Plan**

FIGURE 5.2
**Process for Preparing
Strategic Financial
Plans**

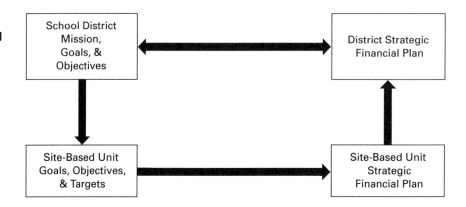

school district. Therefore, the district's strategic financial plan should offer by default the evidence that it yields to the district's mission, goals, and objectives as also shown in Figure 5.2.

Mission

According to Eadie (1989, p. 166), the mission of a government body is "its reason for being," "establishes the legitimate boundaries of organizational activity," distinguishes one government from another, and gives it a purpose. At the same time, Houle (1989, p. 147) sees the mission as "the primary force" that holds a government body together. The mission is the highest level of policy for a school district.

In his 14 principles that became the basis for Total Quality Management (TQM), the first point made by W. Edwards Deming (1986) was that businesses and organizations must create a constancy of purpose to improve their products and services. The mission of a school district sets the initial definition for this constancy of purpose. When administrators, teachers, and other employees are not sure about the purpose, or mission, of the district or if it keeps shifting, their performances and results will likely not be consistent or exhibit any improvement, and they may even fail to meet expectations.

Therefore, when preparing or reviewing mission statements, leaders in a school district have to begin with its "reason for being" or purpose. In most states a district's primary reason for being comes from the state constitution and/or legislative action. For example, as discussed in chapter 4, the New Jersey Constitution requires school districts to offer a "thorough and efficient" education to all children. Such a directive presents a school district with a legal, constitutional mission statement that can then be supplemented by the school board. For example, in addition to a constitutional or state legislative directive, a school district may have mission statements declaring that it will: (a) prepare citizens who are able to participate in a democratic form of government; (b) enable students to become productive members of society; and (c) guarantee a healthy school environment that supports each student's social, physical, and emotional development.

A set of clear mission statements should serve as a guide for the leaders and decision makers in the school district and, more important, ensure continuity from year to year. For example, when a school district (or federal or state education agency) is requested to consider a new endeavor, the first question to ask is whether or not it falls within the mission of the school district (or public education). If it does not, then either the request must be denied or the mission must be revised.

This approach to examining the requests to offer new programs, services, and activities prevents school districts (and government agencies) from taking on inappropriate or "trendy" endeavors at the expense of existing ones. In addition, it protects districts from exceeding their financial limits. This is not to suggest that change be inhibited but rather that a procedure be followed to protect students and the public who depend on existing services. When a proposed endeavor does not fall within the mission of the district and is implemented anyway, the district will not enjoy the benefits derived from having a constancy of purpose.

Goals

The goals of a school district and those of the programs and services offered by the district must support a mission statement, be stated in ideal terms, and be future oriented or visionary. A classic definition offered by Etzioni (1964, p. 6) is that goals should express "a desired state of affairs that the organization attempts to realize." A weakness often observed in many organizations is the existence of an excellent goal that has no relevance to the mission of the organization. Without such a connection, the goal has no basis.

Objectives

Objectives are written for goals and should be *action oriented.* While goals are ideal and future oriented, objectives must be realistic and attainable. When objectives are being met, their visionary goals are becoming a reality.

Because objectives are accomplished through programs and services, they should provide information sufficient for identifying and developing such programs and services. For example, in response to a goal to assist all students regardless of personal abilities, an objective would be to offer the special support programs and services required to meet the needs of all students.

The establishment of objectives should be sensitive to the observations made by Reich (1992) in his discussion of high-volume and high-value enterprises. In high-volume enterprises the intent is to mass-produce goods and services. He explains that these enterprises are being replaced by high-value enterprises, where services are tailored to meet the particular needs of people and businesses. Likewise, a school district should attempt to ensure that programs and services defined by their educational objectives be oriented to the individual needs of their students and not the mass production of instruction.

Programs, Services, and Activities

Programs and services are justified by the school district's objectives and delivered through site-based activity units. Each program or service should have its own set of goals (ideal and visionary) with supporting objectives (action oriented). The objectives of a program or service should then be consulted to determine the personnel needed and what each will accomplish. These accomplishments must be identified in advance and used to set benchmark and end-of-year targets to be met by the program or service.

Program Targets: Outcomes and Outputs

Walker (1999) explains, "the measure of performance is not compliance with the rules and procedures, but the achievement of real results. Results (or outcomes) are not to be confused with mere **outputs**. Outputs give us a sense of how much work has been done, but results give us an indication of the real effects of the work" (p. 9).

The proposed outcomes and outputs for a program or service are their targets. Outcome targets are effectiveness measures that focus on *qualitative* ends, such as student achievement on a standardized test. Many outcome measures will not be evident until after an extended period of time. Therefore, the time period must be long enough to exhibit the effects of the treatment or service but not so long that remedial changes cannot be made.

As a result, the school year should be divided into time periods, or benchmark periods, with proposed outcome targets to be attained by the end of each period. When benchmark targets are set and checked, the expectations of the first standard of the ISLLC (1996) may be attained. Under this standard, administrators are to ensure their school's "vision, mission, and implementation plans are regularly monitored, evaluated and revised" (p. 11).

ISLLC

Output targets regard *quantitative* ends and are referenced for efficiency measures, such as how many hours of instruction were offered. Efficiency measures do not question if an hour of instruction is good or bad, just how many hours were offered. The output measures should also be given benchmark targets to be checked periodically. For example, attendance must be taken on a daily basis and attendance benchmarks should be set for weekly, monthly, grading period, and annual reports. If attendance is falling below the target level, the administrators should seek out the cause.

Proposed outcomes (e.g., student achievement) and outputs (e.g., number of hours of instruction) must correspond to a program's objectives as well as to the legal expectations of government. At the same time, the targets proposed for a program and service offered by a school district must be sensitive to the difference between a high-volume mass-production enterprise and a high-value enterprise that seeks to meet the individual needs of people, as suggested by Reich (1992).

When clearly stated outcomes and outputs exist, direct supervision of programs or services should not be critical to their success. Rather, the monitoring and support of programs and services can be conducted on the basis of reports, both written and verbal, with supporting documentation. In addition, administrators should use budget reports and outcome and output data to conduct a number of cost–benefit analyses, which corresponds to a suggested exercise at the end of Standard 3 of NCATE (NPBEA, 2002b). For example, a **cost-effectiveness** measure might examine the cost of attaining a program's outcome (benefit) while a **cost-efficiency** measure might calculate the cost of the work output (benefit) delivered by the program. Comparing the results generated from these analyses across programs, time periods, and the proposed costs in the strategic financial plan should be revealing and may suggest a need for budget revisions.

Finally, setting outcome and output targets at the time the budget is presented for approval allows the school board and the public to react to them. If the public or members of the board expect other results, this can be discussed and defended or adjusted at the beginning of the year. When proposed outcome and output targets are not identified, at the end of the year anyone can argue that the outcomes and outputs are not good enough. If this occurs, school administrators and teachers can only defend themselves or offer excuses. When effectiveness and efficiency targets are set, approved, and achieved, teachers will be protected from people who are dissatisfied with their performance.

THE CREATION OF GOVERNMENT BUDGET POLICY

Too often budgets are perceived as an unnecessary evil and are not recognized for the important role they play in a free republic. This is unfortunate because it has taken centuries for the publicly approved budget to gain credibility with those in power and challenges to its noble purpose continue, likely from those who do not comprehend its significance.

ISLLC

In fact, when administrators must defend their budgeting process to those within as well as outside their school district, they may find it quite helpful to call on the historical reasons for its being. This corresponds to the ISLLC's (1996) call for administrators to have a knowledge and understanding of the "principles and issues relating to fiscal operations of school management" (p. 14). In addition, they continue that administrators are to facilitate processes and engage in "activities ensuring that fiscal resources of the school are managed responsibly, efficiently, and effectively" (p. 15). In other words, while a familiarity of budget mechanics is suitable for staff managers, this will not suffice for school leaders who must be attentive to the management, effectiveness, efficiency, and political responsibilities associated with the financial operations of the school district.

The Origin of Public Budgets

A budget was first demanded in 1215 in England under Article 12 of the Magna Carta. The purpose was to provide the governed with a means to control the amount of taxes they had to pay King John. To accomplish this, Article 12 placed constraints on King John's right to tax nobility by requiring him to obtain approval from his barons before he could levy taxes on them (Chatfield, 1974).

King John's more immediate successors respected Article 12; however, King John did not. It was then largely ignored over the 16th and 17th centuries. In 1689 Parliament recalled the 12th Article to gain public support for the English Bill of Rights. In the 18th century, the budget policy in England required the chancellor of the exchequer to present to Parliament the expenditures for the previous year and an estimate of expenditures for the coming year. This report led to the tax levied by the Parliament (Chatfield, 1974).

Budgets and the Constitution

Alexander Hamilton, who was the first secretary of the U.S. Treasury and an admirer of the English form of government, presented the first budget to Congress for approval in 1789 in the same manner as his English counterpart, the chancellor of the exchequer. Consequently, Hamilton set the precedent that led to current practices (Chatfield, 1974).

When the framers of the U.S. Constitution provided for a republic with a representative form of government at the federal level, they stipulated in Article I, Section 9.7, that "no money shall be drawn from the treasury, but in consequence of appropriations made by law." An **appropriation** is an act by federal government officials or the public to allocate a sum of public money for a specific use. The appropriation is typically presented in a budget format, preferably with a narrative that shows the amounts to be spent by general budget categories or expenditure classifications. Upon final approval, the government may impose a tax levy to collect the money needed by the appropriation. Thus, when elected officials, or the public, pass a budget appropriation, it is law.

Article I, Section 9.7, of the Constitution continues, as per English tradition, that "a regular statement of the account of receipts and expenditures of all public money shall be published from time to time." In other words, as in Article 12 of the Magna Carta, the public has a right to know how much money has been collected, spent, and remains.

The connection between the appropriation and reporting directives of the Constitution and the individual states is made through Article IV, Section 4, which holds that every state shall be guaranteed a republican form of government. In a republic, the power is vested in the people through either a public vote or a vote of their elected representatives. The Constitution, however, does not set forth any specific financial or budget rules for state and local governments to follow. States still have the right to fashion their own rules but under the terms of a republican form of government.

Currently, in the spirit of the republican form of government, state and local governments have budget policies. Typically, the procedure for these policies requires a report of receipts and expenditures for the previous year, the approved budget for the current year, an estimate of expenditures for the coming year, and a recommended tax levy. The proposed budget is presented to the voters or their legally elected representatives for approval. This common policy evolved independently of a specific national directive but according to the principles set forth in Article 12 of the Magna Carta. In 1994 the Governmental Accounting Standards Board (GASB) issued Concepts Statement No. 2 proposing that state and local governments include nonfinancial reports with their annual financial statements so the public can assess their effectiveness and efficiency.

METHODS OF BUDGETING

Because a set of national standards for budgeting was not developed, a variety of methods evolved over the years. These budget methods are categorized into three basic groups: **line-item budgeting**, **program budgeting**, and **performance budgeting** (Garner, 1991). Within program budgeting two popular practices that have been used are the **Planned Program Budgeting System (PPBS)** and **Zero-Based Budgeting (ZBB)**.

In recent years a budgeting process has evolved that uses elements from all three of the above methods, including PPBS and ZBB. This process, which is described in this book as **strategic budgeting**, is used by many school districts and is a vital part of a strategic financial plan. To fully grasp the elements of this budgeting method, the advantages it offers, and the weaknesses it avoids, an operational knowledge of each of the three basic methods as well as PPBS and ZBB is necessary.

Line-Item Budgeting

The line-item budget, which may be referred to as an object-of-expenditure budget, is the oldest of the budgeting methods. In the traditional format, estimated expenditures are itemized by budget category; however, the purpose of the expenditures is not provided (Hartman, 1988). The object-of-expenditure format lists expenditures by a budget object name but, again, does not address purpose (Cope, 1989).

In its simplest form, the line-item budget proposal requests a percentage increase to the total amount budgeted in the current fiscal year. Salary increases would receive a percentage of the increase with the balance to be spread over the remaining budget categories. In some cases, the amount remaining after the salary allocations are made may be divided equally among the expenditure categories, although an administrator may be permitted to assign money to categories unequally.

In her research in the 1980s, Cope (1986) found that one-third of the local governments used the line-item method while another 43% used this budgeting method with other supporting information. Cope (1989) believed the use of the line-item method seemed to be growing and attributed this to the creation of computer spreadsheet programs. The suspicion is that a large number of school districts still use this method with little or no supporting information to justify a proposed budget.

The major reason for the popularity of the line-item budget is that it is control oriented. This means that a school board can approve specific expenditure amounts per budget category and check to see if they were spent as intended. If a budget change is needed, a board can transfer an amount from one category to another and then confirm that it was made and spent as directed. Because of this control feature, the line-item budget format is used in the strategic budget method.

Program Budgeting, PPBS, and ZBB

In the program budgeting method, program objectives are set, and then managers develop a plan and a line-item budget to achieve them. The PPBS method uses a systems approach that requires a review of the plans, objectives, and budgets periodically and annually. Effectiveness and/or efficiency evaluations, therefore, apply to the achievement of a program's objectives not to specific target performances.

An organization using a program budget method may require the development of several program plans with objectives and budgets. In these cases, managers at different levels in the hierarchy review the proposals. Higher ranking officials then decide which programs or combination of programs to fund or recommend to elected officials, such as the school board, for funding.

The program budgeting method known as the Planning, Programming, Budgeting System (PPBS) was preceded by Planned Program Budgeting, which was also known as Planning, Programming and Budgeting (PPB). The first effort to implement a form of the PPBS method was by the U.S. Air Force in the 1950s. Later, in 1961, Secretary of Defense Robert McNamara brought PPBS into the federal government for implementation in 1963 by Charles Hitch, assistant secretary of defense (Merewitz & Sosnick, 1971). In August 1965, President Johnson formally announced the introduction of PPBS into all levels of the federal government and on October 12, 1965, Bulletin 66-3 was sent to the heads of the federal executive departments for the implementation of PPBS (Knezevich, 1973). In his book, *The Essence of Security,* McNamara (1968, p. 95) claimed that the new planning system allowed the Department of Defense "to achieve a true unification of effort. . . ."

Then, in June 1971, according to Merewitz and Sosnick (1971, p. 301), "the U.S. government quietly abandoned its compulsive version of PPB." In September 1971, Knezevich (1973, p. 15) explains that the Director of OMB, George P. Schultz, "called for a significant revision in many of the components of PPB."

Several reasons have been given for the rapid decline in the popularity of PPBS. Matkin (1985, p. 12) believes the method was too expensive, that it "increased dissension and discord between program staffs," and that staffs saw "each other as rivals for the same pot of money." Chatfield (1974) suggests that it was due to misuse and misunderstanding, and unless someone like McNamara was behind it, it will not work. At the same time, Freeman and Shoulders (1996) recognize difficulties with presenting clear goals and objectives that everyone agrees on, creating an adequate database, having a staff with a high level of technical ability, developing objective measures of performance, and threatening power bases created by those holding the purse strings.

ZBB, or Zero-Based Budgeting, is the other well-known program budgeting method. The creation of this method began in 1962 in the U.S. Department of Agriculture and was implemented in 1964. In 1977 ZBB was brought on a large scale into the federal government by President Carter and then put out of use when President Reagan took office (Cope, 1989; Knezevich, 1973).

Briefly stated, with the ZBB process, every budget in an organization starts at zero each year. All existing programs plus any proposed new programs must be approved for the coming fiscal year. The manager of a decision unit, such as a site-based unit in a school district, prepares a proposal for existing and new programs. Each proposal must have a set of alternatives with budgets, and the manager, or administrator, must rank or describe them in terms of their efficiency. The proposals, which are called decision packages, are processed up through the organizational structure. As the proposals are reviewed at each level, they are ranked according to an efficiency- or priority-rating scale. The proposals and recommendations, or a summary of the recommendations, are then taken to the highest level in the organization (Garner, 1991). A selection of the decision packages is made and a final budget proposal is prepared for the decision makers, such as the school board.

The ZBB process requires that all programs be reviewed and justified each year. If a program cannot be satisfactorily justified, or justified at the existing level of funding, then the program should be discontinued or have its budget reduced. This competition for financial support is intended to encourage managers to seek out less expensive alternatives for a program and to create new programs or products for funding (Garner, 1991). Realistically, however, a proposal that advocates adding new services and, through budget default, eliminating old services may not be practical for school districts. For example, a school district could not eliminate high school science programs with laboratories to implement a less costly science appreciation program without labs.

Because of the practical realities, some finance experts suggest that ZBB be perceived more as an attitude than as a formula. Correspondingly, Welsch, Hilton, and Gordon (1988) observed that organizations using ZBB do not start with a zero balance but at a percentage of the current budget. For example, all operating units in an organization would be given at least 70% of the current budget and then 30% or more would have to be justified through the ZBB process. Freeman and Shoulders (1996) suggest the ZBB process be used periodically not annually in an effort to review the level at which the services should be offered.

Performance Budgeting

Performance budgeting uses the line-item method for presenting a financial request with a list or description of proposed accomplishments, preferably stated in measurable terms. Thus, when a board approves a performance budget, a corresponding set of accomplishments for the school district's programs, activities, and services are set forth.

The proposed performances along with the line-item budget permit periodic evaluations. In the past, the time and cost of generating the necessary data to conduct these periodic analyses were major obstacles. Because of recent advances in accounting and budgeting systems, computer software programs, and computer storage capacity, however, the applications of performance budgeting have moved to new levels of sophistication.

Strategic Budgeting

The basic practices, as well as differences, among the above budgeting methods are: (a) the line-item budget is control oriented; (b) PPBS sets the organization's goals, objectives, and budgets at the top, whereas performance budgets and ZBB build from the bottom; (c) PPBS is a system that provides for feedback; and (d) performance budgets set objectives with proposed performance accomplishments. In comparison, the budget for a strategic financial plan: (a) uses the line-item budget for control purposes; (b) requires site-based units to set goals, objectives, and performance targets that are compatible with the district's mission, goals, and objectives; (c) builds the school district budget from the bottom via site-based budget plans; and (d) requires systematic feedback for the evaluation of current plans, targets, and budgets and the preparation of new plans and budgets.

To present a budget proposal with a strategic plan, a line-item budget format with expenditure categories (such as salaries, supplies, and other items appropriate to the unit, as shown in Figure 5.3) is used. This requires site-based teams and administrators to present proposed expenditure amounts by budget category. When preparing proposals, the site-based unit teams should be able to refer to the expenditure allocations for the current year plus the expenditures at the end of

Budget Category	Expenditures for Previous Year	Budget for Current Year	Proposed Budget for Next Year
Salaries for Teachers			
Other Salaries for Instruction			
General Supplies			
Library/Media Supplies			
Textbooks			
Travel			
Communication			
Equipment Repairs			
Miscellaneous			
Total Budget			

FIGURE 5.3
Line-Item Budget Format

the previous year. When there are multiple programs in one site-based unit, a plan may be prepared for each program in the unit with a general budget request. The site-based administrator or team then consolidates the program plans to create the site-based unit proposal.

Budget categories (e.g., those listed in Figure 5.3) are an important feature for school district administrators to consider. This list is limited to categories relevant to the operation of a site-based unit. A site-based budget should not include categories for overhead or for indirect costs such as heat, electricity, water/sewage, or insurance. In the experience of the author, when these items are assigned to site-based teams, their general reaction to budgeting responsibilities is often negative. In cases where the budget categories are limited to those needed in the actual delivery of the program, service, or activity, the attitude toward development and maintenance of a site-based budget is often more proactive.

STRATEGIC BUDGET SYSTEM

The operations of a strategic budget should be perceived as a system. As an example, Figure 5.4 shows an overview of the strategic budget system. System input is determined by the budget proposals from the site-based units. After the approval of proposed budgets, the process stage allocates the money to site-based unit budgets for expenditure. In the output stage, budget reports are prepared for benchmark reviews and an annual report. The review of the benchmark reports provides feedback to the input stage. For example, the analysis of the data may result in a request for amendments to the current budget. If the school board approves the request, then budget allocations are revised. Site-based units may then expend the money according to the amended budget. In addition, the feedback data provided in the annual report are essential to the preparation of budgets for

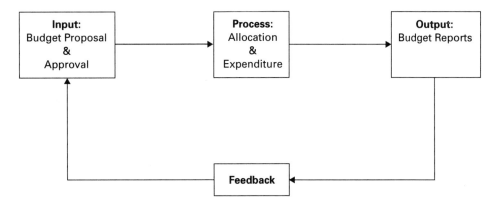

FIGURE 5.4
The Strategic Budget System

the next fiscal year. Further, as NCATE (NPBEA, 2002b) proposes in Standard 1.2, data gained from the strategic planning process should be used in the continuing development of the school's vision.

DECENTRALIZATION OF SCHOOL DISTRICT BUDGETS

When a school district assigns budgets to site-based units for preparation and management, this creates a decentralized budget system. Figure 5.5 exhibits a decentralized structure for a school district's instructional budget supervised by the assistant superintendent for instruction. In this case, the site-based unit budget numbers range from 1–9. The site-based units should have a principal or a teacher serve as a team leader with a site team composed of teachers and people from the community. This practice corresponds to Standard 3 of ISLLC (1996) and Standard 1 of NCATE (NPBEA, 2002b), whereby administrators are expected to communicate and involve stakeholders in the school decision-making process.

ISLLC

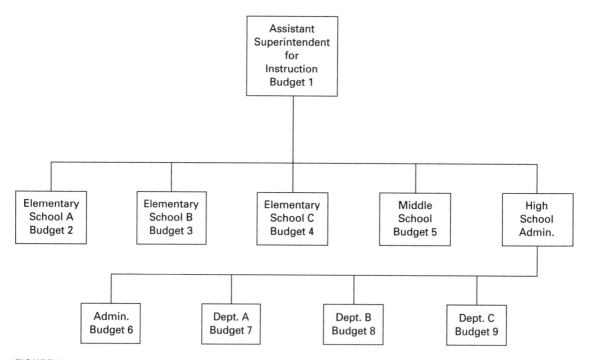

FIGURE 5.5
Decentralization of Site-Based Budgets
Note: In actual practice, plans and budgets are developed for the superintendent's office, the business office, counseling services, the physical plant, transportation, extracurricular activities, and so on.

In Figure 5.5, the elementary and middle schools (budgets 2–5) and the programs in the high school should prepare site-based financial plans. After the financial plans for the high school units (budgets 6–9) are prepared, the principal should review them. Upon the review and approval of the high school plans, a consolidated financial plan for the high school should be prepared.

The assistant superintendent should receive the high school plan and budget, the high school site-based unit plans and budgets, and the plans and budgets for the middle school and three elementary schools. The assistant superintendent should then forward a consolidated financial plan for all budget units, including the assistant superintendent's (budget 1), to central administration and all of the supporting site-based plans to the superintendent. After the superintendent and/or finance committee has reviewed, revised (if necessary), and recommended to the board the school district's financial plan, a public budget document should be prepared for interested citizens, businesses, and related government bodies; it should be published in the newspaper as well.

Before a budget is approved, a school board typically holds a public hearing after the financial plan has been released to the public. In some cases, site-based administrators attend the public meetings to discuss or answer questions about their proposed financial plan. If supporting site-based plans are not included with the district plan, as may likely be the case in large districts, the unit plans should be placed on file in the library for public review. (Note: Site-based plans and district plans do not include personal salaries.)

Upon the board or the public passing the district budget, a tax levy is processed, and money is appropriated to the school district. In states where the public votes to pass the school district's budget, and it fails, local and/or state officials typically hold reviews and hearings to arrive at a compromise.

Budget Calendar

To generate decentralized strategic financial plans, a school district must use a calendar to direct its development. This calendar, which is subject to dates set by state law, is usually prepared by starting with the last deadline for the final budget approval. The calendar timelines are then set by working back from this deadline to the submission of a first draft of a financial plan by the site-based units for internal review.

The budget calendar should be broken down into subcalendars for different groups; for instance, a subcalendar providing a detailed schedule for the site-based units and a master calendar for the board. A public calendar should announce the date or dates for public hearings and official actions by the board.

PREPARATION OF SITE-BASED PLANS

To facilitate the preparation and processing of site-based plans, the district should provide each unit with a standardized form that requires a narrative. A heading on the form should identify the school district, the fiscal year, the site-based budget unit, and budget administrator. In the narrative, the site-based units should state their goals, objectives, activities, and effectiveness/efficiency targets.

For a program narrative, the author and some school districts have found it effective to use a standardized outline. Figure 5.6 shows a similar format on which a unit must list its goals and related objectives. The form then requires each unit to identify the activities/services offered under each objective along with the outcome and output targets. Using such a format requires the unit to align their goals and objectives to their targets. The alignment demonstrates that site teams have thought through the sequence of elements for the plan and developed relevant targets.

The unit's objectives should be presented in priority order from the highest to the lowest. As exhibited in Figure 5.6 under the first objective, the proposed activity or service targets may use grading periods for timing the benchmark reviews. Reviews of the targets and budget are then conducted after the end of each grading period. The end-of-year budget, outcome, and output reports should also be carefully reviewed. The findings in these reviews may lead to revisions in the plan and budgets of the current year and should serve as input for the next fiscal year.

FIGURE 5.6
Format for Presenting a
Strategic Financial Plan

Financial Plan 2000–2001
(School District)
(Site-Based Unit)

Goal 1:
    Objective 1:
        Activity/service:
        Targets:
            Outcomes (end of 1st grading period):
            Outputs (end of 1st grading period):

            Outcomes (end of 2nd grading period):
            Outputs (end of 2nd grading period):

            Outcomes (end of 3rd grading period):
            Outputs (end of 3rd grading period):
    Objective 2:
        Activity/service:
        Targets:
            Outcomes:
            Outputs:

Goal 2:
    Objective 1:
        Activity/service:
        Targets:
            Outcomes:
            Outputs:

To aid in their preparation of strategic financial plans, site-based units should receive a packet with a planning calendar, the forms for presenting their plan and budget, outcome and output data for the current year and previous two years, and budget reports for the current year to date and for the previous two years. The budget reports should show percentage breakdowns for each expenditure category in reference to the total amount allocated to the unit. Admittedly, setting up the process and preparing the plans in the first year can be quite a task; however, the following years allow site teams to review, refine, update, and restate their initial plans. As school administrators gain experience, the preparation and use of site-based plans become less time consuming.

Optional Plans

A school district may wish for their site-based units to present optional plans for the administration and board to consider. For example, an elementary school could propose options that would provide: (a) 12 classes with average enrollments of 30 students, (b) 15 classes with average enrollments of 26 students, (c) 18 classes with average enrollments of 21 students, and (d) 20 classes with average enrollments of 18. Each alternative could then include a budget proposal. This presentation permits the board to examine several options and the circumstances associated with each.

SITE-BASED BENCHMARK REVIEWS

Site-based unit administrators and teams need to conduct efficient reviews of their plans within a short time period just after their benchmark period has passed. These reviews must ensure that the administrators and teams focus on their accomplishments to date. For example, benchmarks may reference among other things student achievement, attendance, class trips, extracurricular activities, curriculum development, personnel induction programs, professional development activities, physical plant maintenance, technology training, transportation schedules, and student assembly programs.

A form should assist administrators and team members with their review. Figure 5.7 gives an example of such a form, which is similar to one used by both the author and some districts. The form begins with one unit's objective. Then, in the first column of the form, the program or activity is listed, followed by columns showing the proposed outcome and/or output targets and actual accomplishments. A final column provides for amendments to the plan, which could be changes in outcome or output targets, target deadlines, and/or budget allocations. An example in Figure 5.7 shows an output target of a class trip in November that was canceled, rescheduled, and approved for February. In turn, this should ensure that the budget allocation for the trip would be retained. If the trip was not rescheduled, a budget change would be required and entered into the amendments column.

(NAME OF BUDGET UNIT)
BENCHMARK REVIEW
(Dates covered by review)

Objective:

Program Activity	Proposed Outcomes	Outcomes Achieved (to date)	Proposed Outputs	Outputs Attained (to date)	Amendments to Plan
1.			Class trip Nov. 6	Trip Canceled	Class trip Rescheduled Feb. 2
2.					

FIGURE 5.7
Report Format for Benchmark Reviews

FINAL THOUGHTS

School district personnel must recognize that a strategic financial plan is an opportunity to act proactively. The plan simply tells everyone why the district exists, what it is going to do, how it intends to do it, and how much it will cost. Administrators can then direct the plan toward crystallizing the district's visionary goals. Most important, without a plan with site-based unit goals and supporting objectives with targets, claims to success would be difficult if not impossible.

One key to making a successful strategic financial plan is to adapt it to the district. For example, a plan and process for an urban school with over 30,000 students will be quite different from one for a rural district with only 3,000 students. Therefore, a prototype will not fit all districts.

A second consideration is that stakeholders in the district must be involved in the process. With stakeholders on the site-based unit teams, the school district will enjoy many advantages. For example, when the public is part of the team, they become aware of the goals and objectives of the district and its programs, have input on program targets, develop an awareness of the financial needs of the district, and assist in the preparation of the budget. When this occurs in a positive setting, the team members are more likely to support the district and its programs and, possibly, defend it from its never-ending list of critics.

Another feature that should be set up carefully is the communication channel for the review and approval process. When strategic financial plans are processed up through the organizational hierarchy for review and reaction, an interaction should occur between the site-based units, the administration, and the board of education. In some school districts, reviews of the plans may provide site teams with an opportunity for discussing their plans with personnel in central administration or even with the school board members. In these cases, communication becomes more personal. When benchmark and annual reports are presented to the board for reaction, communication may be maintained. These interactions can benefit employee morale and community relations plus it corresponds to the spirit of Article 12 of the Magna Carta.

Finally, site-based unit plans should not be set so rigidly that they cannot be adjusted. A good coach knows that even the best game plan may have to be changed while the game is being played; not after it is over. Of course, a good coach also knows to always have a game plan.

DISCUSSION QUESTIONS

1. If a school district does not have a defined sequence of statements (mission, goals, objectives), what are the inherent dangers presented to the educational leadership, students, and budgets?
2. Compare the advantages and disadvantages of the line-item, program, PPBS, ZBB, performance, and strategic budget methods.
3. Describe the outcome and output targets that could be proposed for the following site-based units: an elementary school, a social studies program, physical education, counseling services, the media center, an extracurricular football program, personnel services, food services, and school maintenance.

APPLICATION PROBLEMS

1. Prepare a set of mission, goal, and objective statements for a school district.
2. Prepare a set of goal and objective statements for an elementary school.
3. Assume the state law requires school districts to present their budgets to the public by February 15th for a vote on March 15th. Prepare a calendar for the preparation of instructional strategic financial plans, their reviews, and the promotion of their budgets for the site-based units and district presented in Figure 5.5.

CLINICAL PRACTICUM EXERCISES

Beginning with this chapter, a clinical practicum exercise is presented at the end of each chapter. The purpose of these exercises is to serve as a bridge between the content of the course and practices in the workplace as suggested by the NPBEA (NPBEA, 2002a). For these exercises, students are to select a school district to serve as a research subject for study. This study will require visits to the school district to collect information. This information is in the public domain, is not personal in nature, and will not violate anyone's privacy or confidentiality.

In response to the clinical exercises below, the suggested format is to: (a) state the question, (b) answer the question, and (c) discuss your answer in reference to the content presented in the text. If supporting material is discussed and can be made available, it should be referenced in the discussion as an appendix and attached to the end of the report. Note that one of the objectives of part 3 is to show that the material in this book has been read, comprehended, and applied.

Using the information in this chapter as a reference, report your findings on the following:

1. the school district's mission, goals, and objectives;
   a. Where are they publicized?
2. the use of site-based units;
3. the contents of a strategic financial plan or other plan for the district and site-based units;
4. the budget method used;
5. the forms and approval process used for the strategic or other academic plan and budgets;
6. the district budget calendar; and
7. benchmarks or other formal reviews.

WEB ADDRESSES

National Council for Accreditation of Teacher Education
http://www.ncate.org

National Policy Board for Educational Administration
http://www.npbea.org

REFERENCES

Chatfield, M. (1974). *A history of accounting thought.* Hinsdale, IL: Dryden Press.

Cope, G. H. (1986). Municipal budgetary practices. *Baseline data report, 18,* 910–924.

Cope, G. H. (1989). Budgeting methods for public programs. In J. L. Perry (Ed.), *Handbook of public administration* (pp. 162–175). San Francisco: Jossey-Bass.

Deming, W. E. (1986). *Out of crises.* Cambridge: Massachusetts Institute of Technology, Center for Advanced Engineering Study.

Eadie, D. C. (1989). Building the capacity for strategic management. In J. L. Perry (Ed.), *Handbook of public administration* (pp. 162–175). San Francisco: Jossey-Bass.

Etzioni, A. (1964). *Modern organizations.* Upper Saddle River, NJ: Merrill/Prentice Hall.

Freeman, R. J., & Shoulders, C. D. (1996). *Governmental & nonprofit accounting: Theory & practice* (5th ed.). Upper Saddle River, Cliffs, NJ: Merrill/Prentice Hall.

Garner, C. W. (1991). *Accounting and budgeting in public and nonprofit organizations: A manager's guide.* San Francisco: Jossey-Bass.

Governmental Accounting Standards Board. (1994). *Concepts statement no. 2, service efforts and accomplishments reporting.* Norwalk, CT: Author.

Hartman, W. T. (1988). *School district budgeting.* Upper Saddle River, NJ: Merrill/Prentice Hall.

Houle, C. O. (1989). *Governing Boards.* San Francisco: Jossey-Bass.

Interstate School Leaders Licensure Consortium (1996). *Standards for school leaders.* Washington, DC: Council of Chief State School Officers.

Knezevich, S. J. (1973). *Program budgeting (PPBS).* Berkeley, CA: McCutchan.

Matkin, G. W. (1985). *Effective budgeting in continuing education: A comprehensive plan to improving program, planning and organizational performance.* San Francisco: Jossey-Bass.

McNamara, R. S. (1968). *The essence of security: Reflections in office.* New York: Harper & Row.

Merewitz, L., & Sosnick, S. H. (1971). *The budget's new clothes.* Chicago: Markham.

National Policy Board for Educational Administration (2002a). *Standards for advanced programs in educational leadership* [Online]. Retrieved February 17, 2003, from http://www.npbea.org

National Policy Board for Educational Administration (2002b). *Standards for advanced programs in educational leadership for principals, superintendents, curriculum directors, and supervisors* [Online] Retrieved February 17, 2003, from http://www.ncate.org

Reich, R. B. (1992). *The work of nations.* New York: Vintage Books.

Walker, D. M. (1999). The accountability profession faces enormous challenges and opportunities at the turn of the century. *The Government Accountants Journal, 48*(4), 8–11.

Welsch, G. A., Hilton, R. W., & Gordon, P. N. (1988). *Profit planning and control* (5th ed.). Upper Saddle River, NJ: Merrill/Prentice Hall.

Woodard, J. W. (2001). Three factors of successful work force planning. *Journal of Government Financial Management, 50*(3), 36–38.

Chapter 6

The Financial Framework for a School District

Governmental bodies, including school districts, divide their financial operating structures into separate entities called accounting funds. An **accounting fund** is an independent operating unit that has its own accounting and budgeting systems and set of financial reports.

One of the purposes for breaking a school district's financial operating structure into accounting funds is to segregate its resources. For example, in a school district using the accounting funds set forth by the Governmental Accounting Standards Board (GASB, 2001), one of its funds would contain money received from different governments for regular instruction, a second fund would contain government money for special education instruction, a third would be used for money to construct a new building, a fourth would be set up for money collected or received for food services, a fifth would be for student money collected by a school's different grades, and so on.

Although a strategic financial plan could be prepared for each fund, typically one is only prepared for the larger and more complex instructional funds. Other funds may prepare a business plan while some funds follow directives specifying how the money in the fund must be spent.

Therefore, funds create a financial operating structure through which all of the business transactions of the school district are processed. As explained in this chapter, accounting funds should be integrated into the management structure of the school district in order to assign the responsibility of managing, or supervising the management of, school resources to appropriate administrators.

While state governments designate the types of funds used by school districts, most have adopted the Generally Accepted Accounting Principles (GAAP) presented by the GASB. Consequently, the funds suggested in the GAAP of the GASB are referenced in this chapter to describe the different types of funds, how they are to be used in a school district, and how they can be integrated into a management structure.

ACCOUNTING FUND CATEGORIES

The GAAP of the GASB divide funds into three groups: (a) government funds, (b) **proprietary funds**, and (c) **fiduciary funds**. These funds create a framework for the financial operations of a school district.

Most of the money received by a school district comes from taxes collected by the local, state, and federal governments. This government money is deposited into one of the government funds for expenditure.

Money placed in proprietary funds comes from the sale of goods or services by the school district, although some deposits may come from transfers from a government fund. With respect to the proprietary funds, the school district is the apparent owner, or proprietor, of a business. A school board, therefore, has the authority to use the money in these funds as they deem best within the guidelines of the state law. The use of a strategic business plan (discussed in chapter 11), which is similar to a strategic financial plan, is recommended for these funds.

Fiduciary funds are for resources held by the school district in trust for others or for the school district. Consequently, a school district must spend the money in these funds according to the conditions set in the trust. Owing to the trust restrictions, the preparation of financial plans is not typical. Instead, budget reports are generated for review by the school board and, in some cases, by the donors or group for whom the money is held in trust.

NAMES AND PURPOSES OF ACCOUNTING FUNDS

The names of the funds assigned to the three categories presented in the GAAP of the GASB (2001) are as follows:

Governmental funds:
1. General Fund
2. Special Revenue Fund
3. Capital Projects Fund
4. Debt Service Fund
5. Permanent Fund

Proprietary funds:
6. Enterprise Fund
7. Internal Service Fund

Fiduciary funds:
8. Pension Trust Fund (and those of other employee benefits)
9. Investment Trust Fund
10. Private Purpose Trust Fund
11. Agency Fund

The preceding list of funds reflects minor revisions set forth for all state and local governments by the GASB in 1999. Under Statement 34 (GASB, 1999), these funds were phased into operation from July 1, 2001, to July 1, 2003. Thus, when comparing financial reports for the fiscal years prior to and following the 2001–2003 time span, there may be some minor differences.

A description of the GASB accounting funds in terms of their use by school districts is as follows.

Governmental Accounting Funds:
- *General Fund*—to account for all financial resources of the school district except those accounted for in another fund; primary receipts are from tax revenues and tuition, and expenditures are for regular instructional programs and related activities.
- *Special Revenue Fund*—for proceeds from revenue sources legally restricted for specified purposes; such as state and federal grants for special education, vocational education, math/science programs, and so on. Money may not be transferred from this fund to other funds, such as the general fund, to ensure the revenue is spent as intended. At the end of the year, an unexpended balance should not exist as all receipts should have been spent on the programs offered.
- *Capital Projects Fund*—to account for revenues received for the acquisition or construction of major capital projects, such as money received from the sale of bonds and state grants to build and furnish a new school. Earnings from the investment of money held in this fund should be spent on the project or used to reduce the debt; not for general fund expenditures.
- *Debt Service Fund*—for the accumulation of receipts for the payment of general long-term debt and related interest incurred through the capital projects fund. A debt service fund receives the tax money collected from taxpayers for the payment of bond or other loan receipts placed in the capital projects fund. Earnings from the investment of money held in the fund are to be spent on the retirement of debt and not transferred to another fund for expenditure.
- *Permanent Fund*—a new fund created in the 1999 GASB Statement 34 directive, it is for resources given to and that will benefit the school district. The restriction on money placed in this fund is that only the interest earnings from the donation, and not the principal, may be spent.

Proprietary Accounting Funds:
- *Enterprise Fund*—to account for operations where the intent is that the cost of providing the goods or services to the public is recovered or financed primarily through user charges; such as the sale of food in a cafeteria.
- *Internal Service Fund*—to account for operations through which goods or services are sold by the school district to a site-based unit in the school district or to a local, county, state, or federal government. The charges

rendered are on a cost reimbursement basis and not for generating a profit. An example of an operation in this fund would be a central supply store from which a site-based unit within the school district purchased supplies from money allocated to it in a government fund. Another example would be money received from another governmental body, such as the municipal recreation department, for the rental of a room or gym. Note that if money is received from a nongovernmental organization or business for room rent, it is deposited in the enterprise fund.

Fiduciary Accounting Funds:

- *Pension Trust Fund*—for money held in trust for pensions and other employee benefit plans.
- *Investment Trust Fund*—for investment pools used by the school district.
- *Private Purpose Trust Fund*—for money received where a donor directs that the principal and/or interest earned must be used to benefit individuals, private organizations, or the school district.
- *Agency Fund*—for custodial purposes and involves the receipt, temporary investment, and/or payments to individuals and organizations. Examples of an agency fund may be:
  - *Payroll Fund*—holds cash for payroll checks and withholdings for taxes and benefit payments.
  - *Unemployment Trust Fund*—holds money in reserve for unemployment compensation claims.
  - *Student Activity Fund*—a special agency fund used for resources owned, operated, and managed by the student body under the supervision of the school, such as homerooms, yearbook sales, choral and band groups, student clubs, and student council.

School districts must have one general fund and usually a special revenue fund. If any of the other funds are not needed, they should not be used (GASB, 2001). For example, if a district deposits all teacher pension money directly into a state retirement account, it would not need a pension fund. At the same time, except for the general fund, a school district may create more than one type of accounting fund to meet its particular needs. For instance, a large school district may create a special enterprise fund for food services.

AN ILLUSTRATION OF FUND OPERATIONS

To illustrate how funds operate as separate entities, a comparison is made between a person who owns three businesses and a school with three accounting funds. First, assume a person owns a hardware store, a gas station, and a taxi service. In this case, each of the three businesses represents a different activity and operates independently; that is, each has a set of accounts with a business plan (as opposed to a strategic financial plan) to earn a profit (the primary mission of a business). A set of financial reports is prepared containing information on how much is owned, how much is owed, the accumulated wealth, and the current profit/loss of each business for the owner.

When one of the businesses makes a sale or spends money, it enters the transaction into its own set of accounts. For example, the sale of gas by the gas station is entered into its accounting records while receipts from delivering people to their destinations is entered into the books of the taxi service.

If the businesses interact with each other, each enters the accounting transaction into its own accounting records. For example, if the taxi service buys fuel from the gas station, the taxi service would enter it as an expense in its accounting records and the gas station would enter it as a sale in its records. If the hardware store sells the gas station an air compressor, an entry would be shown in the books of each business as follows: a sale for the hardware store and the acquisition of an asset (air compressor) for the gas station.

Funds operate in the same way; that is, they must enter their business transactions into their own set of accounts, including their transactions with each other. For example, when a school receives revenue from the state government to offer a special program to students, the revenue receipt is entered into the records of a special revenue accounting fund. When students pay for meals in the cafeteria, the sales are entered into the records of the fund used for food services. If a contribution is received for a scholarship, it is placed in a fiduciary fund.

Likewise, when money is spent for the special program funded by the state, it must come from the special revenue fund. When food is purchased for the cafeteria, it must be charged to the accounting fund used for food services. If money is used to provide a scholarship, it must come from the fiduciary fund. If the school uses money in the general fund to buy food for the cafeteria, money is transferred from the general fund to the fund used for food services. A record of the transfer is made in the general fund and another entry is made in the fund used for food services.

Therefore, as with separate businesses, each accounting fund enters its transactions into its own set of accounts, and a set of financial statements is prepared for each accounting fund. Then the statements for all of the accounting funds in a school district are combined to exhibit the comprehensive financial position of the school district.

Returning to the owner in the example of the three businesses, this person would not likely try to manage all three businesses personally but would hire a manager to run each one. In fact, if the businesses were quite large, the owner may have to break each business into departments with separate managers. In such a case, the owner would seek out people with the appropriate expertise and education to run each business and department. It is likewise true that people with the appropriate expertise and education should manage accounting funds and site-based units. Too often this is not the case!

BUILDING BLOCKS FOR THE FINANCIAL FRAMEWORK

The accounting funds are the building blocks in the construction of a financial framework for a school district. Each of the accounting funds has been assigned a number by the National Center for Educational Statistics (NCES; Fowler, 1990) to facilitate the generation of a common report for all states. These numbers, which are discussed further in chapter 8 and also shown in Resource B at the end of the book, are as follows:

Fund Number	Fund Name
10	General Fund
20	Special Revenue Fund
30	Capital Projects Fund
40	Debt Service Fund
45	Permanent Fund
50	Enterprise Fund
55	Internal Service Fund
60	Pension Fund
65	Investment Trust Fund
70	Private Purpose Trust Fund
80	Agency Fund
90	Student Activity Fund

Note: In the fund numbers above, numbers for the permanent fund and the student activity fund used by school districts are not included in the list suggested by NCES.

As already mentioned, the GAAP direct that a school district should use the minimum number of accounting funds legally required and necessary to institute a sound financial program. At the same time, except for the general fund, it may use more than one particular type of accounting fund (GASB, 2001).

When more than one type of accounting fund is used, names as well as numbers are assigned to clearly identify their different activities. For example, schools with a large cafeteria operation often create a food services fund in addition to the proprietary fund. Further, a food services fund may be subdivided, providing records for different financial operations; for instance, separate accounts showing the receipts and expenditures for breakfast, lunch, and catering services. The same may be true for school districts with large athletic programs. In addition, a school district could have three internal service funds. For example, a district may have a fund for building maintenance (called the Physical Plant Fund), a fund for classroom supplies (called the Central Supplies Fund), and another fund for miscellaneous receipts and expenditures (called the Internal Service Fund). Figure 6.1 illustrates how a set of accounting funds with assigned fund numbers may be expanded.

For example, if the set of accounting funds in Figure 6.1 were used by a school district, the local tax money received would be placed in general fund 10. As the

FIGURE 6.1
**Illustration of an Expanded
Set of Accounting Funds**

Fund Number	Fund Name
10	General Fund
20	Special Revenue Fund
30	Capital Projects Fund
40	Debt Service Fund
45	Permanent Fund
50	Enterprise Fund
52	Food Services Fund
54	Athletic Fund
56	General Internal Service Fund
57	Supplies Fund
58	Physical Plant Fund
60	Pension Fund
65	Investment Trust Fund
70	Private Purpose Trust Fund
80	Agency Fund
90	Student Activity Fund

money is spent, it would be spent through the accounts used by the accounting and budgeting systems (chapters 7 and 8) in fund 10 and reported in the financial statements for fund 10.

PUTTING THE FINANCIAL FRAMEWORK INTO THE MANAGEMENT STRUCTURE

Because accounting funds are for specific programs, services, and activities, they should be assigned to the appropriate administrative divisions or offices within the school district's management structure. This is to ensure a link between financial resources and personnel with the expertise to develop and manage the plan for a program, service, or activity. When this occurs, a financial operating structure is created within the management structure.

Figure 6.2 uses the expanded fund numbers shown in Figure 6.1 and applies them to a management structure for a large school district with multiple schools and cafeterias. In this case, the administrator assigned to an accounting fund would be ultimately responsible for the preparation of all financial plans; the supervision of all fund budgets, receipts, and expenditures; and the reviews and reports of the fund programs, services, or activities.

As shown in the application in Figure 6.2, both the board of education and the superintendent have complete authority over all funds, whereas the superintendent alone has direct supervision over the fiduciary funds and fund 45, which is for reasons related more to appropriate business practice and community

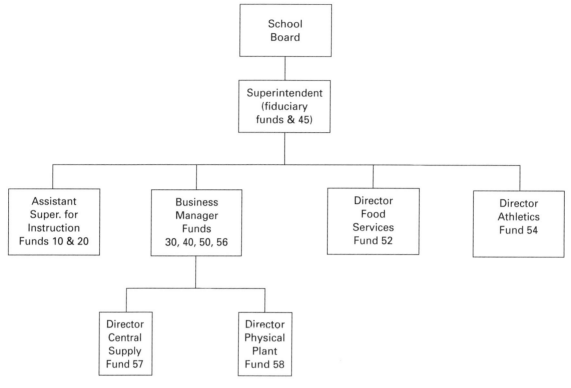

FIGURE 6.2
A Financial Operating Structure

relations than to programmatic necessity. The instructional funds (general fund 10 and special revenue fund 20) are assigned to the assistant superintendent for instruction while the business manager is given the responsibility for the capital project fund 30, debt service fund 40, general enterprise fund 50, and general internal service fund 56. The four proprietary funds (food services fund 52, athletic fund 54, supplies fund 57, and physical plant fund 58) are assigned to the respective directors of these self-supporting activities. Of course, the supervision of these directors varies from district to district. In some cases the directors are under the school business administrator and in others the school principal is responsible for their supervision.

The oversight of the different accounting funds also varies from district to district. This is because the arrangements are dependent on the size of the district, available personnel, preferences of the board and superintendent, and so on. The point, however, is that in many settings, they depart from the early practice in which the school district's superintendent and business manager bore the responsibility for all accounting funds, budgets, and business activities.

EXTENDING THE FINANCIAL OPERATING STRUCTURE TO SITE-BASED UNITS

After assigning accounting funds to offices and personnel in the management structure, the financial operating structure should be extended to include the decentralized site-based units discussed in the last chapter. To demonstrate this, the decentralized site-based units and the budget numbers shown in chapter 5, Figure 5.5, are used in Figure 6.3. As shown in Figure 6.3, the site-based budget units may receive budget allocations from funds 10 and 20, which are under the supervision of the assistant superintendent (as per Figure 6.2).

In the management structure shown in Figure 6.3, the elementary schools, the middle school, and the high school's administration and three departments are assigned budgets 10-2 to 10-9 while budget 10-1 is for the assistant superintendent. With respect to fund 20, the elementary and middle schools are given budget numbers 20-2 to 20-5, Department A in the high school is assigned budget 20-6, and the assistant superintendent is given budget 20-1 for general administrative allocations. If more than one revenue award is made from fund 20 to a site-based unit, each award would need to have its own budget number. For example, the elementary schools would need to have separate budgets for special

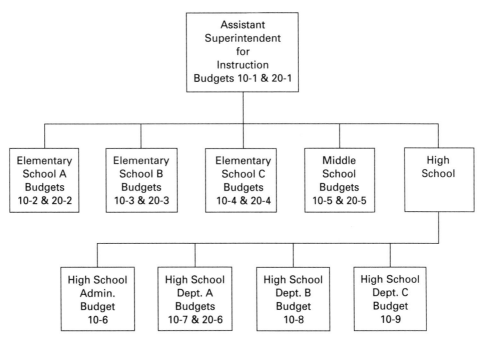

FIGURE 6.3
Site-Based Units in Two Accounting Funds

education and remedial program awards. Through this arrangement, the school district can ensure that the revenues will be spent for each program as intended by the state and federal government. At the end of the year, an audit can verify that the awards were spent as intended.

FINAL THOUGHTS

The single entry method of bookkeeping, which was the method of choice of state and local governments until recent years, did not separate district money into funds but used one set of accounts and one financial report for all business operations in a school district. Therefore, the separate programs and activities offered by a district could not have separate strategic financial plans, budgets, and reports. As a result, an analysis of costs by program, cost-effectiveness or efficiency analyses, the tracking of costs, audits, and so on, were not possible unless local administrators went to considerable effort.

The use of accounting funds with budgets for site-based units permits the generation of meaningful reports for school districts. With such accurate information, generating valid accountability reports and audits is possible. Further, informed judgments are possible when making decisions about such things as the costs associated with an increase or reduction of class sizes, the reallocation of resources, the costs related to an adjustment of priorities, and so on.

In addition, the use of funds with separate sets of accounts, budgets, site-based units, and financial reports produces some related operating benefits. To illustrate, the following three cases are described.

In the first case, a district allocated money to site budgets for janitorial services and instructional supplies. The allocation for janitorial services was based on the size of the school (square footage) and special facilities in the building. The allocation for instructional supplies was based on the number of students and types of programs/classes offered in a school. The principals of each school paid a physical plant accounting fund from their site-based administrative budgets for custodial services and building alterations, and the site-based units for programs and services paid the central supply accounting fund from their allocations for paper, pencils, and other supplies. Because of these allocations, school principals ceased to lobby central administration throughout the year for extra janitorial services, alterations, and supplies. Thus, central administration relieved themselves of some internal turmoil and also received support for the supervision of custodial services since the customer (school principal) now had a financial stake in their delivery. Further, the building administrators and teachers tended to be more conservative when spending their own budget allocations for supplies.

In another case, a newly employed business manager set up site-based budgets for all schools, programs, and support activities. Initially the change was treated with great suspicion. After a time, however, the school principals, program heads, and teachers realized the budgets were theirs to prepare and manage. After two years the business manager reported that the principals, program heads, and teachers had become intensely involved to the point where they "shop around for the best deals," spend hours figuring out how to save money, and pull together in a healthy team effort creating a positive influence at their schools.

In the final example, the business manager and superintendent were responsible for preparing and making all budget reports to the school board. As often is the case, the meetings focused almost entirely on expenditures. After instituting a decentralized budgeting process with site-based units, the site-based budget administrators and site team leaders were asked to periodically attend monthly board meetings to discuss their budgets and programs. Surprisingly, the board meetings became more involved with the program offerings and less with the expenditure reports. At one meeting the school board decided to allocate more money from the reserve to a program budget without requesting more money. Organizational communication improved to the point where the board became more informed about school programs and the program administrators had a better grasp of the bigger picture.

DISCUSSION QUESTIONS

1. How would you describe the purposes of government, proprietary, and fiduciary funds?
   a. What are the purposes of the funds in each category?
   b. Why is this arrangement important to school districts, policymakers, and the public?
2. School districts can create their own funds when necessary. As a school district administrator, what special enterprise and internal service funds might you establish? Why?
3. As the principal of elementary school A in Figure 6.3, would you have separate teams for site budgets 10-2 and 20-2, or would you have one team for both budgets? Why? What would be the advantages?

APPLICATION PROBLEMS

Using the fund numbers in Figure 6.1, identify the fund number into which the money would be placed for the following receipts. If a transfer is made, also identify the fund number from which the money is taken. The answers are provided at the end of the chapter, following the References.

1. Tuition is received from another school district.
2. A statement is received showing investment income earned from money set aside to retire a bond issue.
3. Daily cafeteria sales are deposited.
4. Repairs are made to the administrative offices by the physical plant and paid from a budget in the general fund.

5. Money is received for a federal vocational grant.
6. A site-based unit in the high school uses its allocation in the general fund to purchase instructional supplies from central supply.
7. Students pay Tri Hi Y club membership dues.
8. Money is received from a bond sale to build a new elementary school.
9. The high school receives money for an academic incentive student award program from a local corporation.
10. Money is deposited from the gate receipts of the football game.

CLINICAL PRACTICUM EXERCISES

In response to the clinical exercises below, the suggested format is to: (a) state the question, (b) answer the question, and (c) discuss your answer in reference to the content presented in the text. If supporting material is discussed and can be made available, it should be referenced in the discussion as an appendix and attached to the end of the report. Note that one of the objectives of part 3 is to show that the material in this book has been read, comprehended, and applied.

Using the information in this chapter as a reference, report your findings on the following:

1. the accounting funds used by the district and their purpose.
2. the administrative positions responsible for the supervision of the accounting funds.
3. the administrative positions assigned to supervise the budgets within each fund.

WEB ADDRESSES

National Center for Education Statistics
http://nces.ed.gov

REFERENCES

Fowler, W. J., Jr. (1990). *Financial accounting for local and state school systems.* Washington, DC: U.S. Department of Education [Online]. Retrieved April 4, 2002, from http://nces.ed.gov

Governmental Accounting Standards Board (1999). *Basic financial statements and management's discussion and analysis for state and local governments.* Norwalk, CT: Author.

Governmental Accounting Standards Board (2001). *Codification of governmental accounting and financial reporting standards.* Norwalk, CT: Author.

ANSWERS TO APPLICATION PROBLEMS

1. Deposit is made to general fund 10.
2. Entry of earnings is recorded in debt service fund 40.
3. Deposit is made to food services fund 52.
4. Money is transferred from general fund 10 to physical plant fund 58.
5. Deposit is made to special revenue fund 20.
6. General fund 10 transfers money to supplies fund 57.
7. Deposit is made to student activity fund 75.
8. Deposit is made to capital projects fund 30.
9. Deposit is made to trust fund 65.
10. Deposit is made to athletic fund 54.

Chapter 7

Contents and Process
of the Accounting System

School leaders are not expected to be accountants; however, being knowledge-able about the terms, process, and reports used by the accounting system gives them a distinct advantage. This chapter explains how the accounting system works and how it interacts with the budgeting system.

Accounting is the process that records, classifies, and summarizes business transactions and provides a history of the business activities of a school district. To this end, the accounting system, at the close of each fiscal year, creates financial statements that exhibit the results of a school district's business operations and the status of its resources.

One of the more important features of the governmental accounting system, as compared with profit accounting, is that budget information is also recorded. This permits the governmental accounting system to record all budget transactions, to classify the transactions into the proper budget accounts, and to summarize all budget transactions into monthly budget reports for site-based units and accounting funds; profit accounting systems do not enter budgets into the accounting records.

WHAT IS DOUBLE ENTRY ACCOUNTING?

Under the GAAP, school districts must use the double entry form of accounting, which replaced the single entry method that is limited to keeping records of budget receipts and expenditures for only the current year. Thus, the single entry method simply responded to budget expectations demanded under Article 12 of the Magna Carta and put into practice by Alexander Hamilton.

The double entry method uses an algebraic formula developed *800 years ago* that requires all transactions to have a minimum of two entries in the accounting records. In addition, this method requires that the entries be processed through a system of journals, ledgers, and reports that serve as a check on all transactions. Deviations from the system's procedures may leave the books out-of-balance and indicate an effort to abuse the resources of the school district. Most important, however, these procedures allow for the efficient recording and processing of a large number of daily transactions leading to the creation of valid financial reports. For example, a school district with a budget exceeding $12 million is not unusual; however, a $12 million budget will process an average of $1 million a month in transactions.

The double entry accounting method, which is used in each of the accounting funds, maintains records of **assets** (what is owned), **liabilities** (what is owed), and a fund balance (what is left if the liabilities are paid off through the liquidation of the assets). The governmental double entry accounting system also maintains records of all budget receipts, allocations and expenditures, current surplus, and the accumulated surplus. The balances of all accounts, receipts, and budget expenditures are reported every month and in the financial statements at the end of the year.

THE DEVELOPMENT OF GOVERNMENTAL ACCOUNTING PRINCIPLES

The earliest record of the double entry accounting method was found in the 1211 bank ledgers in Florence, Italy. The first complete set of accounting records was discovered in the treasurer's books dated 1340 for the city of Genoa and the first book on double entry accounting, *Summa de Arithmetica Geometria Proportioni et Proportionalita* (Review of Arithmetic, Geometry, and Proportions), was written by Luca Pacioli in 1494.

One theory on the impetus to create the double entry form of accounting suggests that it was prompted by the opening of the trade routes to the Middle East. Because of the large volume of trade, there was a need to accurately record, process, and protect a great number of daily business transactions. For the same reason, the double entry method has been given partial credit by some historians for the success of the industrial revolution (Chatfield, 1974; Garner, 1991; Kam, 1986; Lee, 1984; Yamey, 1984). In the latter part of the 20th century, the United States found itself in a situation where the large number of daily business transactions being processed by state and local governments required an accounting system that could handle the volume accurately and efficiently (Garner, 1996).

Even though the double entry method was in existence when the United States won its independence, the accounting method of choice by the federal, state, and local governments as well as many profit companies was the single entry method. The stimulus for a national accounting policy based on a double entry method occurred in 1933 and 1934 when the Securities Acts were passed in response to the Great Depression. The purpose of these acts was to develop a means whereby the public would be protected from investing money in profit companies that misrepresented or failed to reveal their financial standing. As a result, the **Securities and Exchange Commission (SEC)**, an independent federal agency, was established in 1934 to oversee the accounting and financial reporting standards for all businesses, nonprofit agencies, and governments.

The SEC determined that rather than having the federal government regulate the accounting practices of private companies and all governments, the accounting profession should set reporting standards, ensure compliance, and always represent the best interests of the public. The accounting profession, however, concentrated its efforts on profit companies and each state continued to set its own governmental accounting policies. Consequently, the accounting practices varied from state to state, and in some states from one local government to another, and even from one department within a state office to another (Freeman & Shoulders, 1996; Garner, 1991).

The succession of financial problems in New York, Cleveland, and Chicago from 1974 to 1980 caused the federal government to attempt to amend the Securities Act of 1934. The controversial amendment would have given the federal government the authority to oversee the financial reporting activities of state and local governments through a standards council. The unpopular amendment was seen as an assault on federalism. Although this effort failed in the early 1980s, the amendment caused the accounting profession to seek a solution to the problems associated with state and local governmental accounting practices (Chan, 1985).

In 1984, the Financial Accounting Foundation (FAF) established two national accounting standards boards. The Governmental Accounting Standards Board (GASB) was created to set national accounting principles for all state and local governmental bodies. The **Financial Accounting Standards Board (FASB)**, which was already in existence in 1984, was designated to continue setting accounting principles for all other entities, including nonprofit organizations. The Generally Accepted Accounting Principles (GAAP) compiled for state and local governments by the GASB included directives of the National Council on Governmental Accounting (NCGA) and the American Institute of Certified Public Accountants (AICPA).

In May 1986, the AICPA passed Ethics Rule 203 recognizing the GASB as the standards setting body for state and local governments. In November 1989, the FAF Trustees clarified a jurisdictional division between the GASB and the FASB in terms of a standards hierarchy. In January 1992, the decision of the FAF Trustees was implemented by the AICPA Auditing and Standards Board by issuing the Statement of Auditing Standards No. 69, The Meaning of "Present Fairly in Conformity with Generally Accepted Accounting Principles" (GASB, 2001).

Indirect support for implementing an accounting system based on GAAP came from the Securities and Exchange Commission via the Exchange Act 15c2-12 of 1989 that was amended in November 1994. This act required that sound financial statements be prepared and proper accounting principles (GAAP) followed by municipalities intending to issue securities or to have securities on the open market. In other words, to gain a sound credit rating for the sale of bonds, school districts' financial statements must be based on the GAAP. Finally, as discussed in the previous chapter, the GASB made a number of important revisions to its principles in 1999 for implementation from 2001 to 2003.

It is interesting to note that since the late 1980s, Christiaens (2002) reports, European countries as well as other countries around the world are introducing the use of accounting into the public sector. The impetus for these reforms—from budget control practices (known as an authorization system) to the use of accounting principles—comes as a result of a call for greater accountability and for performance measuring and reporting. In addition, more recently the establishment of International Public Sector Accounting Standards (IPSAS) has been proposed.

USING THE COMPUTER TO RUN THE DOUBLE ENTRY ACCOUNTING SYSTEM

The double entry accounting system is not difficult for school districts to operate or manage because of the availability of user-friendly computer software. Essentially, a personal computer and a data entry clerk have replaced the bookkeeper. The data entry clerk makes the entries into the computer, and the computer software processes the entries through the accounting system and prepares the financial reports.

The key to recording entries is to use the forms that appear on the computer screen. Although the number of forms used and their composition vary from one software program to another, the routine followed by the data entry clerk is the same. The data entry clerk may be located in the business office; however, in large districts with site-based budgets and a local computer network, a data entry clerk is located at each school in the district.

Computer Illustration

To describe how computers are used for entering transactions into the accounting system, a three step illustration of the process follows.

> **Step 1**–*Preparing and Processing the Purchase Order:* Assume that a site-based administrator wishes to issue a purchase order. To start the process, the administrator writes the name and number of the budget unit, a list of items or services to be ordered, their costs, and the vendor's name on a form and gives it to the data entry clerk.
>
> The data entry clerk enters the information into the purchase order form on the computer screen and notes the form number (for example, 6633). The information entered into the computer usually includes budget numbers for the site-based unit, budget account numbers (described in the next chapter), name and address of the vendor (in many cases this information is recalled from memory storage), name and catalogue number of the item or service, quantity to be purchased, unit cost, total cost (often calculated by the computer), shipping costs (if applicable), grand total cost (often calculated by the computer), and any special ordering comments.

The data entry clerk then enters the code number of the person authorized to make the order. This entry should also indicate that a signature appears on a hard copy, which then is retained for auditing purposes.

After the information is entered on the screen, the data entry clerk makes the entry command. The computer checks the budget account to ensure the amount of money to be spent is available. Then, assuming a proper balance does exist, the request is forwarded via the computer network to the purchasing clerk in the business office (if a computer network is not used, the request is forwarded in hard copy to the business office).

The purchasing clerk also checks that the balance in the budget account can cover the expenditure. If the budget account has a sufficient balance, the purchasing clerk directs the computer to print the purchase order, which makes the entries to the proper accounting and budgeting accounts. A business officer signs the purchase order to indicate it is approved. The purchase order can then be mailed to the vendor.

Step 2–*Receipt of Goods or Services:* When the items or services ordered have been received, the site-based administrator, or whoever receives the order, informs the data entry clerk. The data entry clerk recalls the form to the screen by using the purchase order number (for example, 6633) and places a mark in the box to indicate receipt of the order or service. In response, the computer program makes the appropriate accounting entries. The receiving slip or memo, indicating the goods or services have been delivered, should be mailed to the business office for control purposes.

Step 3–*Receipt and Payment of Invoice:* When the invoice is received (usually in the business office), it is attached to the receiving slip or memo and a payment voucher is prepared for approval. The approval, usually made by the business manager, indicates the goods or services have been received and the invoice agrees with the purchase order. If the invoice amount differs from the purchase order amount, inquiries should be made.

After the business administrator approves the voucher, the materials are forwarded to the accounts payable clerk in the business office. To prepare the check, the accounts payable clerk recalls the purchase order form (6633) to the screen, checks all information, enters the amount of payment, and directs the computer to print the check. When the accounting clerk enters the command to print the check, the computer makes the entries to the proper accounts. All materials associated with the purchase (including the receiving slip or memo) are forwarded with the check for signature (possibly by the business manager, the board treasurer, or both) and then mailed.

This illustration is typical of most transactions conducted by the school district. When combined with recording the budget allocations and payroll transactions, up to 95% of the business transactions are entered into the accounting system by the data entry clerk. An accountant must then record the few remaining entries into the system; for example, the reversing or deletion of an entry, adjustments, and closing entries.

When monthly budget and accounting statements are needed, the data entry clerk instructs the computer to print them. However, when a school district has a local area network, a site-based manager can call their budget report to the computer screen (not other budget reports) for review at any time and, if needed, print a copy.

ACCOUNTS USED BY THE ACCOUNTING SYSTEM

Accounting accounts (as opposed to budget accounts) are divided into two types: **real accounts** and **nominal accounts**. The balances in real accounts are carried over from one fiscal year to the next; for example, the end-of-year cash balance is the beginning balance for the next fiscal year. On the other hand, nominal accounts are temporary accounts used for one fiscal year. For example, an expense account records an allocation of money and then the charges to the account over the fiscal year. At the end of the fiscal year, the account is closed to a zero balance so that in the new fiscal year it can be opened again with a new allocation.

Real Accounts

There are three types of real accounts: assets, liabilities, and fund balance. Assets are accounts that log how much money a school owns (cash) or is owed (receivables), what it can use to conduct daily business (equipment), and what it has retained for future economic benefit (buildings). Assets may be divided into two groups: current and fixed assets. Current assets are cash or anything that can be converted to cash within a short period of time without disrupting business operations. Fixed assets are property and equipment that cannot be readily converted to cash and that promise future economic benefit.

Liabilities represent what a school owes. There are two groups of liabilities: current and long-term liabilities. Current liabilities are short-term credit arrangements that must be paid within the fiscal year. Long-term liabilities are credit arrangements that extend beyond the current fiscal year, such as a bond debt that is payable over several years.

Fund balance accounts show how much a school would have left if its assets were used to pay off its liabilities. The two major types of fund balance accounts are the *unreserved fund balance,* meaning the board can spend it as they wish, and the *reserved fund balance,* meaning the money is set aside for a specific purpose or debt.

Nominal Accounts

There are two types of nominal accounts: *revenues or income* and *expenditures or expenses. Revenue* is the account name used when money comes from tax receipts, donations, bond sales, and loans, whereas the term *income* typically represents money earned from the selling of goods and services. When money is spent, the use of an *expenditure* account indicates the charge is against a revenue source; however, using an *expense* account indicates the money comes from an income source. Although these distinctions are not always formally recognized, they are often used in general conversations and on some financial statements.

To properly relate to the use of revenues/income and expenditures/expenses in the accounting process, they should be viewed in reference to their effect on the fund balance (not cash as is often the case); that is, expenditures/expenses reduce the fund balance while revenue/income add to it. Therefore, at the end of the fiscal year, when the amount of money received exceeds the amount spent, there will be a fund balance surplus. An example of this principle is shown in the following problem.

Problem 7.1: If expenditures = $47,000 and revenues = $52,000, the effect on the fund balance would be _____?
(Answer given at the end of the chapter.)

ENCUMBERING MONEY

There are several special accounts needed to make the accounting system work. Two of these, used in governmental accounting and not in profit accounting, are the "encumbrances" and "reserve for encumbrances" accounts.

An **encumbrance** is a nominal account used when a purchase order is released. The amount of a purchase order is first recorded in an encumbrance account and causes the amount of money for the purchase to be set aside, meaning the money has been committed or promised. This entry also causes the amount to be subtracted from the available balance in the budget account. When the goods or services ordered by the purchase order are received and paid for, an expenditure is recorded for the amount paid and the amount of the encumbrance is canceled.

Problem 7.2: If encumbrances = $9,500, expenditures = $37,000, and revenues = $52,000, the impact on the fund balance would be _____?
(Answer given at the end of the chapter.)

The reserve for encumbrances account is used each time a purchase order or payment causes an entry to be made to an encumbrance account. Because the reserve for encumbrances account is a fund balance account (real account), the entry places the committed amount of the purchase order in reserve. The amount set aside in the reserve for encumbrances is deleted when the invoice is paid and the encumbrance canceled.

When an amount is held in the reserve for encumbrances account at the end of the year, it is carried over into the next fiscal year through an account called the Reserve for Encumbrances–Prior Year. The amount remaining in the encumbrance account is closed out as an expenditure against the revenue received for the current fiscal year. When the invoice is paid in the new fiscal year, it is charged against the money set aside in the Reserve for Encumbrances–Prior Year account and not against the revenue for the new fiscal year.

Therefore, the reserve for encumbrances account relieves a school district from having to collect and pay all invoices before the end of the fiscal year. Therefore, they need not have all purchase orders processed 60 to 90 days before the last day of the fiscal year, which was the practice under the single entry method.

CONTRA ACCOUNTS

Another special account is called a *contra account*. **Contra accounts** are used to temporarily reduce the balance of an asset in the financial records. For example, assume that a school district collects the local property taxes and as of July 1, 20XX, $5,000,000 is to be received. This amount is entered into an asset account called *local taxes receivable*. Realizing it will not collect the full amount, the school district estimates an amount ($100,000) that will not be collected. Upon board approval, the estimated amount ($100,000) is entered into a contra account called *Allowance for Uncollectible Taxes*. On the accounting statement the estimated uncollectible amount is subtracted from the taxes receivable amount ($5,000,000) to present the amount ($4,900,000) the school actually expects to collect. The report in the financial statement under assets would show:

ASSETS		
Taxes Receivable (Current)	$5,000,000	
Less: Allowance for Uncollectible Taxes	100,000	$4,900,000

When making the contra entry, the double entry record also causes $4,900,000 and not $5,000,000 to be entered into the revenue account. This ensures that the amount of the estimated uncollectible taxes will not be allocated and spent. If more or less than $4,900,000 is collected during the year, an accounting entry changes the amounts in the contra and revenue accounts.

THE DOUBLE ENTRY FORMULA

The algebraic formula used by the double entry accounting method is as follows:

$$\text{Assets} = \text{Liabilities} + \text{Fund Balance}.$$

This means that the total assets (what is owned) is equal to the liabilities (what is owed) plus the fund balance (what the school would have left if the assets were to pay off the liabilities). Because of this logic, the formula is more easily understood as follows:

$$\text{Assets} - \text{Liabilities} = \text{Fund Balance}.$$

In this case, the assets (what is owned) minus the liabilities (what is owed) equals what a school would have left over after all debts are paid.

Problem 7.3: If Assets = $97,000 and the Fund Balance = $84,000, then the Liabilities would equal _____?
(Answer given at the end of the chapter.)

To keep the algebraic formula balanced, a change (or entry) must be made in at least two accounts: either an equal amount must be added and subtracted from one side of the formula, an equal amount must be added to both sides of the formula, or an equal amount must be subtracted from both sides of the formula; thus the reason this method is called *double entry*.

ACCOUNT NUMBERS

The recording of accounting entries and the processing of the entries by the computer (or an accountant) require that a number be assigned to each asset, liability, fund balance, revenue, and expenditure account. The accounting numbers and names of accounts are referred to as the *Chart of Accounts*. The chart of accounts does not include the budget numbers discussed in the next chapter. Thus, there are two sets of numbers: budget numbers and accounting numbers. Both sets are important when conducting business operations and cost analyses for a school district.

As noted in the last chapter, each fund uses a set of accounts. In other words, the same accounts with the same accounting numbers are used by each accounting fund. As a result, each accounting fund has a cash account with the same accounting number.

All school districts in a state usually use the same chart of accounts. Typically, a chart of accounts follows a numbering scheme that presents the accounts in the following order: assets, liabilities, fund balance, revenues, and expenditures. In addition, the asset accounts are given numbers in reference to the length of time they can be converted to cash (lower numbers represent the shortest amount of time) while liabilities are numbered according to their currency (the more immediate liabilities have lower numbers).

The chart of accounts, which was prepared by the National Center for Educational Statistics (Fowler, 1990) for all state Departments of Education and school districts, is presented in Resource A at the end of the text. Note that assets, budget, liabilities, and fund balance accounts are assigned numbers within a range; for instance, current assets are given numbers ranging from 100 to 199. If an additional account is needed, it can be given a number and a name in the appropriate category.

While the school administrators in central administration and the school business office reference accounting numbers in their work, site-based administrators and data entry clerks do not often use them. Rather, they use the budget numbers presented in the next chapter on a regular basis.

OVERVIEW OF THE ACCOUNTING PROCESS

An overview of the accounting process is shown in Figure 7.1. This is the traditional process followed by accountants, and it is conducted by the computer software program discussed in the prior illustration. Specifically, when a business

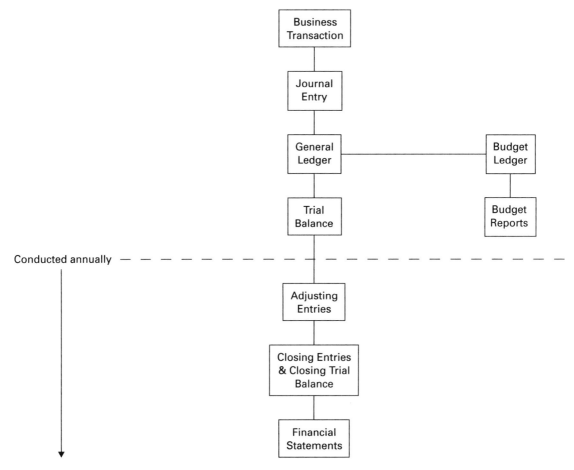

FIGURE 7.1
The Accounting Process

transaction occurs, it is recorded in an accounting journal. The amount of the entry is entered into at least two of the accounts shown in the chart of accounts (for example, when a debt is paid, one account would be the cash account 101 and the other, accounts payable 421). The journal entries are then sorted (called posting) and recorded into their separate general ledger accounts (like an index card in the computer). As a result, if an administrator wished to check on an entry, for example the amount recorded for a purchase order, either the journal entries for that purchase order number or the accounts in the ledger can be displayed on the computer screen or printed out in hard copy.

After the posting to the general ledger, the amounts for the budget accounts are forwarded (posted) to a budget ledger for entry into a budget account number.

Posting to the budget ledger is how the accounting system is connected to the budget system. When site-based budgets are used, the budget numbering system simply provides for an additional posting of the transactions to budget subledgers. While the budget reports present the balances of the budget ledger accounts, the trial balance is a statement (see Figure 7.1) that presents the balances of the accounting accounts in the general ledger.

At the end of the year, necessary adjustments to the accounts are entered, and then closing entries are made. Once the books are closed, administrators must be aware that no further business can be conducted because the nominal accounts have a zero balance. Upon the completion of the closing trial balance, the financial statements are prepared and may be reviewed. Usually after these statements are reviewed, they are presented for an audit by an accountant. After an audit, the statements are presented to the board and then released to the public.

After a fiscal year has ended, it typically takes a school district one to two months to close the books and prepare the financial statements. Then another two months should be allowed for the audit report to be received. The report containing all of the financial statements made available to the public is called the Comprehensive Annual Financial Report (CAFR).

LINKING THE ACCOUNTING AND BUDGETING SYSTEMS

The budget ledger uses budget account numbers (see chapter 8). The accounting system is connected to the budget system through special accounts in the accounting system designated as *control accounts*. When an amount is posted to a control account in the general ledger (shown in Figure 7.1), the amount is also posted to the budget ledger. The control accounts and their accounting numbers shown in Resource A are: appropriations 601, expenditures and expenses 602, encumbrances 603, estimated revenue 301, and revenue or income 302. The following figures (Figures 7.2, 7.3, 7.4) exhibit how the accounting system places

Budget Unit 10				
Budget Acct. Number	Appropriations	Expenditure	Encumbrances	Available Balance
610 Supplies	$1,000.00			$1,000.00

FIGURE 7.2
Appropriation Posted to Budget Report

Budget Unit 10				
Budget Acct. Number	Appropriations	Expenditure	Encumbrances	Available Balance
610 Supplies	$1,000.00		$100.00	$900.00

FIGURE 7.3
Appropriation Posted to Budget Report

encumbrances and expenditures into budget accounts. Budget number 610 is used to represent the supplies budget account.

1. When a budget has been approved, the total amount is entered into the appropriations control account 601 in the accounting journal and then posted into the general ledger to the appropriations account 601. Because 601 is a control account, the allocation is then posted to the various budget ledger expenditure accounts. The amount placed into each budget account comes from the information entered into the computer by the data entry clerk. In the example shown in Figure 7.2, an appropriation of $1,000 is posted to Budget Unit 10's supplies account 610 to create an available balance of $1,000.

2. After the fiscal year begins, assume the administrator responsible for Budget Unit 10 authorizes an order to purchase $100 of supplies. The data entry clerk enters the order into the computer system for Budget Unit 10, account 610. This computer entry: (a) makes a journal entry to the encumbrances control account 603 for $100, (b) posts the amount to the general ledger encumbrance control account 603, and (c) transfers the charge to the budget ledger for Budget Unit 10, account 610. This is illustrated in Figure 7.3, reducing the amount in the available balance column to $900.00.

Budget Unit 10				
Budget Acct. Number	Appropriations	Expenditure	Encumbrances	Available Balance
610 Supplies	$1,000.00	$110.00		$890.00

FIGURE 7.4
Appropriation Posted to Budget Report

3. Assume the estimate on the purchase order was not accurate and the supplies along with an invoice for $110 were received. A payment voucher for $110 is prepared and approved and a check is drawn for $110. When the payment is recorded into the accounting system: (a) the amount of $110 is entered into the journal for the expenditure control account 602 and an amount of $100 (the amount of the purchase order estimate) is entered into the encumbrances control account 603, (b) the amounts are posted to both control accounts in the general ledger, and (c) the charges are posted to the budget ledger for Budget Unit 10, account 610. The amount of $110 is entered as an expenditure (as shown in Figure 7.4) and the encumbrance entry for $100 cancels the amount encumbered. The report now shows an available balance of $890.

CLOSING THE BOOKS

Before the accounts can be closed at the end of the fiscal year, adjustments may be necessary. Because these affect operations, school administrators must be aware of their potential impact. Adjustments are made if necessary, as discussed below, as follows: (a) to accrual entries for revenue and expenditure accounts; (b) to the **depreciation** of capital assets, such as buildings and equipment; and (c) to inventories for goods purchased for consumption and goods purchased for resale.

Accrual Adjustments

Two methods may be used when accounting for the receipt and expenditure of money. One approach, called the **cash accounting** method, simply records income or revenue when money is received (not earned) and recognizes expenditures when money is actually spent (not when goods or services are received). The other approach, called the **accrual accounting** method, recognizes income or revenue when it is earned (not when cash is received) and expenses when services are received and goods are used (not when they are paid). A modified accrual approach is when a cash method is used in one instance (such as the receipt of money) and accruals in the other (such as expenditures). As explained later, some funds use the modified accrual method whereas others use full accruals.

There are four possible accrual adjustments that may be made. With respect to receipts, when money has been received in the current year but will not be earned until the next year, an accrual adjustment is made to recognize the money received as revenue earned in the next year (not the current year when the cash is received). Example: Money for football season tickets is received in May but will not be earned until the next fiscal year. The accrual adjustment would cause the money to be recognized as income the next year when the games are played and not the current year.

Another adjusting entry is required when money has been earned in the current year but will not be received until the next year. The accrual entry will cause this money to be recognized as revenue for the current year. Example: A payment from a federal grant will not be received until the next fiscal year. The accrual entry would record the receipt as revenue earned in the current year when services were rendered (not next year when a check is received).

Adjustments are also made for expenditures. One adjustment is for money paid in the current year for goods or services to be received the next year. The accrual entry would charge the payment against next year's budget. Example: To gain a discount, a textbook order is paid before the end of the year; however, the delivery will not be made until the next fiscal year. The accrual entry will charge the expenditure against next year's budget, not the current year's.

The second expenditure entry involves the receipt (and use) of goods or services this year that will not be invoiced or paid for until next year. Example: A school district has a building repair made on June 25th (the fiscal year ends June 30). The cost of the repair is known but the invoice is not received until July 10th. The accrual entry will cause the repair to be charged against the current budget when the repair was made and not in the following fiscal year.

Capital Assets and Depreciation

Capital assets are buildings, land, and equipment whose purchase price or value is greater than a predetermined amount, such as $500 or whatever amount the state or school district sets. When the cost of an item is less than $500 and has not been purchased for resale, it is considered a consumable supply item and is recorded as a supply expenditure.

To spread the cost of a capital asset over its expected life (except land), it is depreciated each year. To calculate depreciation, the cost of the asset minus its estimated salvage value at the end of its useful life is divided by the number of years of its estimated useful life. For example, if a machine cost $21,000, has an estimated salvage value of $1,000, and is estimated to have a life of 10 years, the annual depreciation would be $2,000 or ($21,000 − $1,000)/10 years = $2,000.

Depreciation does not involve the expenditure of any money or the setting aside of money in a savings account. Rather it is simply a means to allocate a large expenditure of money over the time period when the asset will be used. Therefore, the cost for educating children should include the annual $2,000 depreciation expense for the use of the equipment. Such an inclusion of costs would allow more accurate expenditure comparisons to be made among school districts along with the formal recognition of the deterioration of assets. In fact, the exclusion of the use of capital costs in accounting shows an underestimated amount of the cost of expenditures that were made for education. This, in turn, causes a failure to recognize some extreme differences in the inequities that exist among school districts, within school districts, and from one generation to the next.

When fixed assets are depreciated, the financial statements present their book value through the use of a contra account—accumulated depreciation. For example, if a truck with a salvage value of $1,000 had been depreciated for three years, the value of the $21,000 truck less the accumulated depreciation of $6,000 ($2,000 $\times$ 3 years) would be $15,000 and shown in the financial statements as follows:

ASSETS

Truck	$21,000	
Less: Accumulated Depreciation	6,000	$15,000

The GASB (1999) proposes that capital assets purchased through the government funds should be accounted for in a statement of net assets. At the same time, the proprietary and trust funds should show their capital assets and depreciation in the financial statements prepared for their funds.

Further, the GASB recommends that governmental capital assets be accounted for at their original historical cost while donated assets be recorded at their market value. And finally, they suggest that all capital assets should be depreciated over their useful life. To depreciate an elementary school built in 1935 at an historical cost of $10,000, however, is not likely relevant. As a result, the recognition of capital assets and the accounting of their depreciation still needs attention.

Inventory: Resale and Consumption

In an enterprise fund, goods may be purchased for resale. In such cases, the calculation of the goods unsold (inventory) must be made before the books are closed. When goods are purchased for consumption but remain unused, some states require school districts with a central supply fund to conduct an inventory at the end of the year. In both cases the amount of the inventory reduces the expenditures charged to a budget at the end of the fiscal year.

One of the many advantages for conducting an inventory is to prohibit the removal of supplies and other items from a school district. If supplies are inventoried periodically, the security offered to these resources will be enhanced.

FINAL THOUGHTS

The double entry accounting system offers a variety of controls for the protection of the resources of a school district. Likely the most important issue to a school administrator is preventing overexpenditures from being processed against budget accounts. Another is protecting school resources from improper use or manipulation through the inherent advantages offered by the double entry algebraic formula.

These and other accounting controls, however, are only effective if administrators require employees to follow proper procedures and to examine all records and financial statements. An old practice of office managers, including the author, is to ensure that everyone abides by the rules for processing and recording financial transactions, regardless of how pointless they may seem. Violations of procedures

ISLLC

are often attempts to manipulate the system by an individual who wishes to conduct fraudulent activities or test the administrators and the system. In this regard, Standard 6 of the ISLLC (1996) becomes appropriate. This standard states that administrators are expected to facilitate the processes and engage in activities "ensuring that the school community works within the framework of policies, laws, and regulations enacted by local, state, and federal authorities" (p. 21).

Also, educational leaders should recognize the importance of the effort to standardize the numbers of the chart of accounts for the accounting and budgeting systems by the National Center for Educational Statistics. By using a common accounting framework with the same accounting and budget numbers, it becomes possible to eliminate many inconsistencies among financial reports. For example, valid and reliable financial data gained from reports prepared in previous years or from a regional, state, or national data bank is invaluable to policymakers. Further, the responses to the calls for financial accountability will not likely be held in high regard if the reports are confusing and appear contradictory.

DISCUSSION QUESTIONS

1. Explain what *double entry* means.
   a. How is this method different from the single entry method?
   b. How does the double entry method of processing of information enhance the security of a school district's resources?
2. How might the centralization and annual inventory of consumable supplies benefit a school district?
3. What is the reason for depreciating capital assets?
4. What advantages do accrual entries offer a school district?
5. With respect to the entering and processing of business transactions by a data entry clerk, what are the duties of a site-based administrator, such as a school principal?
   a. What rules and procedures might this person set for the teachers and a data entry clerk?

APPLICATION PROBLEMS

The answers are provided at the end of the chapter.

1. If the school district's assets equal $97,000 and the fund balance is $13,000, the total liabilities are _____?
2. At the end of the year, the following balances exist: Fund Balance $4,000, Revenue $58,000, Expenditures $53,000, and Encumbrances $2,000. After the accounts are closed, the new balance of the Fund Balance account will be _____?

3. Using the account numbers in Resource A, identify the names of the following.
   a. 101
   b. 111
   c. 241
   d. 431
   e. 770
4. If a school building cost $12,000,000 to build, the estimated life of the building is 40 years, and the salvage value is estimated at $2,000,000; how much would the building be depreciated each year?
   a. If 500 students attended the school in the past year, what is the cost of the building per student for the year?

CLINICAL PRACTICUM EXERCISES

In response to the clinical exercises below, the suggested format is to: (a) state the question, (b) answer the question, and (c) discuss your answer in reference to the content presented in the text. If supporting material is discussed and can be made available, it should be referenced in the discussion as an appendix and attached to the end of the report. Note that one of the objectives of part 3 is to show that the material in this book has been read, comprehended, and applied.

Using the information in this chapter as a reference, report your findings on the following:

1. the method of accounting and chart of accounts used by school district;
2. the process for the entry of purchase orders into the computer software;
3. the processing of delivery slips and invoices; and
4. procedures followed for the payment of invoices.

WEB ADDRESSES

National Center for Education Statistics
http://nces.ed.gov

REFERENCES

Chan, J. L. (1985). The birth of the Governmental Accounting Standards Board: How? Why? In J. L. Chan (Ed.), *Research in governmental and nonprofit accounting* (Vol. 1, pp. 3–32). Greenwich, CT: JAI Press.

Chatfield, M. (1974). *A History of Accounting Thought.* Hinsdale, IL: Dryden Press.

Christiaens, J. (2002). Symposium introduction. *Journal of Public Budgeting, Accounting & Financial Management, 14*(4), 560–564.

Fowler, W. J., Jr. (1990). *Financial accounting for local and state school systems.* Washington, DC: U.S. Department of Education [Online]. Retrieved April 4, 2002, from http://nces.ed.gov

Freeman, R. J., & Shoulders, C. D. (1996). *Governmental & nonprofit accounting: Theory & practice* (5th ed.). Upper Saddle River, NJ: Merrill/Prentice Hall.

Garner, C. W. (1991). *Accounting and Budgeting in Public and Nonprofit Organizations: A Manager's Guide.* San Francisco: Jossey-Bass.

Garner, C. W. (1996). An inquiry into the feasibility of a national accounting policy for public schools. *Journal of Public Budgeting and Financial Management, 8*(2), 208–223.

Governmental Accounting Standards Board (2001). *Codification of governmental accounting and financial reporting standards.* Norwalk, CT: Author.

Interstate School Leaders Licensure Consortium (1996). *Standards for school leaders.* Washington, DC: Concil of Chief State School Officers.

Kam, V. (1986). *Accounting Theory.* New York: Wiley.

Lee, G. A. (1984). The development of Italian bookkeeping: 1211–1300. In C. Nobes (Ed.), *The development of double entry* (pp. 137–155). New York: Garland Publishing.

Yamey, B. S. (1984). The functional development of double entry bookkeeping. In C. Nobes (Ed.), *The development of double entry* (pp. 333–342). New York: Garland Publishing.

ANSWERS TO PROBLEMS IN THE TEXT

7.1 An increase of $5,000

7.2 An available balance of $5,500

7.3 $13,000

ANSWERS TO APPLICATION PROBLEMS

1. $84,000
2. $7,000
3. **a.** cash
   b. investments
   c. machinery and equipment
   d. contracts payable
   e. unreserved fund balance
4. $250,000
   a. $500

Chapter 8

Contents and Process of the Budgeting System

ISLLC

Standard 3 of the Interstate School Leaders Licensure Consortium (ISLLC, 1996) proposes that administrators ensure that their financial resources are aligned to the goals of the school and that the systems are regularly monitored and modified. To meet this expectation, school administrators must know how the budgeting system works. Further, a working knowledge of this system is necessary if administrators wish to ensure, as suggested by the ISLLC, that the "fiscal resources of a school are managed safely, efficiently, and effectively" (p. 15). Under Standard 3, the National Council for Accreditation of Teacher Education (NCATE) expects leadership candidates to understand the finance structure and be able to allocate resources equitably and to ensure that they are used to support student achievement (NPBEA, 2002).

ISLLC

When managing the financial resources of a school or school district, an old maxim for administrators to follow is that the three most important tasks are to: (a) document, (b) document, and (c) document! Documentation is one of the major benefits provided by the budget system. This is because budget numbers are connected to every budget transaction. Each transaction can be traced to the form used for generating the computer entry, to the person who authorized the budget action, to the use of the money, and to the person or company that cashed the check. When the accounting and budgeting systems are properly installed, following a money trail is not a difficult task.

The budgeting system actually uses two sets of budget numbers within each fund. One set is for revenues, the other for expenditures. Revenue numbers are used to identify the source of the money placed in a fund. Expenditure numbers are used to record each budget allocation and then the expenditure of the allocation. Thus, the benefit of budget documentation relates directly to the design and application of the numbering scheme.

A uniform set of budget numbers should be used by all school districts in a state. Like accounting numbers, the GASB (2001) does not suggest a list of budget numbers to be used; however, they do recommend a numbering outline. In 1990, the National Center for Educational Statistics designed a list of revenue and expenditure account numbers that correspond to the suggested outline of the Governmental Accounting Standards Board (GASB). The numbers set forth by the National Center for Education Statistics (NCES) are referenced for the numbering scheme discussed in this chapter.

BUDGET NUMBERING FORMAT

The NCES budget numbers (Fowler, 1990) were designed by a committee trying to set national standards for state Departments of Education and school districts. As explained in the forward of the document, the budget names and numbers should be used by school districts in the annual reports they submit to their state Department of Education. In turn, these departments must use the same numbers in their reports to the federal government. Thus, using this set of budget names and numbers helps to ensure that all fiscal data is reported in a comprehensive and uniform manner by all school districts in the country.

The committee that prepared the budget names and numbers for the NCES in 1990 (reprinted in 1995) was careful to ensure that their numbering schematic complied with the Generally Accepted Accounting Principles (GAAP). Although the GASB made a number of changes in their standards in 1999, their suggested format for the classification of account and budget numbers was not significantly revised. Thus, the schematic set forth by the NCES will likely be relevant for some time.

The NCES budget numbering schematic consists of one set of names and numbers for revenues and one for expenditures. The revenue numbers are composed of two subsets: xx-xxxx. The first two numbers represent the fund into which the revenue is placed, and the remaining four numbers identify the source of the money, as follows:

Fund	Revenue
xx	xxxx

Expenditure names and numbers used by the budgeting system are composed of four subsets of numbers, for example, xx-xxx-xxxx-xxx; although an additional subset may be added to designate a site-based unit. Again the first two numbers represent the accounting fund from which the expenditure is made, and the remaining 10 numbers identify the program, function, and object of the expenditure, as follows:

Fund	Program	Function	Object
xx	xxx	xxxx	xxx

Therefore, the first numbers considered in either a revenue or an expenditure number are those designating the accounting fund (as listed in Resource B). This list does not contain any duplicate or special funds described in the previous chapters but corresponds to the major types of funds proposed by the NCES (Fowler, 1990) and the GASB (2001), with the exception of the student activity fund. This fund has been added to the list for reference and discussion purposes since it should be used by all school districts.

REVENUE BUDGET NUMBERS

Revenue budget numbers identify the source of money received by a school district. The five categories used for the revenue sources are listed in Figure 8.1. The first four categories represent revenues received from local, intermediate, state, and federal sources, while the fifth provides numbers for miscellaneous sources. Although the category numbers range from 1000 to 6999, as shown in Resource C the numbers within each category identify every possible type of revenue that a school district could receive. If other types of revenues are received by a school district, a new number and the name of the source can be added to the list.

To record a revenue award into the accounting and budgeting systems, an accounting clerk enters the accounting fund and revenue number into the computer. For example, if an award was received from the state for foundation aid and placed in the general fund, the budget number entered into the computer as per Resources B and C would be 10 (general fund)–3110 (foundation aid).

> **Problem 8.1:** Using Resources B and C, what revenue number would be used for a revenue award received for the general fund from the state for transportation aid?
>
> (Answer given at the end of the chapter.)
>
> **Problem 8.2:** What revenue number would be used to indicate that a receipt is for a capital project from the sale of bonds?
>
> (Answer given at the end of the chapter.)
>
> Note: A school district could use revenue number 5110 to represent one bond sale and 5111 to represent another bond sale.

FIGURE 8.1
Revenue Number Categories

Range of Numbers	Revenue Source
1000–1999	Local sources such as local taxes, admission receipts, rentals, and cafeteria sales.
2000–2999	Intermediate sources such as county tax revenue.
3000–3999	State revenue sources such as state grants.
4000–4999	Federal revenue sources.
5000–6999	Other sources such as fund transfers, bond sales, and loan receipts.

CONTROLLING REVENUE RECEIPTS

Receipts of cash, checks, and wire transfers must be secure from the time they are received by a school employee to the time they are deposited in a bank. The protection provided to these receipts, as well as to employees who handle the money, begins with a policy approved by the school board. The rules and procedures developed for implementing the policy should designate the administrative positions allowed to receive money, describe how money is transmitted from position to position, designate the positions that may make bank deposits, set deadlines for the length of time the money may be held until deposits are made, require that deposits be recorded into the accounting system daily, designate the position that reconciles the bank statements, and set a time limit for bank reconciliations (such as within one week of the receipt of the bank statement). Note that the policy should identify positions and not people. Although such a policy may seem extreme, cases of fraud can be cited when one or more of the above conditions has been ignored.

Site-based administrators must also be concerned with the development of rules and procedures for carrying out board policies. For example, the site administrator for food services (such as a Director of Food Services, or in some states the responsibility is assigned to the school principal) is ultimately responsible for the collection of cafeteria money; school principals are responsible for all money collected in their school from students (such as class dues, club dues, yearbook sales, and class trips); and athletic directors are responsible for all gate receipts and deposits. In the event of any theft or embezzlement, the person in charge is always suspect and ultimately held accountable when a district policy or law has been violated. To reduce their potential liability, the following suggestions should be considered by administrators.

First of all, at least three people should be involved with the receipt, recording, and depositing of money. That is, an employee who receives money must provide receipts to the individuals making a payment (mail including cash and check payments should be opened, recorded, and processed by two employees). Next, another employee should either deposit the money in the bank or deliver it to the business office for deposit. After the deposit is made, a data entry clerk should enter the amount on the bank deposit receipt into the accounting records. Another employee, who is not involved with either the receipt or expenditure of money, or a board treasurer, should reconcile the bank statements. In the case of wire transfers (a deposit from one bank to another via electronic transfer), the transmittal and deposit should be verified by one employee, entered into the accounting records by a second person, and confirmed in the bank reconciliation by a third person.

Second, school administrators should have employees use transmittal forms when money is handed from one employee to another. When money is transferred, both employees sign the form indicating the amount and date of transfer, and each person retains a copy.

Finally, the revenue budget reports should be reviewed by all parties receiving, processing, recording, and depositing money. Their verifications that the records are accurate should be recorded and placed on file by the site-based administrator. At unannounced times, the business office should conduct internal audits of receipt and transmittal records. Administrators must not only protect the resources of the school, but they must also protect their honest employees.

Fidelity Bonds

A **fidelity bond** is an insurance policy that covers employees who handle money. In the event of any fraud or embezzlement, the insurance company covers the loss caused by a bonded employee. Fidelity bonds are often effective because a bonding agency will press charges whereas too often school districts will not.

Although the cost of a fidelity bond is reasonable, a school must demonstrate to the bonding company that proper financial controls are in place; particularly at the time the loss takes place. In cases where controls were not in place, a bonding agency may not make restitution or may only make minimal restitution. Therefore, a fidelity bond is not a substitute for receipt control.

EXPENDITURE BUDGET NUMBERS

The five sets of expenditure budget numbers set forth by the NCES (Fowler, 1990) are for:

1. accounting funds;
2. programs, such as regular and special education programs;
3. functions, such as instruction, media services, and business services;
4. objects, such as salaries or supplies;
5. and instructional, operational, subject matter, job, or cost center units.

Program Budget Numbers

Program budget numbers have three digits with the first digit classifying the program in the broadest sense of the word, such as regular, special, and vocational programs as shown in Figure 8.2. A second program digit can denote the grade level or area in a program category, and the third digit may further define the program in terms of student classifications, type of service offered, or student population.

FIGURE 8.2
Categories for Program Expenditure Numbers

1st Digit—Nine Categories
- 100—regular programs
- 200—special programs
- 300—vocational programs
- 400—other instructional programs
- 500—nonpublic school programs
- 600—adult and continuing education programs
- 700—debt service
- 800—community service programs
- 900—enterprise programs
- 000—undistributed expenditures

FIGURE 8.3
Categories for Function Numbers

Range of Numbers	Function
1000–1999	Instruction
2000–2999	Support Services
3000–3999	Noninstructional Services
4000–4999	Facilities Acquisition/Construction
5000–5999	Other

Derived from the numbers suggested by the NCES, a comprehensive list of program numbers is presented in Resource D.

Function Budget Numbers

The **function budget numbers** are four digit numbers used to further define the budget program areas presented above. Figure 8.3 shows the five areas that function numbers represent. For example, the first set of function numbers is for instructional activities. When a number within the 1000 range follows a 100 program number, the expenditure would be for regular instruction. If a program number is 300 (vocational education) and the function number is 1000, the expenditure would be for instruction in a vocational education program. A list of four digit function numbers is shown in Resource E.

> **Problem 8.3:** Using Resources B, D, and E, what would be the expenditure for budget number 10-140-1000?
> (Answer given at the end of the chapter.)

Object Budget Numbers

Object budget numbers are three digit numbers used to further define program allocations and expenditures. For example, in the previous exercise, the number 10-140-1000 needs more definition. Was the expenditure for salaries or supplies? The object number provides that information. Figure 8.4 shows the range of

FIGURE 8.4
Categories for Object Numbers

Range of Numbers	Object of Expenditures
100–199	Salaries
200–299	Benefits
300–399	Professional–Technical Services
400–499	Property Services
500–599	Other Services
600–699	Supplies & Materials
700–799	Property
800–899	Other Goods & Services
900–999	Other Uses of Funds

budget numbers for nine object categories, while Resource F lists the numbers and objects used within these categories.

> **Problem 8.4:** Using the Resources, what expenditure number would be used to pay a bus driver (full-time employee) to take the football team to another school when the money is to come from the gate receipts of the home games?
>
> (Answer given at the end of the chapter.)

> **Problem 8.5:** What would the following expenditure number represent: 40-701-5100-910?
>
> (Answer given at the end of the chapter.)

Site-Based Budget Numbers

A list of site-based unit budget numbers, such as those used shown in Figure 6.3 in chapter 6, are not likely included in a master list of numbers used by school districts. This is because the differences in the organizational structures of school districts are too great, such as a small rural district versus a large metropolitan district, to present a specific list of numbers. Therefore, the basis for a numbering system for site units is typically determined at the local level.

The site-based unit budget numbers may consist of two or three digit numbers and appear as a prefix or suffix to the other expenditure budget numbers. The numbers assigned to budget units should follow a pattern: for example, numbers from 01 to 19 for district-wide units, such as central administrative units; 20 to 49 for high school units; 50 to 74 for middle school units; 75 to 84 for elementary schools; and 85 to 99 for miscellaneous units in proprietary and fiduciary funds. Each fund then uses the same set of site-based unit numbers.

CONTROLLING THE DISBURSEMENT OF MONEY

As with the receipt of money, disbursements should be guided by board policy with administrators developing rules and regulations to implement the policy. In addition, the rules and regulations may have to be modified for each site unit.

First of all, when processing expenditures, recognizing the difference between authorization and approval signatures is crucial. An authorization signature indicates an expenditure request is appropriate to the financial plan or the needs of the school or unit. Therefore, the person making the authorization must be knowledgeable about the strategic financial plan to validate that the purpose of the purchase is appropriate, such as supplies for a class or repairs to a building. The approval signature, on the other hand, verifies that the person authorizing the purchase has been approved to make the purchase and that there is a sufficient balance in the allocation to the expenditure account to cover the order.

Next, the rules and regulations for disbursements should divide the responsibilities among three employees as follows: (a) the person who authorizes a disbursement, (b) the person who approves the disbursement and oversees the recording of the entries into the accounting records, and (c) the person who signs the checks for the payment of the goods and services. This set of rules is designed to address the old accounting tenet that collusion and conspiracy are much more difficult when three or more people are involved.

As noted above in revenue control, the person reconciling the bank statement should not be involved in both disbursements and receipts. Further, amounts of wire transfers from the school district to another bank should be verified in the accounting records, the bank reconciliation, and a transmittal letter. For example, the bank account in one school district was being used to launder money via wire transfers. Because the account was not monitored, the violation was learned through an embarrassing FBI raid on the school district's administrative offices.

School regulations should stipulate that the person who authorized the expenditure should inspect and accept the shipments or services when received. This individual should also review the invoices before payments are made. This is particularly important since all of the goods ordered may not have been received or may have been damaged, or a service may not have been completed satisfactorily.

In addition, if an invoice is greater than the amount stated on the purchase order, the site-based administrator should be on record as accepting the overcharge or given the option of returning the goods (which this author has done). The internal audit by the building administrator and business manager should verify that the goods and services ordered and reported received were actually received. The regulations should also insist that audits periodically inventory the receipts and verify any services rendered. These checks are important because of the numerous cases involving collusion between an employee and a vendor. In one case, for example, the amounts on the invoices exceeded the purchase orders by an average of 60%. Although collusion was obvious, it could not be proven.

The business manager or position designated in the business office should provide the final approval for the payment of invoices. The person signing the checks should not authorize the payments, enter transactions in the accounting records, receive goods, or reconcile the bank statement. When site-based administrators review the budget report, all expenditures in the report should be checked against the records on site for accuracy, and the verifications should be placed on file.

When these and other basic rules are not established and followed, the stories of embezzlement, fraud, abuse, and ruined careers are too numerous to mention. One school board felt they were saving the taxpayer money by having the school district bookkeeper authorize and approve all purchase orders, verify receipts, receive invoices, make out the checks, reconcile the bank balances, and make deposits. The savings were small compared to the million dollars embezzled and the ruined reputations of the school board members, school administrators, and school auditor.

EXPENDITURE FORMS

Budget control is enhanced when different forms are used for the expenditure of budget money. These forms allow expenditures to be categorized, which helps school administrators process, control, and trace transactions. The forms, which are printed via computer software programs, should contain the organization's name and address on all copies, a form number, and lines for authorization and approval signatures. The following forms are recommended.

Purchase Order—presents a proposed business transaction between the school and a vendor. This form must have an affirmative action statement on the copy sent to the vendor.

Quick Purchase Order—is the same as a purchase order except it may be used when a purchase is for less than a specified dollar amount, such as $50 or $100 or $250. They are considered "quick" because the order is sent from the site-based administrator (such as a school principal) to the vendor with a copy to the business manager. The approval by the business office and the entry into the accounting system are completed after the order has been made. In some cases a phone approval by the business office may be required before an order is released. Again, as with the purchase order, the quick order must have an affirmative action statement on the copy sent to the vendor.

Requisition—is used internally to draw a check without an invoice. For example, a check may have to be sent with a purchase order when a vendor requires payment in advance, given to a speaker as an honorarium at the end of a visit, or given to an employee who needs cash to take a trip.

Internal Purchase Order—is processed when one site-based budget unit (such as an elementary school) is requesting goods or services from another (such as central supply).

Travel Form—is presented along with original receipts for personal travel reimbursement or relief from a cash advance.

Wage Payroll Form—is used to record the hours worked for payments to temporary employees.

Vouchers—are internal forms used to process a request or when a hard copy of a request for an order is needed. For example, teachers may use vouchers to submit a request for supplies, for transportation for a class trip, and so on.

FINAL THOUGHTS

Although the budget numbers and procedures may be common for all school districts in a state, the responsibilities assigned to the positions in the organizational structure of the districts are likely to be different. Therefore, the rules and procedures developed for implementing the policies, for providing controls, and for utilizing the budget data will vary from one school district to another. This is the challenge that requires administrators to be informed and creative. One set of rules cannot fit all situations.

An important benefit of the site-based budgeting practice is the equitable allocation of money within a school district. Concern about the equal distribution of resources within a district was the issue brought before the court in Washington, DC in *Hobson v. Hansen* (1967, 1971). Guthrie, Garms, and Pierce (1988) explain how the cases caused the Washington, DC, schools to decentralize their budgets. They also explain that, in turn, the U.S. Office of Education issued the "so-called comparability regulations, demanding that school districts distribute resources equitably in order to remain eligible for federal funds" (p. 199). Although the court ruling limited their directive to equal minimal funding, the plight was for the district to be able to decentralize their budgets to show compliance. Using site-based budget units can provide this evidence.

Finally, a concern often heard from educators is regarding the many tasks set forth for site-based administrators and the danger of their getting bogged down with the minutiae of budget management. So that administrators can focus on teachers and children, some school districts have assigned a business assistant to coordinate the daily budget operations of site-based units. These assistants are located in either the school or a common building, where they are responsible for managing several budget units and often work under the supervision of the school district's business manager. At this time, the benefits of employing these coordinators, who are not certified business managers, seem to outweigh the cost.

DISCUSSION QUESTIONS

1. Using the revenue numbers in Resource C, identify:
   a. a revenue that would be placed in the general fund and in the special revenue fund.
   b. a revenue that would be placed in the capital projects fund and in the debt service fund.
   c. a revenue that would be placed in the enterprise and in the internal services funds.
   d. a revenue that would be placed in the student services fund.

2. Assume that the teachers in an elementary school are responsible for collecting money from students for their class accounts and also for cafeteria tickets. What procedures should the principal of the school set up for the collection and transmission of this money to the principal's office and then to the business office?

3. What is the purpose of fund, program, function, and object numbers?

4. Assume that an elementary school principal is the site-based administer for all budget allocations to the school for funds 10 and 20. What procedures should the principal implement for expenditure requests, processing the requests, receipts of goods and services, and reports to the business office?

5. In a faculty meeting with the teachers, the principal receives a complaint about the use of the complex budget numbers along with the rules and procedures

related to the collection and expenditure of money. What justifications might the principal offer in regard to the legal and organizational benefits of the numbers and procedures?

APPLICATION PROBLEMS

The answers are provided at the end of the chapter.

1. Using Resources B and C, indicate the fund and revenue numbers used to record the following receipts.
   a. Daily receipts from the cafeteria are deposited.
   b. A check is received—a Chapter I grant for handicapped students.
   c. Money is received from the Gillman Elementary School for the fifth grade class trip.
   d. Tuition is received from Mr. Roy Ellenberger who resides in the neighboring school district.
   e. The PTA makes a donation to the school for the purchase of new playground equipment at the Fudrow Elementary School.
2. Using Resources B, D, E, and F, indicate the fund, program, function, and object numbers used in the following transactions.
   a. Instructional supplies are ordered for the high school.
   b. A purchase order is released for classroom supplies for the state funded evening shop program.
   c. Food is purchased for the cafeteria from food receipts.
   d. The home instruction counselor, Mrs. Patricia McLoughlin, is reimbursed for travel expenses.
   e. Programs are ordered from a printer for the high school play (to be paid from ticket receipts).

CLINICAL PRACTICUM EXERCISES

In response to the clinical exercises below, the suggested format is to: (a) state the question, (b) answer the question, and (c) discuss your answer in reference to the content presented in the text. If supporting material is discussed and can be made available, it should be referenced in the discussion as an appendix and attached to the end of the report. Note that one of the objectives of part 3 is to show that the material in the book has been read, comprehended, and applied.

Using the information in this chapter as a reference, report your findings on the following:

1. the budget numbers used for revenues, expenditures, and site-based units;
2. rules and procedures related to receipts (including the use of cash transmittal forms), expenditures, receipt of goods and services, and the processing and payment of invoices;

3. the rules and procedures for the use of authorization and approval signatures;

4. the use of fidelity bonds;

5. conducting internal audits; and

6. different types of business forms used (such as purchase orders).

WEB ADDRESSES

National Council for Accreditation of Teacher Education
http://www.ncate.org

National Center for Education Statistics
http://nces.ed.gov

REFERENCES

Fowler, W. J., Jr. (1990). *Financial accounting for local and state school systems.* Washington, DC: U.S. Department of Education [Online]. Retrieved April 4, 2002, from http://nces.ed.gov

Governmental Accounting Standards Board (2001). *Codification of governmental accounting and financial reporting standards.* Norwalk, CT: Author.

Guthrie, J. W., Garms, W. I., & Pierce, L. C. (1988). *School finance and educational policy: Enhancing educational efficiency, equality and choice* (2nd ed.). Upper Saddle River, NJ: Merrill/Prentice Hall.

Hobson v. Hansen 269 R. Suppl. 401 (D.D.C., 1967).

Hobson v. Hansen 327 R. Suppl. (D.D.C., 1971).

Interstate School Leaders Licensure Consortium (1996). *Standards for school leaders.* Washington, DC: Council of Chief State School Officers.

National Policy Board for Educational Administration (2002). *Standards for advanced programs in educational leadership for principals, superintendents, curriculum directors, and supervisors* [Online]. Retrieved February 17, 2003, from http://www.ncate.org

ANSWERS TO PROBLEMS IN THE TEXT

8.1 10-3120

8.2 30-5110

8.3 The expenditure is from the general fund (10) for grades 9–12 (140) for instruction (1000).

8.4 50-990-2700-110

8.5 This number designates money placed in the Debt Service Fund for the payment of the principal of an incurred debt, such as a bond issue.

ANSWERS TO APPLICATION PROBLEMS

1a. 50-1620
1b. 20-4512
1c. 90-1740
1d. 10-1310
1e. 70-1920
2a. 10-140-1000-610
2b. 20-630-1000-610
2c. 50-910-3100-630
2d. 20-219-2122-580
2e. 50-410-3200-550

Part 3

Preparing and Administering Site-Based and District Plans

Chapter **9**

Preparation and Administration of Instructional Strategic Financial Plans

Using strategic financial plans with site-based budgets for instructional programs, services, and activities is not a recent development. Rather, colleges and universities have used this form of budget planning for over 50 years, and more recently it has been implemented by many school districts across the country. As the two examples below indicate, however, the practices can take a variety of forms.

Example 1: The central office in one school district, whose board now requires that site-based budgets be used, prepares budgets for the general and special revenue funds for each site-based unit. The site administrators, who have no input into their own budgets, are then required to spend their allotments by the end of October. If all the money is not spent, the remainder is recovered by the business office and expended by administrators in the central office.

Example 2: The central office in this district deposits into the general and special revenue fund budget of each site-based team the amount of money available to them for expenditure over the coming fiscal year. The teams are given expenditure account names and numbers for use in their budgets, although other accounts may be used by teams if desired. The accounts used by the teams do not include those for transportation, maintenance, custodial services, and salaries, although the total salary allocation is indicated on their budget reports.

In the first case, the school district assigns its site administrators functional (not leadership) tasks, one of which is to spend all of the money provided to their units by the end of October. There are no plans, no teams, and the assignments are often not taken seriously. In the second case, the site administrators are expected to lead teams that will maximize the budget allocation. Each team must manage its money throughout the fiscal year to achieve the unit's objectives.

The purpose of this chapter is to show how site-based teams and the district apply the information discussed in the previous chapters to the preparation and administration of instructional financial plans. The ultimate end for the plan, of course, is expressed by the National Council for Accreditation of Teacher Education (NCATE) in Standard 3.1 (NPBEA, 2002), whereby administrators are instructed to display how their financial resources will be used for promoting student achievement. Although many references may be suggested for additional reading on this objective, the book *The Educational Leadership Challenge: Redefining Leadership for the 21st Century* (2002) published by the National Society for the Study of Education offers interesting insights and ideas. Specifically, these chapters (see References) should be consulted: Goldring and Greenfield (2002) for a discussion on the evolution of school leadership; Lugg, Bulkley, Firestone, and Garner (2002) for an overview of the changing terrains encountered by school leaders; and Leithwood and Prestine (2002) who conducted a case study of a school district that took the Illinois state standards and used district and building teams to develop their own standards and benchmarks for each grade level.

AN OVERVIEW OF THE PROCESS AND SITE-BASED AGENDA

Before delving into financial accounts, procedures, reports, and administrative techniques, an outline of the basic administrative process is important to the development of a site-based unit's strategic financial plan and should be reviewed. The following suggested outline is based on the information described in the previous, and current, chapters.

1. Using the school district's strategic goals and objectives, site-based units prepare their units' goals, objectives, and target outcomes and outputs with benchmarks.
2. Site-based teams are informed of the sources of revenues and the estimated amounts available for their instructional programs, services, and related activities.
3. Site-based teams allocate their revenue to the expenditure categories.
4. Site-based budget plans are consolidated and presented to the central office for the preparation of the district budget.
5. The district budget is prepared and presented to the board for approval and adoption.
6. Upon adoption, budgets are placed in operation.
7. Team members implement and monitor the plan to meet benchmark targets and ultimate outcomes and outputs.

A basic agenda outline suggested for a site-based team might include the following:

1. Along with the budget reports, the team collects or is provided with past effectiveness and efficiency performances for its program, service, or activity.
2. The team is provided with any outcome and output expectations of the state and school district.
3. The team analyzes past performances in reference to proposed future performances to identify strengths and weaknesses.
4. The team prepares options for achieving outcomes and outputs with an estimated cost for each option. In this regard, as NCATE (NPBEA, 2002) under Standard 3.0 proposes in a suggested exercise, school and district administrators should analyze their budgets to identify how the allocations support a school improvement plan and/or the district strategic plan. Likewise, their budget proposals should be analyzed to ensure that they promote improvement and benefit the strategy of the district.
5. The team selects an option, sets its unit outcomes and outputs with benchmark targets, and prepares a budget.
6. The site plan is submitted to the district.

ISLLC

When preparing their plans, site-team leaders must keep their visionary goals in mind. As Cloke and Goldsmith (2002) point out, attaining these goals is the ultimate purpose of the strategic method of management. At the same time, according to the Interstate School Leaders Licensure Consortium (ISLLC, 1996), administrators should ensure that the "operational plans and procedures to achieve the vision and goals of the school are in place" and that their "operational procedures are designed and managed to maximize opportunities for successful learning" (p. 15).

Thus, creating appropriate targets is a critical component of the plan. While designing the targets is beyond the scope of this book, it must be done carefully. For example, as explained previously, strategic budgeting combines several techniques, including performance budgeting. Under the performance method, performance targets are expected to address multiple measures related to a known standard. Further, these measures should have performance assessments that encourage acquiring depth as well as breadth of knowledge, skill, and performance. The effectiveness and efficiency targets should not be limited to a single cognitive measure.

When administrators and team members are on target, moving toward achieving their goals, and staying within their budget plan, they have the luxury of assuming a proactive position and delivering **value-added benefits** to their constituents. When this occurs, administrators and team members have achieved an admirable level of competence.

SOURCES OF INSTRUCTIONAL REVENUE

Financing instructional programs is limited to the use of two funds: the general fund and the special revenue fund. Although a school district will have a number of other funds, most school administrators and instructional site-based teams will focus their work on these two funds, introduced and described in chapter 6.

The general fund is the primary operating fund for a school district and, as such, receives the revenue designated for the regular instructional programs and related services and activities. The Governmental Accounting Standards Board (GASB, 2001) explains that this fund accounts for all of the financial resources of a governmental body except those that have been assigned to another fund.

Because the special revenue fund receives money restricted for designated programs and services, the school district must prove that the money is spent as intended. Thus, formally identifying these restricted revenues in the budget system is important. For example, in one district a restricted revenue award of nearly $40,000 was improperly deposited and expended in the general fund. This error was revealed in the audit report and the district had to refund the money to the governmental agency that made the award.

Because the quantity of revenue numbers and names shown in Resource C is overwhelming, revenue numbers that are most appropriate to the general fund are listed in Resource G. To show how these accounts may be expanded to include other sources of revenue, the numbers and names were supplemented; for example, in the 3000 series, revenue numbers from 3110 to 3170 and from 4561 to 4564 were added to break the classifications into detailed categories.

Likewise, Resource H presents the revenue numbers and sources likely to be found in the special revenue fund. These revenues are primarily from state and federal governments. As with revenues in Resource C, those in Resource H were supplemented to demonstrate how the numbers may be expanded. For example, the 3220 and 4500 series were expanded. Also, although local tax revenue is generally placed in the general fund, these revenue numbers may be needed in the special revenue fund for states where the board or taxpayers restrict money for special programs.

The Major Revenue Source: The Property Tax Levy

The major revenue provided to most school districts is from the local tax levy. When planning their programs and services, school leaders must be sensitive to the status of the local tax levy. Will the levy be greater than, the same as, or less than the current year's? To gauge the potential of the local tax levy and to discuss this with members of their teams, educational leaders must understand how it is calculated.

Calculations for determining the tax levy begin with an estimate of the amount of money needed for operating the school district. This estimated amount can be found in the district budget, created from the consolidation of its site-based budgets. The amounts of money expected from other revenue sources (such as tuition income and state assistance) and the amount taken from the general fund's unreserved fund balance (surplus) are subtracted from the total amount needed by the district. This adjusted balance is the total that should be requested by the tax levy for the general fund. To calculate the *total* local tax levy, the revenue needed for the debt service fund must be added to the amount needed by the general fund. The formula used to calculate the tax levy is as follows:

$$\text{Property Tax Rate} = \frac{\text{Total Request from Local Tax Levy}}{\text{Assessed Value of Property}}$$

Example: For the general fund, Renrag School District must collect $5,963,936 from the local tax levy and another $293,649 for payments due on the bond issue (explained in chapter 10) for the debt service fund. The total budget request from the local tax levy, therefore, is $6,257,585. The assessed value of the taxable property in Renrag is $617,364,278. The tax rate to be paid by the property owners in Renrag is:

$$\text{Property Tax Rate} = \frac{\$6,257,585}{\$617,364,287} = \$.010136 \text{ per dollar}$$
of assessed value or
10.136 mills per
$1,000 of assessed value.

Note: A mill = $.001 or 1/10 of a cent.
Thus, the property tax for a home with an assessed value of $100,000 would be $100,000 × $.010136 = $1,013.60 or 100 × 10.136 mills.

Recognizing that property taxes may be levied only on plots deemed *taxable* is important. For example, land and buildings owned by the government, a college or university, a hospital, or charitable and religious organizations may not be taxed. For this reason a considerable amount of property in some cities and towns may not provide financial support to the local school district.

PRESENTING THE DISTRICT BUDGET TO THE PUBLIC

After the tax rate is calculated, the school district budget must be approved and then adopted before the local tax levy can be imposed. This process requires preparing a proposed budget for board action and, ultimately, presenting the budget to public taxpayers and getting their reactions. This report should not only be limited to the budget for the general fund but also offer the public the opportunity to review the proposed budgets for all government funds. The publication of the proposed budgets for nongovernmental funds is usually at the discretion of the school board.

The typical proposed budget for the government funds is divided into revenue and expenditure reports that are further subdivided by accounting fund. An example of a revenue section of a proposed budget is presented in Figure 9.1.

The report shown in Figure 9.1 presents the anticipated revenue receipts from: (a) the local tax levy for the general and debt service funds, (b) other revenue sources for the general and special revenue funds, and (c) the budgeted fund balance that is to be taken from the unreserved fund balance in the general fund. This report should also present the actual receipts for the prior year (column 1, 2001–2002) and an updated report (column 2, 2002–2003) on the receipts for the current year.

Renrag School District Budget Statement for 2003–2004			
	2001–2002 Actual ($)	2002–2003 Revised ($)	2003–2004 Anticipated ($)
General Fund			
Budgeted Fund Balance		100,000	130,000
Revenues from Local Sources:			
Local Tax Levy	5,384,629	5,737,570	5,963,936
Tuition	1,120,443	1,064,593	1,081,967
Miscellaneous	119,204	46,000	55,500
Subtotal	6,624,276	6,848,163	7,101,403
Revenues from State Sources:			
Transportation Aid	52,242	55,964	55,964
Special Education Aid	412,926	414,161	425,243
Bilingual Aid	7,811	8,336	8,674
Aid for At Risk Pupils	95,896	97,176	98,994
Subtotal	568,875	575,637	588,875
Total General Fund	7,193,151	7,523,800	7,820,278
Special Revenue Funds			
Revenue from State Sources:			
Restricted Entitlements	51,659	47,793	47,793
Revenues from Federal Sources:			
P.L. 100–297 Chapter 1	4,642	50,703	50,703
P.L. 100–297 Chapter 2	5,606	4,908	4,908
I.D.E.A. Part B (Handicapped)	52,263	59,290	59,290
Other Estimated Federal Revenues	6,350	7,098	7,098
Total Revenues from Federal Sources	118,861	121,999	121,999
Total Special Revenue Funds	170,520	169,792	169,792
Debt Service			
Revenue from Local Sources:			
Local Tax Levy	317,908	307,158	293,649
Total Debt Service Fund	317,908	307,158	293,649
Total Revenues/Sources	7,681,579	8,000,750	8,283,719

FIGURE 9.1
Report: Proposed Revenue Receipts

The proposed budget presented to the taxpayers at a public meeting or in a newspaper should also include the anticipated expenditures of the revenues. These expenditure amounts should be generated from consolidating the site-based budget plans. An example of such a report is shown in Figure 9.2 for each government fund. Again, the public should be able to examine the amount expended in the previous year and an updated report for the current year. Note

Renrag School District Budget Statement for 2003–2004			
Budget Category	**2000–2001 Actual ($)**	**2002–2003 Revised ($)**	**2003–2004 Anticipated ($)**
General Fund			
Regular Program—Instruction	2,660,169	2,787,823	2,936,646
Special Education—Instruction	432,600	462,307	494,728
Basic Skill/Remedial—Instruction	72,052	95,896	95,896
Bilingual Education—Instruction	6,899	7,811	7,811
School-Spon Cocurricular Activities—Instruction	248,722	259,545	271,940
Undistributed Expenditures:			
Instruction	254,986	230,560	330,792
Attendance and Social Work Services	13,543	14,196	14,373
Health Services	109,570	111,281	108,559
Other Support Services: Students—Regular	102,991	113,117	115,353
Other Support Services: Students—Special	209,329	233,664	251,435
Improvement of Instructional Services	148,556	156,466	162,005
Educational Media Services—School Library	115,213	138,531	75,957
Support Services—General Administration	404,034	428,519	440,608
Support Services—School Administration	324,983	385,162	388,587
Operation and Maintenance of Plant Services	936,103	927,607	970,880
Student Transportation Services	164,468	168,000	155,000
Business and Other Support Services	867,303	899,552	887,435
Food Services	10,000	10,000	10,000
Total Undistributed Expenditures	3,561,079	3,816,655	3,910,984
Equipment	111,630	93,763	102,273
General Fund Grand Total	7,193,151	7,523,800	7,820,278
Special Revenue Fund			
State Projects:			
Nonpublic Textbooks	16,307	13,861	13,861
Nonpublic Handicapped Services	13,607	14,544	14,544
Nonpublic Nursing Services	21,745	19,388	19,388
Total State Projects	51,659	47,793	47,793
Federal Projects:			
P.L. 100–297 Chapter 1	54,642	50,703	50,703
P.L. 100–297 Chapter 2	5,606	4,908	4,908
I.D.E.A. Part B (Handicapped)	52,263	59,290	52,290
Other Special Projects	6,350	7,098	7,098
Total Federal Projects	118,861	121,999	121,999
Total Special Revenue Funds	170,520	169,792	169,792
Debt Service Fund			
Debt Service—Regular	317,908	307,158	293,649
Total Debt Service Funds	317,908	307,158	293,649
Total Expenditure/Appropriations	7,681,579	8,000,750	8,283,719

FIGURE 9.2
Report: Proposed Budget Expenditures

that the totals for the revenues in Figure 9.1 and those for the allocations in Figure 9.2 must be equal. In some districts the site-based plans and budgets are made available for review at public hearings, which the site-based team members attend allowing for their participation in small group discussions.

PLACING THE BUDGETS INTO OPERATION

After the budget is adopted by either a public referendum or a vote of the board members, the revenue and allocation amounts are entered into each fund's estimated revenue and appropriation accounts (shown in Resource A as account numbers 301 and 601, respectively). Next, the amounts are posted to the budget ledger revenue and expenditure accounts. The budgets are now in an operating position. Transactions may be processed against the allocations.

Monitoring Revenues

After the budgets are placed in operation, site teams and administrators use monthly budget reports to administer their plans. The monthly revenue report, prepared at the end of each month, is referred to as the Schedule of Revenues Actual Compared with Estimated. Assuming the proposed budget in Figure 9.1 is adopted, an example of the revenue report for the general fund for Renrag School District as of the end of the first month of the fiscal year is shown in Figure 9.3. Note that the revenues are listed by number, and the amount expected as per the adopted budget is entered in the *estimated* column.

Entries are made in the *actual* column of the revenue report when receipts are recognized in the accounting entries. Because the cash basis method of accounting does not recognize money until it is received, entries cannot be made in this report until the cash, check, or money order is obtained. With respect to the use of the budgeted fund balance, this money is not made available until an accounting entry places it in the actual column. The differences between the estimated and actual amounts are then shown in the *unrealized* column.

Thus, when a budget is adopted, the estimated amounts are entered into the revenue report in the *estimated* column. When a check is received, the amount is placed in the actual column, and the unrealized balance is changed. For example, in Figure 9.3 Renrag School District entered the estimated amounts from its adopted budget. The full amount shown for the local tax levy indicates that the anticipated local tax has been collected or awarded. At the same time, although it has been officially informed it will receive the estimated amounts from the state aid programs, the district cannot make any entries in the actual column until a check is received or the money is wired from the state into its bank account.

When reading the report for the special revenue fund, site-based administrators with state and federal projects should compare the actual money received for their programs to the total amount spent to date. This is because payments for state and federal projects are typically received periodically throughout the year and not all at the beginning of the fiscal year (as some may assume). Specifically,

Report of the Secretary
To the Board of Education
Renrag School District
General Fund—10
Schedule of Revenues
Actual Compared with Estimated
(July 31, 2002)

	Estimated ($)	Actual ($)	Unrealized ($)
General Fund			
Budgeted Fund Balance	130,000		130,000
Local Revenue			
1110 Local Tax Revenue	5,963,936	5,963,936	
1320 Tuition	1,081,967		1,081,967
1990 Miscellaneous	55,500		55,500
Total	7,101,403	5,963,936	1,137,467
State Revenue			
3120 Transportation Aid	55,964		55,964
3130 Special Education Aid	425,243		425,243
3140 Bilingual Aid	8,674		8,674
3150 Aid for At Risk Pupils	98,994		98,994
Total	588,875		568,875
Total General Fund	7,820,278	5,963,936	1,856,342

FIGURE 9.3
Schedule of Revenues Report

since the fiscal year for the federal government does not begin until October 1st, school districts usually have to provide a line of credit for these programs for several months into the new fiscal year. Then when the payment is received, it may only cover the expenditures made to date. The consequence for some school districts is that the business office may have to hold some purchase orders when received owing to cash flow projections. As a result, maintaining a positive cash flow has to be the responsibility of all administrators and not just the business manager's.

In addition, site administrators should recognize how the cash basis method creates a problem when the final payments on state and federal contracts are not received until after a fiscal year has ended. Because the final revenue payments are based on the end-of-year expenditure reports (usually June 30th), the last payment will not likely be received until the next fiscal year.

Monitoring the Budget Plan

In addition to the revenue statement, a monthly report is prepared for the amounts appropriated for expenditure. This report uses the line-item budget format and is prepared for each fund and referred to as the Statement of Appropriations Compared with Expenditures and Encumbrances. The purpose of this statement is to give an up-to-date report on the balances for each budget account. An expenditure report should also be prepared for each site-based unit that receives an allocation.

The typical monthly expenditure report for the school district's general fund will likely be 10 to 20 pages long, and it will be presented to the school board at a monthly meeting for their review and approval via a vote and possibly for signatures on the report of the attending members. Because of the length, only a segment of an expenditure report for a school district is shown as an example in Figure 9.4.

As shown in Figure 9.4, the heading for the monthly expenditure statement identifies the fund (general fund 10) and the date of the report. The expenditure categories that received an appropriation are listed along with the applicable budget numbers and the amounts appropriated, expended, encumbered, and available to be spent. Having the report from the previous month or a report showing monthly/quarterly balances of the previous year may benefit administrators. Thus, with this brief overview, the state of a budget can easily be determined. As discussed in the next section, the same is true for the monthly reports provided to site-based teams when they conduct formal program reviews.

Report of the Secretary
To the Board of Education
Renrag School District
General Fund—10
Statement of Appropriations
Compared with Expenditures and Encumbrances
(for three-month period ending 09/30/02)

Expenditure Accounts	Allocation ($)	Expenditures ($)	Encumbrances ($)	Available ($)
Regular Programs: Instruction				
10-110-1000-110 Pre-kindergarten				
Teacher Salaries	122,109	20,351	101,758	
10-120-1000-110 Gr. 1–5				
Teacher Salaries	873,969	196,319	677,650	
10-130-1000-110 Gr. 6–8				
Teacher Salaries	464,628	77,438	387,190	
10-140-1000-110 Gr. 9–12				
Teacher Salaries	1,188,392	264,508	921,109	2,775
Regular Programs: Undistributed				
10-190-1000-110 Other Salaries				
for Instruction	174,122	27,733	146,319	
10-190-1000-610 General				
Supplies	87,186	33,650	8,096	45,440
10-190-1000-640 Textbooks	26,310	9,311	8,049	8,950
Total	2,936,646	629,310	2,250,171	57,165

FIGURE 9.4
Monthly Budget Report

The use of the undistributed expenditure account shown in Figure 9.4 often draws questions from people who examine the reports. This account refers to allocations that may be spent by more than one program. For example, the undistributed salaries in Figure 9.4 could be for art, music, and other teachers and aides that provide instruction or services to students in Grades pre-k through 8. Likewise, undistributed supplies would mean the allocation is for Grades pre-k to 12. When site-based budgets are created, the art teacher and supply expenditures are allocated to each site unit and the account title in the report would be *consolidated salaries* as opposed to *undistributed salaries*.

Personnel Salaries: Allocation and Turnover

Maintaining accurate salary balances regardless of the complicating effects of personnel turnover is a serious concern for many school districts and site-based units. For example, in one district with an annual budget of $60 million, the amount allocated to salaries was over $40 million. Because the new administrator did not tie their personnel roster to their budget, the district lost complete control over the constantly changing balances. Upon the employment of another administrator, a process similar to the following illustration was established.

First of all, after money is allocated to a fund, salaries are encumbered as per the amounts in the personnel contracts. For example, in Figure 9.4 the allocation for teacher salaries based on the contracts for the fiscal year for Grades 1–5 (budget number 10-120-1000-110) was $873,969. Therefore, on July 1st the amount encumbered for Grade 1–5 teachers should be $873,969.

When teachers are paid, the amount of the payroll is entered into the expenditure column and the encumbered amount is decreased accordingly. The selected section of the Statement of Appropriations in Figure 9.4 exhibits how the report would appear for salaries paid as of September 30th, assuming that the teachers are paid over the 12-month fiscal year. Note in Figure 9.4 that an unexpended balance remains for the Grade 9–12 teachers. This indicates that either (a) all of the salary allocated for Grades 9–12 was not contracted or (b) a person replaced an employed teacher and received $2,775 less in annual salary. In either case, the amount of $2,775 could be reallocated with the permission of the board to another budget category.

After the salaries are encumbered by the accounting system, the budget ledger should be used for managing changes in employment. To describe how to use the budget ledger to track faculty turnover, the following set of examples, beginning on July 1st, have been created. In these examples, one of the teachers employed by the school district is Mr. Thomas Napoli, whose salary of $36,000 is paid over the 12-month fiscal year. As shown in Figure 9.5, on July 1st Mr. Napoli's full salary is entered in the allocation and encumbered columns. Note that the total amount allocated for salaries has been encumbered leaving a zero balance to be spent.

Because the teachers are paid over a 12-month period beginning July 1st, Mr. Napoli is paid $3,000 a month. In the month of September, Mr. Napoli resigned effective October 31st. As a consequence, on November 1st, the personnel

Name	Salary Allocation	Encumbered	Expended	Balance
List of Names				
Napoli, T.	36,000	36,000		
Totals	482,036	482,036	0	0

FIGURE 9.5
Salary Record—July 1, 20xx

roster (see Figure 9.6) shows an allocation for Napoli of $12,000, a zero balance in encumbrances, $12,000 expended, and a $24,000 balance available to spend on salaries in the *Totals Balance* column.

The board hired Mr. David Rines to fill Napoli's vacated position on December 1st for $21,000. As a consequence, on December 1st (Figure 9.7) Rines was added to the personnel roster. An allocation from the total salary balance and an encumbrance of $21,000 must be made to Rines' salary line. As shown, the district has a balance of $3,000 that may be reallocated to other accounts.

Finally, an important point for school administrators to realize is that not all school districts follow the same salary payment schedule. School districts may pay their teachers over a 12-month period, although they are actually being paid for 10 months of service. If the payments begin July 1st and end June 30th, a district may prepay the teachers for the months of July and August. On the other hand, some school districts may withhold money from the teachers paychecks each month over the school year for payment in July and August of the following fiscal year. In other cases, teachers may be paid their salaries over the 10 months they are teaching. Administrators must be aware of the method their district follows in paying personnel so that they can inform new employees properly when hired and ensure overpayments are not disbursed.

In the Napoli case he was prepaid $3,000 for July and August although he actually earned $3,600 a month from September 1st to June 30th. Thus, he was paid

Name	Salary Allocation	Encumbered	Expended	Balance
List of Names				
Napoli, T. (resigned 10/31)	12,000	0	12,000	0
Totals	482,036	[total = 482,036 − 12,000]		24,000

FIGURE 9.6
Salary Record—November 1, 20xx

Name	Salary Allocation	Encumbered	Expended	Balance
List of Names				
Napoli, T. (resigned 10/31)	12,000	0	12,000	0
Rines, D. (Napoli position 12/1)	21,000	21,000	0	0
Totals	482,036	[total = 479,036]		3,000

FIGURE 9.7
Salary Record—December 1, 20xx

$12,000 ($3,000 a month) for July, August, September and October and earned $7,200 ($3,600 a month) for teaching in the months of September and October. As a result, he would have to reimburse the district $4,800 ($12,000 − $7,200) on his last day of service or the district would withhold payment of $3,000 for October and require $1800 from him on his last day. As a result, in the above example, after settling the Napoli account, the salary balance in Figure 9.7 would indicate that an additional $4,800 ($7,800 total) would be available in the balance for total salaries. The recovery of the salary amount would also reduce the amount shown on the personnel roster that was allocated and paid to Napoli from $12,000 to $7,200.

ADMINISTERING THE STRATEGIC FINANCIAL PLAN

As seen in the above reports, the administration of the strategic financial plan involves two basic tasks. The first is to monitor the program benchmarks in reference to the proposed targets set forth in the strategic financial plan. The second is to review expenditures, ensuring that budget allocations are spent as intended, or as amended, in the plan.

Meeting Benchmark Targets

ISLLC

A school district's success is directly related to the care and attention given by the leadership to the articulation of the "objectives and strategies to achieve the vision and goals" of their program (ISLLC, 1996, p. 11). This is achieved at the site-based level via formal effectiveness and efficiency benchmark reviews of the programs, services, and activities.

Benchmark reviews should: (a) check on performances, (b) consider possible revisions, and (c) serve to keep the school and community team members engaged in the operations. After a review, the team leader should transmit a report with recommendations up through the organizational hierarchy to the district school board. For example, the recommendations may concern modifying the strategic plan (e.g., do timelines or assignments need adjusting?).

The ultimate goal for the benchmark reviews is identifying problems as they evolve and not only after they have occurred. If problems must be solved after they have occurred and caused damage, the administrators are likely to be thrust into the crisis management abyss.

Controlling and Fine-Tuning the Budget

There are three basic purposes for expenditure reviews. The first is ensuring the budget allocations are adequate. The second is ensuring the allocations are being spent as the plan intended. The third is determining if each expenditure category will be over- or underspent. If these are not conducted in an aware and deliberate manner, the expenditure reviews may simply become a mathematical exercise. The team leader should include comments and recommendations on the budget in the report submitted to central administrations. (For instance, are any budget transfers needed? Is additional money needed?)

For example, in Figure 9.8, the amount encumbered against the allocation to budget number 10-190-1000-610, general supplies, as of September 30th is $28,096 and the amount expended is $33,650. When the encumbered and expended amounts are subtracted from the allocation of $87,186 for general supplies, the unexpended balance is $25,440. The questions, therefore, in the review of the supplies allocation are as follows: (a) Are the expenditures to date on target? (b) Are all expenditures and encumbrances to date appropriate to the plan? and (c) Is the remaining balance sufficient?

Many experienced administrators know that monitoring and fine-tuning the budget throughout the year is a prerequisite to getting the most from a budget

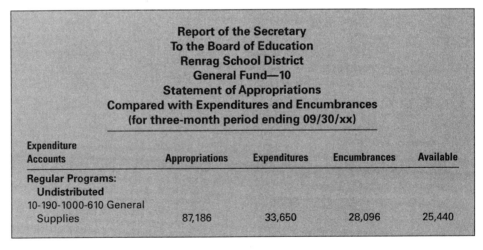

Report of the Secretary
To the Board of Education
Renrag School District
General Fund—10
Statement of Appropriations
Compared with Expenditures and Encumbrances
(for three-month period ending 09/30/xx)

Expenditure Accounts	Appropriations	Expenditures	Encumbrances	Available
Regular Programs: **Undistributed** 10-190-1000-610 General Supplies	87,186	33,650	28,096	25,440

FIGURE 9.8
Allocation of Appropriations

allocation. Probably the worst practice observed by the author is the example given in the introduction to this chapter, where all site-based units had to spend a total year's allocation by the end of October.

FINAL THOUGHTS

ISLLC

When benchmarks are being met, that is, the attainment of objectives is ensured and movement toward the visionary goals is taking place, unit administrators may consider *value-added benefits*. The primary advantage in providing such benefits is that they support the ISLLC (1996) proposal that school leaders should continually strive to enhance community relations.

Briefly, a value-added benefit in the profit sector means the cost of a purchase includes something extra at no additional charge to the customer. A value-added benefit may be a special warranty on a product being purchased, a free service or gift after a specified number of purchases, a contribution to a charity, or the support of a public interest project (such as a donation to an environmental organization) taken from the cost of a product or service. Of course, businesses make sure their customers are aware of these no-cost benefits!

What additional service can a school district offer their constituents for the tax dollars paid? Of course, the concept of value-added benefits is not possible unless a strategic financial plan with stated benchmarks and objectives exists, has been made public, has been implemented, and are being met. Otherwise the public would not know, or possibly believe, that they are receiving a value-added benefit!

Even with limited resources, there are numerous value-added benefits a school district can offer. In one district, for example, a special high school concert was offered to people in a senior citizen complex. The district provided the buses for transportation, high school students volunteered to serve as attendants on the bus and guides for tours of the building, refreshments were served by the parent association, and the marching band, the concert band, and the jazz ensemble provided the music. The event was very successful. In another school district an intramural sports program is offered after school. The program involves a large number of children at a time when supervised activities are badly needed, and the cost is minimal. Both of these cases evolved via the proactive leadership of administrators who met the expectation of the ISLLC (1996) that they "engage in activities that offer the school high visibility, active involvement, and communication with the larger community" (p. 17).

ISLLC

In conclusion, after benchmark and annual reviews are conducted, school leaders must inform the public of their progress. If a district manages their budgets efficiently and creates a surplus, the public should be advised that this will reduce their property tax levy. Likewise when benchmarks are reached, public recognition should be given to the administrators and teachers who met their targets and objectives. In addition, if value-added benefits are provided at no extra cost, the public must be made aware of them. Of course, if school leaders do not have such a plan, they cannot tell the public what they will accomplish, inform them of their progress, and provide them with value-added benefits.

DISCUSSION QUESTIONS

1. What are five of the related services and activities that might be offered through revenue provided in the general fund?

2. Name five programs that might be offered in a school district through the use of the special revenue fund?

3. As noted in the chapter, a school district may use more than one special revenue fund. Under what circumstances might a school district wish to have a second special revenue fund?

4. The assessed value of a home is used to calculate the property tax paid by the homeowner. Does the percentage of the assessment of properties in the district (for example, 10 or 50% of the market value) make a difference in the tax levy paid by a homeowner? Why or why not?

5. Compare the advantages and disadvantages of paying employees over a 12-month period as a prepayment for services to be rendered as opposed to withholding money in an academic year for salary payments in July and August of the next fiscal year?

6. What value-added benefits might a school district offer to the people in your community?

7. If a site team reviewed its benchmarks and determined that one of the classes was not meeting its targets (for example, an elementary school class has a low achievement record, a high level of student absences, and a higher level of spending than their share of the budget would allow); how could the team proceed to revise its plan and assist the teacher?

APPLICATION PROBLEMS

The answers are provided at the end of the chapter.

1. Using the information provided for Renrag School District in the example given on calculating the tax levy, how much more would the district receive if the tax levy was increased by one mill?
   a. How much more would the owner of the home assessed at $100,000 have to pay?

2. You have been assigned to serve as the team leader for your site-based unit. You must prepare for the first meeting with the team, which consists of three teachers and the parents of three students. The team members have never served on a team and have never been told about site-based operations. What material would you collect for the first meeting? Prepare an agenda for the first meeting and an outline of a plan for preparing your proposal.

CLINICAL PRACTICUM EXERCISES

In response to the clinical exercises below, the suggested format is to:(a) state the question, (b) answer the question, and (c) discuss your answer in reference to the content presented in the text. If supporting material is discussed and can be made available, it should be referenced in the discussion as an appendix and attached to the end of the report. Note that one of the objectives of part 3 is to show that the material in the book has been read, comprehended, and applied.

Using the information in this chapter as a reference, report your findings on the following items. As suggested by NCATE, also indicate if the budget allocations support school improvement and, if available, the district strategic plan.

1. Who is responsible for the preparation of instructional plans?
   a. Are benchmark targets set and reviewed?
2. What expenditure categories are used by the site-based budgets?
3. Describe the content and use of the revenue and expenditure reports.
4. How is the school district budget publicized?
   a. Are hearings held? Describe them.
   b. What is required to pass the school district budget in order to levy a tax?
   c. What is the property tax rate in the district?
5. What are the sources of revenue for the instructional programs, services, and activities in both the general fund and the special revenue fund?
6. Is employee attendance tied to the payroll?

WEB ADDRESSES

National Council for Accreditation of Teacher Education
http://www.ncate.org

REFERENCES

Cloke, K., & Goldsmith, J. (2002). *The end of management and the rise of organizational democracy.* San Francisco: Jossey-Bass.

Goldring, E., & Greenfield, W. (2002). Understanding the evolving concept of leadership in education: Roles, expectations, and dilemmas. In J. Murphy (Ed.), *The educational leadership challenge: Redefining leadership for the 21st century* (pp. 1–19). Chicago: National Society for the Study of Education.

Governmental Accounting Standards Board (2001). *Codification of governmental accounting and financial reporting standards.* Norwalk, CT: Author.

Interstate School Leaders Licensure Consortium (1996). *Standards for school leaders.* Washington, DC: Council of Chief State School Officers.

Leithwood, K., & Prestine, N. (2002). Unpacking the challenges of leadership at the school and district level. In J. Murphy (Ed.), *The educational leadership challenge: Redefining leadership for the 21st century* (pp. 42–64). Chicago: National Society for the Study of Education.

Lugg, C. A., Bulkley, K., Firestone, W. A., & Garner, C. W. (2002). The contextual terrain facing educational leaders. In J. Murphy (Ed.), *The educational leadership challenge: Redefining leadership for the 21st century* (pp. 20–41). Chicago: National Society for the Study of Education.

National Policy Board for Educational Administration (2002). *Standards for advanced programs in educational leadership for principals, superintendents, curriculum directors, and supervisors* [Online]. Retrieved February 17, 2003, from http://www.ncate.org

ANSWERS TO APPLICATION PROBLEMS

1. $617,364.29
   a. $100

Chapter 10

Financing School
Facility Projects

ISLLC The Interstate School Leaders Licensure Consortium (ISLLC, 1996) emphasizes that all school administrators should have a "knowledge and understanding of principles and issues relating to school facilities and use of space" (p. 14). The consortium continues by stating that administrators must be committed to providing a safe environment for students and ensuring that "the school plant, equipment, and support systems operate safely, efficiently, and effectively" (p. 15). To meet these expectations, school leaders must be able both to make the financial arrangements for improving the facility and to pay the debt incurred for making such improvements.

In a casual conversation between the author and two superintendents (one from New Jersey and one from Oregon), the discussion shifted to school facilities. One superintendent remarked about the report that the average age of school buildings in the country is over 40 years. The conversation then turned to the problems they experienced when attempting to build new buildings or make major renovations. One superintendent observed that the process of constructing a school building was so long and complex that the administrator who begins the plan might not be in the district when the building opens. This observation was actually his experience since he was beginning a building project but would retire before it was completed. It is interesting, however, that two administrators from quite different states at opposite ends of the country had such similar opinions and experiences.

As the superintendents noted, building a school is an extensive, complicated endeavor. Likely, the more complex aspect of the project for many school leaders is establishing a financial course of action and communicating the plan to board members, administrators, and taxpayers in the district. For example, in a conversation the author had with a taxpayer attending a meeting that proposed the construction of a new high school for the district, the taxpayer expressed concern about the difference between the cost of the proposed building and the amount of the bond issue. Although the actual amounts cannot be remembered, as an example, the issue was why a building that cost $40 million required an approval to sell $44 million in bonds. The person continued to complain that he had posed his concern to a school administrator (the principal), but the administrator was nonresponsive.

In addition to the qualms about financing a new school building, another criticism often heard is regarding the necessity for a new facility. Why must educators have a new facility when some governmental buildings are over 100 years old? If the parents attended classes in a school building, why is it not good enough for their children? In response to these inquiries, which are quite common, the public must understand that the primary function of school buildings in the 19th and early 20th centuries was providing housing for students; that is, protection from the elements and a source of heat in the winter. Then in the early to mid-20th century the consolidation of the one-room and small schoolhouses gave rise to the creation of larger structures. Although the designs of the newer buildings still centered on the need to shelter students, they began to shift to the needs of the teachers plus a range of educational services (Castaldi, 1994).

Beginning in the second half of the 20th century, educators became more interested in the way in which all children learn, in new and creative approaches to teaching, and in applying remarkable technological advances to the teaching of children. Correspondingly, new expectations for school facilities began to take form. In more recent years, continuing discoveries and developments in the teaching–learning process and in technology have placed even more demands on existing school facilities, some of which defy modernization (Castaldi, 1994; Meyer, 1967; Rippa, 1988).

As a result, because of the innovative advances in education over the past 50 years, the current challenge for educational leaders is providing safe learning environments that present opportunities for teachers and students to access the latest and most effective instructional methods and technology. The purpose of this chapter is presenting the necessary activities and process for financing the construction or modernization of an educational facility.

OVERVIEW OF THE PROCESS

Assume that a school board determines that a new school building must be constructed. The general specifications for the building—such as the number of rooms, special facilities, and offices—are usually determined by the school administrators with the assistance of teachers and consultants. Bids with a proposed design of the building are then solicited from architects.

After the board selects an architect, the total cost of the capital project is determined. Because most school districts have a legal debt limit imposed by a state law, state approval may be needed. A state review looks at the assessed value of the taxable properties in the district, the current debt being carried by the district and other local governments, and the proposed debt to be incurred by the project.

After a district is granted the authority to move forward on a building project and is aware of any state and/or federal assistance to be provided, the balance of the money needed for the project must be collected from the local taxpayers. Before the tax can be levied, however, the local taxpayers or their elected representatives on the school board must vote to give the school district permission to sell bonds. If the bond issue is approved, the school leaders can make the arrangements to sell the bonds. Property owners will then be assessed a tax for the payment of the bond principal and interest. If the bond issue is not approved, the project must be terminated.

Low-Wealth Districts

The examination of property values and of current debt of local governments is problematic for many low-wealth school districts. This is because they often have a number of old facilities needing replacement; the assessed value of their properties is low; and often the region has incurred considerable debt for other local government improvements.

As a consequence, some low-wealth school districts are not able to assume the long-term debt necessary for upgrading their facilities and furnishings. Even if it would be permissible for debt to be incurred, it is likely that it would be insufficient to meet the needs of the district; in addition, the interest rate would likely be higher owing to the districts' weak financial reports. For these districts, substantial state and federal aid for the construction of new facilities is a necessity; otherwise, the learning environments of the children will become more outdated, classrooms will be more overcrowded, and courses will continue to be technologically substandard.

BOND FINANCING

Financing a capital project, which is accomplished through the sale of bonds, is not as straightforward as one may expect for a number of reasons. First, in addition to the cost of the land, building, and furnishings, money is needed to cover the costs associated with the project—such as the fees of the architect and of the professional services assisting in the sale of the bonds. Second, some fees may be due before a bond sale can take place. Third, the financial activities and the order in which they take place will likely vary from one district to another.

The Sale of Bonds

Financing through the sale of bonds is the means for enabling school districts to borrow large sums of money for extended periods of time. A bond is a certificate of debt issued by a company or government in exchange for an agreed upon sum of cash.

Bonds offered by a school district are known as *municipal bonds*. The amount of a bond is referred to as its *face value* or **par value**, which is typically $5,000 although bonds may have smaller or larger face values. In exchange for money from an investor, a bond guarantees in writing that the investor will be paid a *stated* or *nominal* rate of interest, usually semiannually on the 1st or 15th day of a month. The face value of the bond will then be paid to the investor upon its maturity, which is usually 5 years or longer.

For example, assume that an investor, Mr. Robert Meehan, purchases four $5,000 bonds with a stated interest rate of 6% to be paid annually. In exchange for the $20,000, the school district will pay Mr. Meehan $1,200 at the end of every year ($20,000 × 6%), as follows:

Time of Payment	Amount
End of 1st year	$1,200
End of 2nd year	$1,200
End of 3rd year	$1,200
End of 4th year	$1,200
End of 5th year	$1,200
	$20,000
Total Amount	$26,000

Thus, the total interest earned by Mr. Meehan would be $6,000.

Bond Bids

When purchasing a bond, investors make offers, called *bids*. To gain a greater return on an investment than the stated rate of interest provided by a bond, an investor offers a school district an amount that is less than the face value of the bond.

Using the example given above, assume Mr. Meehan wishes to earn more than 6% on his investment. To gain the greater return, he could purchase a $5,000 bond for $4,950. He would still receive the annual payments of $1,200 and then the additional $50 when the bond matures. Of course, the school district would receive $4,950 as opposed to $5,000 from the sale.

Making a Bid

Bids, which are commonly referred to as *quotes,* on bonds are made in percentages. For example, a bond quote of 99 would mean a buyer is bidding 99% × $1,000 or $990 per $1,000. A bid at 99¾ equals an amount of 99.75% × $1,000 or $997.50 while 100⅞ equals $1,008.75. An increment of 1/8 equals $1.25 for a $1,000 bond while 1/8 equals 12.5 cents per dollar in stock quotes.

When a bond is purchased for less than its face value (such as 99¾), the amount of the reduction is considered a **bond discount**. If the amount paid by the investor is greater than its face value, the amount that exceeds the face value is the **bond premium**; for example, at 100⅞ the sale is considered to include a premium of $8.75. The seller, or school district, receives the premium. If an investor purchased the bond at the asking price, the bond is sold at par; for example, a school district would receive $5,000 for the sale of a $5,000 bond.

The rate of return for the investor, therefore, is determined by the stated interest and the bid, or purchase, price. This rate of return, which is referred to as the **yield to maturity** (YTM) or the effective interest rate, determines the amount an investor earns.

The formula for calculating the YTM for a bond sold at a discount is as follows:

$$\text{Yield to Maturity} = \frac{\text{Stated Yield} + \text{Discount/Bond Life}}{(\text{Face Value} + \text{Purchase Price})/2}$$

Example: 1. A $1,000 bond is purchased for $900.
2. The stated interest of 6% × $1,000 = $60 annual yield.
3. The purchase prices is $900, therefore the discount = $100.
4. The bond life is 5 years.

$$\text{YTM} = \frac{\$60 + \$100/5}{(\$1000 + \$900)/2} = \frac{\$80}{\$950} = 8.42\%$$

A bond selling for a premium would use the same formula except the premium amount would be inserted instead of the discount and this amount would be subtracted from the stated yield (Zipf, 1997).

In a bear market, bond bids (by an investor) decline (lower than par), the yield to the investor increases, and the amount received by the school district decreases. In a bull market the bids increase, the yield to the investor decreases, and the sale price of the bond increases (better return to the school district). Obviously, school districts prefer to sell their bonds in a bull market, whereas investors prefer to buy in a bear market.

FACTORS INFLUENCING BOND BIDS

The amount of a bid for a bond by an investor is a personal decision that is dictated by the investor's portfolio. Some of the factors considered in this decision are the amount of money being invested, the **present value** of the investment, the length of time it is invested, the risk that the person or government will be able to pay the interest and principal on time, how much could be earned by placing the money in another investment, and the taxes paid on the interest earned.

Present Value

To determine a bid, an investor must be concerned with the *present value* of money; that is, the effect of time on the value of money.

Assume that you are asked to loan someone money, and, in exchange, you will receive $100 in 1 year. How much would you loan the person? Your response must consider the present equivalent value of the $100 in reference to its value to you, the investor, in 1 year (Weygandt, Kieso, & Kimmel, 1999). One reason for the difference is that the value of money today is impacted by inflation; that is, after 1 year, $100 will not have the same value that it has today.

The present value of money must also be applied to the annuity to be paid. An investor will receive annuities, which are interest payments, periodically over the life of the bond. The concern, therefore, is the present value of the annuities received throughout the life of the bond (Weygandt et al., 1999).

For example, assume a loan of $100 for 1 year offers a 5% semiannual interest payment for a total investment return of $5. The investor would receive $2.50 at the end of 6 months and $2.50 at the end of the year. In this case, time affects the present value of the interest earned. As a result, the first $2.50 would have a higher value to the investor than the $2.50 received at the end of the year. Of course, when bonds are sold and purchased for millions of dollars, these calculations are critical. A tenth, hundredth, or thousandth of a point can cost and earn thousands of dollars a year.

While present value tables for the principal and annuities are used to calculate the amount an investor will offer for a bond, each has a formula for making the calculations. The formula for determining the present value for the principal (excluding the annuity) is as follows:

$$PV = F\frac{1}{(1 + i)^n}$$

P = present value
F = future amount to be discounted
i = interest rate
n = number of investment periods

Assume that in the example given above, Mr. Meehan wishes to receive 8% on his investment as opposed to 6%. Using the above formula for the principal only, his bid would be:

$$PV = \$20{,}000\frac{1}{(1 + .08)^5}$$

$$PV = \$20{,}000\frac{1}{1.4693}$$

$$PV = \$20{,}000 \times .6806 = \$13{,}612$$

Note: When using the PV table, the number .6806 is located under the column for 8% and across the row for five investment periods.

Therefore, if Mr. Meehan was not receiving an annual interest payment, he would bid $13,612 in order to receive an 8% return on his investment. However, since he would receive an annual interest payment, he would have to make the second calculation as follows:

$$PVA = R \times \frac{1 - \left[\dfrac{1}{(1 + i)^n} \right]}{i}$$

PVA = present value of the annuity
R = periodic annuity payment to be received
i = interest rate
n = number of payments

In Meehan's case, because he wishes to receive 8% instead of a 6% annuity payment annually for the 5 years, his bid would include the following:

$$PVA = \$1,200 \times \frac{1 - \left[\dfrac{1}{(1 + .08)^5} \right]}{.08}$$

$$PVA = \$1,200 \times \frac{1 - .6806}{.08}$$

$$PVA = \$1,200 \times 3.9927 = \$4,791$$

Note: When using the PVA table, the number 3.9927 is located under the column for 8% and across the row for 5 periods.

Using the above information, Mr. Meehan's total bid would be:

Present Value − Principal	$13,612
Present Value − Annuity	4,791
Total Bid	$18,403

If the interest payments would be compounded—for example, semiannual payments of $600 instead of an annual payment of $1,200—then in the PVA formula: (a) the interest rate is divided by the number of annual payments, which would be 4% instead of 8%, and (b) the number of payment periods is multiplied by the number of annual payments, which would cause an increase from 5 to 10 periods.

Taxes

Tax exemptions on municipal bonds may also have a considerable influence on a bid. For example, the interest earned on securities sold by the U.S. Treasury (such as "T-bills," notes, and bonds) is exempt from taxes by local and municipal governments but not by the federal government. Interest earned on bonds sold by a school district may be exempt from federal, state, and local taxes.

The federal tax exemption on the earnings from municipal bonds was changed considerably in 1986 in the Tax Reform Act. This act provided that for bonds issued after August 15, 1986, the federal government could tax interest earnings on some types of municipal bonds and on any profit realized from the purchase or sale of the bonds. In addition, municipal bonds were divided into three types depending on the purpose of the issue (Zipf, 1997).

The first type of municipal bond is the *public purpose* bond, which would be used for the construction of a school building. These bonds have been exempt from federal taxes. Although the U.S. Supreme Court has provided that federal taxes may be levied on the interest income of all municipal bond types, at this time Congress has not elected to do so (Zipf, 1997).

The second type of bond is the *private activity bond,* which is subject to federal taxes and may be exempt from state and local taxes. These bonds are used to finance projects that may generate income, such as a sports complex (Zipf, 1997). They would be sold through a proprietary fund, not through the capital projects and debt service funds.

The last, or third, type of municipal bond is for nongovernmental purposes, such as student housing. They are also exempt from federal taxes, and there is a maximum on the amount that may be issued (Zipf, 1997). These bond issues would not use the capital projects and debt service funds but would also be sold through a proprietary fund.

Bond Ratings and Risk

A **bond rating** focuses on risk, which is based on an evaluation of a school district's potential to repay a debt. With respect to an assessment of this risk, bond investors depend heavily on the opinion of a bond-rating agency. Basically, the greater the risk, the lower the rating, the lower the bid, and the greater the earnings on the investment. For a bond sale that is less than $1.5 million, a bond rating is usually not necessary.

Two of the larger agencies that provide bond ratings are Moody's Investors Service and Standard and Poor's. The bond ratings used by these two agencies are as follows:

Moody's: Best to the lowest are Aaa, Aa, A, Baa, Ba, B, Caa, Ca, and C;
Standard and Poor's: Highest to the lowest are AAA, AA, A, BBB, BB, B, CCC, CC, C, and D.

Junk bonds are those being sold by companies that do not have a strong financial record. These bond ratings are below Moody's Baa and Standard & Poor's BBB (Zipf, 1997). If a number is placed after the bond-rating letter, it simply further classifies the risk; for example, an A1 is higher than an A3.

The review for a bond rating takes into consideration a number of variables including the economic base of the community, the public debt of the community, the financial history and performance of the school district, and the district's potential for meeting their legal obligations (demonstrated by an audit and a set of financial statements based on the Generally Accepted Accounting Principles or GAAP). The school district pays for the review; for a district that has had a recent bond issue, the review will cost less than for a new review.

BOND CLASSIFICATIONS

Bonds can be classified in terms of the life of the issue. A **term bond** issue is when all of the bonds mature on the same date. In these cases, there is usually a *sinking fund,* or reserve account, into which money is collected to pay for bond interest periodically and the principal at maturity. The money in a sinking fund is invested, but with restrictions, and the interest earned from the money in the fund must be used to pay the bond issue (Freeman & Shoulders, 1996).

For a number of reasons, term bonds are not popular and in most states they are not allowed to be sold by school districts. Rather, the preferred type of bonds is a **serial bond**, which is an issue retired at the end of a series of time periods. For example, after 5 years, bond issues may be retired every year over a 20-year period.

Bond Ownership

In 1983 Congress began requiring that the name and address of the owners of municipal bonds be recorded either on the bond certificate, called a **registered bond**, or by the district's fiscal agent, referred to as a **book entry bond**. Before 1983, municipal bonds could be sold without a name on them and were referred to as coupon or bearer bonds. In these cases, the interest payments were made to the person presenting the coupon at the time the payment was due.

Today most bond sales are book entry bonds. If a bond is resold, the information is filtered to the fiscal agent so that the name and address of the new owner can be recorded (Zipf, 1997).

PROFESSIONAL SERVICES FOR THE SALE OF A BOND ISSUE

Once a bond sale is approved, the selection of a buyer may be a major consideration. One type of sale is that made to private investors. In these cases, the purchase arrangements are made between the buyer and seller, a bond rating is not necessary, and the interest paid may be somewhat greater. The other type of sale is made to the public through the open market, where the bonds may be resold at any time; however, the terms of the resale do not affect the issuer of the bond. Although the interest paid on the open market may be less than in a private sale, the costs of selling bonds on the open market is greater.

The process of selling bonds on the open market is an extremely complex endeavor that requires considerable time and the services of highly specialized professionals. When serving as an agent of the school district, school administrators must be aware of the services performed by the various professionals. The following descriptions refer to the professionals who provide the services as opposed to the chronology of events that take place in a sale.

Financial Advisor

At the beginning of the process, a school district may hire a financial advisor or consultant. This may occur even before an approval is sought from state officials and put before local taxpayers. In these cases, the cost of the advisor will have to be paid from a budget in the general fund. When hiring an advisor, a school board may request applications or proposals from people who wish to serve as the advisor, and then they interview several candidates. Before an advisor is chosen, however, the person's record on advisement should be checked out.

A financial advisor may come from a bank, an independent firm, or even a state agency. For projects involving a large bond issue, applications from possible advisors may be requested from state and regional firms or banks. Financial advisors may be compensated with a flat fee, a percentage of the cost of the project, or an hourly fee.

Financial advisors may assist in many activities throughout the process, for instance: preparing documents promoting the project for state and public approval, timing the bond issue, drawing up a long-term financial plan, determining terms of the bond issue, and financial strategizing and writing of grant applications, the prospectus for potential investors, and the application for a bond rating. They may also assist in overseeing the sale of a bond issue and the selection of an underwriter. A word of caution, though—the financial advisor should not serve as the underwriter. The underwriter must represent both the investor and the school district whereas an advisor should only be concerned with the best interests of the district.

Bond Counsel

The bond counsel acts as a legal advisor to the board and is concerned with the legal interests of the investors. The bond counsel works with the mechanics of the issue: preparing the documents needed for the public hearings, the prospectus, bidding materials to be sent to underwriters, legal advertisements, and legal advice to investors on the bond issue—such as its validity, source of payments, bond security, and tax exemptions. A bond counsel is paid by the school district, and the fee is based on the size of the sale, time spent on the bond issue, and the risk of the issue. In addition to the legal concerns related to the bond issue, a counsel might also assist in the development of the financial plan, the preparation of documents, government approvals, and so on.

Although a request for applications may be sought, school boards usually solicit the services of a bond counsel. In some cases the decision to employ a bond counsel is based on reputation or a visit to the firm. Because the bond counsel has a legal obligation to the investors, a school board may also retain an attorney to oversee the sale as well as the services of the bond counsel.

Bond Underwriters

Bond underwriters are known as the *middlemen* because they represent both the school district and the investors. An underwriter may be a commercial bank or investment firm. Very large issues may be taken on by an *underwriting syndicate*, which consists of two or more firms that join forces to sell the issue.

An underwriter purchases bond issues from the school district and sells them to dealers, brokers, or private investors. Underwriters make money from the spread between the amount paid to a school district for an issue and the amount at which it is sold.

Fiscal Agent

A fiscal agent is responsible for preparing the bonds for the underwriter, maintaining the records of the investors, taking care of the interest and principal payments, keeping an inventory of blank bond certificates if necessary, helping the school district with a **bond recall**, and preparing periodic reports on interest and principal payments. The fiscal agent for a school district is usually a bank or trust company and is selected by the board based on their services and cost.

The fiscal agent may also serve as the underwriter. This arrangement may provide some advantages, including influencing the amount charged to the school district. The charges by the fiscal agent are dependent on the amount of the issue. If multiple issues are sold, the cost of the first issue may be greater than that of later issues. Otherwise the costs vary according to the size of the issue, the type of registration (registered bonds versus book entry bonds), and the call provisions.

PREPARING A FINANCIAL PLAN

There are a number of actions to be considered by school leaders when preparing a bond issue. As noted above, a prospectus for investors is prepared and will likely be released with information on bond issues by other school districts and municipal governments. Thus, the information in the document should be of interest to the educational leaders of the district. This information may include the maturity schedule and purpose of the issue; information about the community and school district; local maps, data on the school system, and the school budget; and statistics on family income, level of education of the population, housing, and employment. In other words, the intent is to provide potential investors with a picture of the district and community that will encourage them to offer the best possible bid.

Another decision must be made about bond insurance. Although insurance may make an issue more desirable, it will not likely be a benefit unless the school district received a low credit rating—such as an A rating or below. In these cases, a school district may also obtain a letter of credit from a bank to send to potential investors. This letter, like insurance, guarantees the payments of principal and interest to investors.

Because the money for a large project may be spent over a period of several years, school leaders must decide whether to sell all of the bonds when the issue is approved or to have multiple sales. In many cases the entire issue is sold when it is made available. When this occurs, the money being held in the capital projects fund can be invested to earn interest. This strategy can present numerous problems, one of which relates to **arbitrage** penalties and another to penalties administered by state offices when bond sales exceed the needs of the district.

Arbitrage

Arbitrage means that the interest earned by a school district from the investment of borrowed money is greater than the interest being paid for the loan. For a number of reasons, the federal government's 1986 Tax Reform Act along with changes in the code of the Internal Revenue Service do not permit the generation of arbitrage earnings. Specifically, in some cases, the federal government could take the earnings that exceed the cost of borrowing the money; plus if the directives are ignored, a school district could lose its tax-exempt status (Granof, 1998; Razek & Hosch, 1995). Most states, therefore, prohibit the generation of arbitrage earnings. Expectations, in general, are that any interest earned from the investment of bond and debt service money is to be used to reduce the debt from the bond issue.

One approach, although it requires more effort and depends on the size of the issue and the current interest rates, is to prepare a financial plan that involves more than one sale of the series bonds. For example, if a project requires only 10% of the money from an issue within the first 2 years, then possibly 12 to 15% of the bonds should be sold with a second issue made after the end of the 2nd year. Further, because bond issues usually have an amount added for unknown contingencies, it should not be called on unless needed, and then as close to the end of the project as possible. If the contingency is not needed, the bonds would not be sold and school officials would not have to take the risk of having to explain a surplus.

In one case, a school district sold its entire bond issue for $12 million when it was approved. The total project, however, came in at just under $10 million. While the school leaders would have liked to take credit for being thrifty, they had a problem explaining the $2 million surplus. The taxpayers were not pleased, regardless of the explanations!

In another case, the school administrators intentionally increased the amount of a bond issue to ensure that a balance remained at the end of the project. The administrators then used the money for other projects. This practice violates the legal process whereby when a bond issue is approved by the public or their representatives, the project to be financed by the bond sale is defined. To use the money otherwise breaks the public trust and can be a "career ender" for administrators.

THE TAX LEVY FOR THE DEBT FUND

The amount of an annual tax levy is based on the amount of the principal and interest payments to be made in the fiscal year. For example, in the illustration in the last chapter, a payment of $293,649 was due on the last payment of a bond issue (principal and interest). The assessed value of the taxable property in Renrag was $617,364,278. Thus, the tax rate to be paid by property owners for the bond redemption and interest would be:

$$\text{Property Tax Rate} = \frac{\text{Principal} + \text{Interest}}{\text{Assessed Property Value}} \quad \text{or} \quad \frac{\$293,649}{\$617,364,278} = .0005$$

Thus, a tax of .0005 cents per dollar of assessed value or .5 mills per $1,000 of assessed value would be levied for the debt fund. A property with an assessed value of $100,000 would be assessed an additional $50 for the bond and interest payments due in the fiscal year. The deposit of the tax receipts and the payments to the investors from the expenditure accounts would be processed though the accounts in the debt fund.

Short-Term Loans

If money is not available in the capital projects fund for the payment of expenses for a project (for example, expenses incurred prior to the bond sale), then the payment may have to come from the general fund. However, taking money from the general fund, even for a short period of time, may place unfortunate constraints on the district budget. The alternative is for the district to borrow money against the pending bond sale. This loan is called a **bond anticipatory note (BAN)** and is placed in the capital projects fund. The amount of the bond sale must cover the BAN. The BAN and the interest on the BAN must then be paid from the first receipts of the bond sale.

School districts may also borrow money against future tax receipts **[tax anticipatory note (TAN)]** and future revenues **[revenue anticipatory note (RAN)]** such as money to be received from state or federal aid for construction. TANs and RANs are short-term loans with notes that must be paid when the district receives the money. They may also be used by the general and special revenue funds in the case of a cash-flow problem.

Surplus

When a project is completed, any residual amount in the capital projects fund should be transferred to the debt service fund and applied to the outstanding debt. If any money remains in the capital projects fund and the district wishes to spend it on another project, approval may be provided by the board, or possibly the state government, and reported to the public.

Bond Recall

Finally, because the market interest rates may change dramatically (for example, in 1982 the rates were above 11%, 10 years later they fell to below 7%, and 10 years after that they fell below 4%), a school district may wish to buy its bonds back and then reissue new bonds. A district may recall its bonds if the bond issue has a "call feature." If so, these bonds are referred to as "callable bonds." This feature permits the school district to redeem the bonds at a predetermined amount before the bond matures. In some states, school districts are required to offer only callable bonds.

WORKING WITH THE ACCOUNTING FUNDS

The acquisition of capital assets for a school district is usually conducted through the capital projects and debt service funds. The receipts from a bond sale are placed in the capital projects fund for expenditure on the project, and tax receipts to pay off the bond debt are deposited into the debt fund. If capital assets are purchased by local tax money collected to meet the expenses in the current fiscal year, they are purchased through the general fund (GASB, 2001). This is because (in the spirit of Article 12 of the Magna Carta) revenue placed in the general fund must meet the current needs of government.

When a school district finances a capital project associated with a proprietary fund (such as a new sports complex to be paid from ticket and user receipts), the loan and debt payments would be processed through that fund. The records of the assets and long-term bond liabilities are maintained in the accounts of that fund. If a school district receives a donation for a capital project (such as a new library), it is placed in the fiduciary fund. The donation, payment, and records of the asset must then use the accounts of that fund (GASB, 2001).

When the capital projects fund is utilized, the revenue numbers and accounts names in Resource I (taken from Resource C) are used. As shown, the revenue accounts are limited to receipts from different levels of government, bonds, loans, and investment-related activities. The receipts are then allocated to the appropriate expenditure accounts for the project. Receipts from the sale of fixed assets may appear in this fund when the money from the sale is spent on the replacement of the assets.

With respect to the debt service fund, the revenue numbers and account names used in the fund are listed in Resource J. Although the accounts used in this fund may also be in other funds, they are limited to the payment of debt created from the sale of bonds or loans. After the money is allocated to the expenditure accounts, payments may be made on the debt. Note that in the 5000 series the revenue numbers for the sale of bonds are listed. These accounts are needed for a bond recall; meaning, the money from the sale of the new bonds is used to pay for the recalled bonds.

LEASE-PURCHASE AGREEMENTS

When a school district cannot obtain approval to incur a long-term debt for the construction of a new facility, they may determine to acquire a building through a lease-purchase agreement. Basically these agreements require a school district to pay a monthly fee for the use of a building and then after a stated number of years, the ownership of the building is transferred to the district. Under this form of acquisition, the school board, and possibly a state agency, needs to approve the agreement. Therefore, an advantage of the lease-purchase is the elimination of a bond issue and possibly the corresponding public approval.

A major disadvantage of a lease-purchase agreement, however, is that the total cost for acquiring a building may be greater than the cost to build one. Another may be that the facility is not conducive to a sound learning environment or it may not meet state code. In these cases the school district may have to take money from the budget in the general fund to modify the building.

Another disadvantage, and likely the most serious, in a lease-purchase agreement is that the monthly payments are a current expense to be charged to the general fund. Without a bond issue and a public endorsement of long-term debt obligation, an additional tax levy for the payment of the lease and use of the capital projects fund is not appropriate. Because the monthly fee for the lease may be significant in relation to the amount of revenue placed in the general fund, the budgets in the general fund may be placed under considerable financial stress.

Relief from the financial stress caused by a lease-purchase payment is often harmful. This is because a property tax increase to cover the lease requires an increase in the tax levy for the general fund. For example, in one case the author observed severe public criticism of a superintendent over a school district's proposed budget increase and, in another, a nasty dispute between the school board and the teacher's union was blamed on the increase in teachers' salaries. In a review of the budgets of both districts, the analysis revealed they had excessive charges for lease-purchase agreements on buildings. In the first case, the superintendent, who was employed as the superintendent when the lease-purchase agreement was made, could only ask for understanding; it was not granted. In the second case, the board could either take on the teachers in a contract dispute over salaries and benefits or explain to the taxpayers the reason for a large tax increase was due to the lease agreement. They chose to provide a minimum salary increase and to assess a charge for health benefits to the teachers in the contract. The rift caused a teacher strike and immense harm in community–school and teacher–board relations that will last for several years.

FINAL THOUGHTS

As noted in the beginning of the chapter, the process to finance a building project is long and complex. From the time a facility review is conducted to determine if a new building or the remodeling of a facility is needed to the grand opening for public tours, site-based leaders and teams should be kept involved and informed when possible. Their involvement could include activities such as serving as a resource for project specifications, reviewing of plan details, participating in meetings and presentations on the proposed facility (sometimes to serve as a witness), and assisting with progress meetings, the final inspection, and the open house.

For instance, in one school district the public was dramatically opposed to the board's placement of a bond request on the ballot for the construction of a new high school. The bond referendum did not pass by a landslide. In response, the board and administration set up teacher and community teams to study the problems, to make recommendations, and to assist with the project. After two years, the bond referendum was placed on the ballot and passed. A beautiful high school was built and renovations were made in the other schools. The district maintained its ties to the community, which gained a positive attitude toward the district. Less than 10 years after the construction of the building, another bond issue for a new wing was approved.

Involving people in the community is essential when proposing a project costing millions of dollars. The imposition of a new tax levy for a multimillion dollar facility can be very threatening to some property owners. People are often intimidated because if they cannot pay their property taxes, local law enforcement officials have the right to take their property. Technically, the properties of the taxpayers serve as collateral for the bond issue.

Finally, as mentioned in the beginning of the chapter, new educational facilities are a necessity and not a luxury for many communities. The utilization and teaching of new technologies are tied directly to the economic viability of graduates with respect to employment and admission to colleges and universities. Finding a means to finance these very costly facilities is an immediate concern of many local school leaders; some of whom have tried a number of innovative tactics.

In an example of an effort to reduce the cost of a new high school, a district plans to purchase 30 acres on which to construct a 230,000-sq. ft building with athletic fields. The city property was essentially abandoned and so the school district can acquire it at a reasonable cost. To defray its costs, the district intends to allow some of the land to be used for retail and housing units and to work with a local development authority to finance the project. In another case, a vocational school included a shopping mall in their building. In still another case, a school took over a military installation and upgraded the buildings for classrooms and offices. In yet another, a school district purchased a building that housed a supermarket and converted the large interior into a prekindergarten school. The open space, parking lot (some of which was converted to playground space), and air conditioning offered advantages. These, and other creative ideas, have to be considered if school leaders wish to provide the expensive facilities needed by our educational system.

DISCUSSION QUESTIONS

1. Why could a $40 million building require a $44 million dollar bond issue?
2. Why might a $44 million bond issue only reap $43 million for a project?
3. If a bond issue is not approved for a school building and a school district is faced with the possibility of going into a split session (students attend a half day of school), would a lease purchase be justified?
   a. What might be the undesirable effects of a lease?
4. What could be the specific tasks of site-based administrators and teams in the proposal, planning, construction, and opening of a new facility?

APPLICATION PROBLEMS

The answers are provided at the end of the chapter.

1. Assume a bond principal and interest payment of $1,278,875 was collected in the current year (assessed property value of $917,364,287).
   a. What would have been the tax levy made on the property owners (in cents and in mills)?
   b. How much would an owner of a home assessed at $62,000 have paid on this tax levy?

CLINICAL PRACTICUM EXERCISES

In response to the clinical exercises below, the suggested format is to: (a) state the question, (b) answer the question, and (c) discuss your answer in reference to the content presented in the text. If supporting material is discussed and can be made available, it should be referenced in the discussion as an appendix and attached to the end of the report. Note that one of the objectives of part 3 is to show that the material in the book has been read, comprehended, and applied.

Using the information in this chapter as a reference, report your findings on:

1. the use of capital projects and debt service funds;
2. (if active) the sources of revenue in the funds;
3. (if a bond issue has been released) the tax levy for the debt service fund for the current year and the balance owed on the bond issue;
4. (if the school has released a bond issue) the type of bonds sold (public vs. private) and the professional services used in the sale; and
5. (if a building was constructed or is being constructed) the involvement of teachers and site teams.

REFERENCES

Castaldi, B. (1994). *Educational facilities: Planning, modernization, and management.* Boston: Allyn & Bacon.

Freeman, R. J., & Shoulders, C. D. (1996). *Governmental & nonprofit accounting: Theory & practice* (5th ed.). Upper Saddle River, NJ: Merrill/Prentice Hall.

Governmental Accounting Standards Board (2001). *Codification of governmental accounting and financial reporting standards.* Norwalk, CT: Author.

Granof, M. H. (1998). *Government and not-for-profit accounting: Concepts and practices.* New York: Wiley.

Interstate School Leaders Licensure Consortium (1996). *Standards for school leaders.* Washington, DC: Council of Chief State School Officers.

Meyer, A. E. (1967). *An educational history of the American people* (2nd ed.). New York: McGraw-Hill.

Razek, J. R., & Hosch, G. A. (1995). *Introduction to governmental and not-for-profit accounting* (3rd ed.). Upper Saddle River, NJ: Merrill/Prentice Hall.

Rippa, S. A. (1988). *Education in a free society* (4th ed.). New York: Longman.

Weygandt, J. J., Kieso, D. E., & Kimmel, P. D. (1999). *Accounting principles* (5th ed.). New York: Wiley.

Zipf, R. (1997). *How the bond market works* (2nd ed.). Paramus, NJ: New York Institute of Finance.

ANSWERS TO APPLICATION PROBLEMS

1a. $.0014 or 14 mills
1b. $86.80

Chapter 11

Financing Noninstructional Operations

Noninstructional operations provide goods and services, including fiduciary services, to the public and governmental bodies. The receipt and expenditure of the money for these operations are processed through the proprietary and fiduciary funds. Proprietary funds are used for selling goods and services to the public through enterprise funds and to governmental units, including site-based units in the school district, through internal service funds. When school districts receive donations or are given money to hold in trust, the money or assets are placed in a fiduciary fund.

The financial responsibilities assigned to school leaders for noninstructional operations vary from school district to school district. Regardless of the assignments, they are typically not burdensome, but, at the same time, how they are handled can be critical to an administrator's career. For example, several young administrators collected money from students for a school trip; however, they used a surplus from the money they received to pay for several economically disadvantaged children. The use of the surplus, of course, was not included in the directives set forth by the school board when the trip was approved. When the violation was discovered, charges had to be levied by the school board. The parents who paid for the trip appealed to the board to forgive the charges. Sadly, the board believed they had no choice but to terminate their employment. Their point was that the young administrators knowingly violated a public trust and such a discrepancy could not be dismissed, not even lightly.

Often the assignments for noninstructional operations are vague and do not offer a clear description of the duties for the personnel working in the units. For example, in some districts the cafeteria and athletic directors are supervised by the school principal whereas in others they report to a position in central administration, such as the assistant superintendent or business manager. In one case, the direct supervision of the food services operation in a large high school was assigned to the principal. With respect to the duties assigned to the person collecting the money, the procedure was for a cafeteria worker to take the daily breakfast and lunch receipts, which were placed in a shoebox, to the bank for deposit sometime in the afternoon. A teller at the bank counted the money and made out a deposit slip. The deposit slip and tickets for free and reduced meals were taken to the business office and recorded as the sales for the day.

Obviously, there are too many hazards in the above case. Several questions would have to be answered by the principal's office in an audit. Specifically, records would have to assure auditors that: (a) all of the money for all food sales was collected, (b) all of the money was deposited, (c) all food tickets received for free and reduced meals were turned in to the business office (not resold), and (d) the charges to the government for free and reduced meals were based on the number of meals served and not on the number of tickets handed out to students.

Although staff employees typically manage noninstructional operations, and the business office records receipts and expenditures, an on-site administrator in a line (as opposed to staff) position of authority, such as the building principal, should ensure that the interests of the children and the school district are properly represented. Even when the responsibility is not assigned to the line administrator, and staff personnel violate directives or the law, the on-site administrator is typically called on to take action or to carry out orders from central administration. In addition, regardless of supervisory assignments, the on-site line administrator is often the person who takes local complaints, resolves on-site disputes and disciplinary problems, reports on resolutions to grievances, and so on.

As a result, school administrators must be knowledgeable about all noninstructional operations within their domain of responsibility. This is supported by the **ISLLC** Interstate School Leaders Licensure Consortium's (ISLLC, 1996) Standard 3 which states that administrators are to ensure that the "fiscal resources of the school are managed responsibly, efficiently, and effectively" and that "a safe, clean, and aesthetically pleasing school environment is created and maintained" (p. 15).

ISLLC The noninstructional operations described in this chapter should be perceived as subsystems within the larger system of the school district. Then as ISLLC (1996) explains, school administrators must ensure that all "organizational systems are regularly monitored and modified as needed" (p. 15). Further, when managing the organization, operations, and resources of the system, administrators are expected to "facilitate processes and engage in activities ensuring that:

- time is managed to maximize the attainment of organizational goals;
- potential problems and opportunities are identified;
- problems are confronted and resolved in a timely manner;
- financial, human, and material resources are aligned to the goals of the school" (p. 15).

This chapter describes the strategic planning process, revenue sources, and administration of noninstructional operations. These operations should be maintained via the same accounting principles used for government funds. This requires using the same set of accounting and budgeting numbers shown in the resource tables and the same procedures to process receipts and expenditures discussed in the previous chapters.

OVERVIEW OF FINANCIAL PLANNING FOR PROPRIETARY OPERATIONS

Because proprietary operations in a school district receive income money in exchange for services or goods, they should have strategic business plans with unit goals, objectives, and benchmark targets. The basic difference between a strategic financial plan and a strategic business plan is in the way the money is received. Financial plans are prepared for revenues that are received in advance of their expenditure. Thus, a budget is prepared and allocations are made for the expenditure of the money.

A business plan, on the other hand, depends on income that is earned throughout the fiscal year. Therefore a business plan cannot allocate money that has not been received into expenditure accounts. Rather, a proposed budget is used as a management document but is not entered into the accounting records. Income is entered when the money is received, and expenses are recorded when money is spent. Cash flow must be carefully monitored. Examples of proprietary operations include: food services, athletic activities, concerts, summer recreational and educational programs, driver training programs, child care services, adult continuing education, cultural arts enrichment programs, reading recovery programs, technology training centers, office and school supply stores, transportation services, and physical plant services and rentals.

When money is received from sales generated by an enterprise or an internal service operation, the receipts should cover the costs. If a profit is realized in a fund, it should be accounted for in a retained earnings or a net assets account as opposed to an unreserved fund balance account. The generation of a profit is appropriate since, ideally, the proprietary operations are expected to earn money for purchasing capital assets necessary for selling goods or services, such as a new refrigerator for the cafeteria or a delivery truck for a central supply store.

If to purchase a capital asset for a proprietary operation a loan is assumed, it is recorded in the accounts of the proprietary fund. Then the payments on the loan are made from the money earned by that fund. For example, if bonds were issued to remodel a cafeteria or football stadium, the money would be deposited in the appropriate enterprise fund to pay the contractors and to buy the new equipment. The payments on the bond principal and interest would then be taken from the money earned and placed in the enterprise fund. If the receipts in the fund could not cover the loan payments, then money would have to be transferred from the general fund to the enterprise fund for the payment.

After a capital asset is acquired, it is recorded and then depreciated in the proprietary fund through which it was purchased. The depreciation expense reduces the income and the profit reported for the operation. Because the depreciation expense does not require an expenditure of cash, it does not reduce the balance in the cash account.

FINANCIAL PLANNING: FIDUCIARY TRUSTS AND DONATIONS

Neither a financial plan nor a business plan is germane to noninstructional operations and activities in the fiduciary funds, which are pension trust, investment trust, private purpose trust, and agency funds (GASB, 2001). As a result, specific rules and procedures need to be in place for the receipt and expenditure of money through the accounts of these funds.

The administration of the pension and investment trust funds is typically the sole responsibility of the business office, and school administrators have little or no reason to work with them. Private purpose trust funds, on the other hand, are used to manage trust arrangements in which the donation and income generated by a donation may benefit the school district, schools, individuals, programs, and other organizations in the school district. The use of these funds when raising and expending money often involves school administrators.

Recall that the permanent fund, which was introduced earlier, is classified as a government fund and is for donations from which only the earnings and not the principal can be spent for "purposes that support the [school district's] programs—that is for the benefit of the [school district] or its citizenry" (GASB 2001, Cod. Sec. 1300.108). On the other hand, a private purpose nonexpendable trust donation is used when money (the principal), or a tangible asset (such as land), may not be spent or sold and does not qualify for deposit into the permanent fund. For example, a gift may require that the interest (not the principal) from the donation must be spent for an award ceremony and plaques honoring outstanding alumni. Because the donation is not for the benefit of the school district's programs or students, it would be placed in the private purpose trust fund as opposed to the permanent fund.

A private purpose expendable trust donation permits the principal and interest to be spent by the school district. These donations, therefore, are placed in the private purpose trust fund and may not be deposited in the permanent fund. In some cases, there may be restrictions on the use of the donation. For example, a parent association may give money to a school for playground equipment. Because of the delicate differences between nonexpendable and expendable donations, a school district may wish to place these receipts into two separate trust funds, such as an expendable and a nonexpendable private purpose trust fund.

The purpose of agency funds is to hold resources in a trust, or custodial, capacity for individuals and organizations, including the school district and its students. A special type of agency fund used by school districts, and shown in Resource B as fund 90, is the Student Activity Fund. This fund is used to hold money in trust for students in different grade levels and clubs in a school district.

Other agency funds are a payroll fund and an unemployment compensation fund. The payroll fund receives money from other funds (such as the general, special revenue, and proprietary funds) for the payment of salaries and wages; for withholdings for taxes, benefits, and social security; and so on. An unemployment fund is used when school districts are permitted to maintain a reserve for unemployment claims. These funds are administered by the business manager.

In conclusion, fiduciary funds do not require much attention from school administrators except to ensure that the trust assignments are not violated and that money is spent appropriately. This may be accomplished quite efficiently, however, when a set of basic rules and procedures are available to direct operations.

REVENUES FOR NONINSTRUCTIONAL OPERATIONS

Because proprietary operations provide goods and services in exchange for money, the revenue accounts used by these funds are limited to sales-related receipts, direct and indirect aid, bond receipts, and transfers from other funds. Resource K exhibits the accounts presented in Resource C that are relevant to the enterprise operations.

Although the internal service operations are similar to enterprise operations in terms of their purpose, their revenue sources are limited to receipts from other funds in the district, other governments, earnings on investments, the sale of assets, leases, the sale of bonds, and loans. Resource L presents the accounts shown in Resource C that are typically used by the internal service funds.

Because fiduciary operations account for money held in trust by or for the school district, a limited number of revenue accounts shown in Resource C are applicable. The revenue accounts that are typically used by these funds are presented in Resource M.

READING FINANCIAL REPORTS
OF PROPRIETARY OPERATIONS

Since proprietary operations do not record a proposed budget appropriation into their accounts as described for government funds, their financial reports do not use the same format. As a result, these financial reports do not include columns for appropriations and encumbrances. Rather, only account balances are shown in the monthly and annual reports. In benchmark reviews, the account balances have to be compared to a separate proposed management budget.

The example in Figure 11.1 is of an annual financial report for a food service enterprise operation. The same format would be used on a monthly basis to report the income and expenses for both enterprise and internal service operations. If budgets are used, which is possible, they can be entered into the accounts and the same procedures and reports described for the general and special revenue funds would be applied.

As shown in Figure 11.1, there are two sections for receipts. The top section of the table presents the total operating revenue received from daily sales less the total **operating expenses**, which is the calculation of the operating income or loss. The second section presents the nonoperating revenues received from federal and state programs. The addition of the total operating income or loss and the nonoperating revenue is used to calculate the net income or loss. Some governments may use the term *increase in net assets* as opposed to *net income*. The amount

Food Service Enterprise Fund
Statement of Revenue, Expense, and Changes in Retained Earnings
for the Fiscal Year Ending June 30, 20x1

Operating revenues:		
Daily sales: breakfast		$ 188,317
Daily sales: lunch		478,060
Sales: other		24,375
Total operating revenues		$ 690,752
Operating expenses:		
Personal Services		
Management salaries	$ 64,217	
Wages	284,256	
Food supplies	428,352	
Other supplies	84,883	
Contractual Services	38,446	
Utilities	14,010	
Repairs and Maintenance	5,876	
Miscellaneous expenses	7,684	
Insurance	5,834	
Depreciation – equipment	6,037	
Total operating expenses		939,595
Operating income (loss):		$(248,843)
Nonoperating revenues (expenses):		
State school lunch program	$117,695	
National school lunch program	95,332	
U.S.D.A.	47,070	
Total nonoperating revenues		$ 260,097
Net income (loss):		$ 11,254
Retained earnings/fund balance July 1, 20x0		4,603
Retained earnings/fund balance June 30, 20x1		$ 16,512

FIGURE 11.1
Annual Financial Report: Food Services Fund

in the retained earnings account, which may be labeled as a *net assets* account, is the surplus or loss from operations. The retained earnings account for the end of the year includes the balance at the beginning of the year plus the profit (or minus the loss) for the current year.

In Figure 11.1, note that depreciation is shown as an operating expense. Although this reduces the profit or increases the loss, depreciation does not represent an actual cash transaction. Rather it is a means to recognize and distribute the costs of the capital assets over the expected life of the equipment or building. In addition, the example suggests that the overhead charges for utilities and insurance are charged to the operation. In some cases, these charges are not levied by a school district; however, they should be shown in reference to allocated space or from separate invoices. When a vendor is contracted to offer the services, the vendor should pay their portion of the overhead expenses.

An optional change to the example shown in Figure 11.1 is to include the **non-operating expenses** (utilities, insurance, and depreciation) under nonoperating revenues and not under operating expenses. In the example, the nonoperating expenses would total $25,881. Although the net income (loss) would remain the same, the operating income would change from a loss of $248,843 to $222,962. Thus, when conducting an analysis of the operation, the operating and nonoperating expenses can now be compared to sales and revenues to obtain a more accurate picture.

READING FINANCIAL REPORTS OF FIDUCIARY OPERATIONS

The financial reports for operations in fiduciary funds simply list the receipts, disbursements, and balances by account. In Figure 11.2 a report for a student activity fund presents the balances in the student accounts at the end of the year. Because

	Balance ($) July 1, 20x0	Receipts ($)	Disbursements ($)	Balance ($) June 30, 20x1
	Student Activity Fund **Statement of Activity** **for the Fiscal Year Ended June 30, 20x1**			
Band Club	2,639	1,290	1,654	2,275
Cheerleaders	726	260	1,618	(632)
Chorus	100	30	105	25
Class of:				
2009	318			318
2008	396			396
2007	200			200
2006	585			585
2005	271			271
2004	1,292	1,313	1,164	1,441
2003	1,737	2,350	2,709	1,378
2002	1,260	2,201	2,598	863
2001		1,061	667	394
Drama Club	1,274	3,206	4,221	259
French Club	224	1,440	1,493	171
Girls Basketball	14			14
Jazz Ensemble	249	5,357	5,569	37
Key Club	951	6,344	6,673	622
Peer Counseling	90	250	265	75
SADD	230			230
Spanish Club	68	80	80	68
Student Council	489	3,660	3,473	676
Yearbook	868	20,041	20,205	704
Total	13,981	48,883	52,494	10,370

FIGURE 11.2
Annual Report: Student Activity Fund

Student Activity Agency Fund Statement of Changes in Assets and Liabilities for the Fiscal Year Ended June 30, 20x1				
	Balance ($) July 1, 20x0	Additions ($)	Deletions ($)	Balance ($) June 30, 20x1
Assets:				
Cash and Cash Equivalents	13,981	48,883	52,494	10,370
Total Assets	13,981	48,883	52,494	10,370
Liabilities:				
Due to Student Groups	13,981	48,883	52,494	10,370

FIGURE 11.3
Annual Financial Statement: Student Activity Fund

the district does not spend the money but, rather, makes the payments as requested, the term *disbursement* rather than *expenditure* is appropriate. These activity reports can be produced via computer software programs upon command and should be made available for review to teachers/advisors of student groups on a monthly basis.

At the end of year, a financial statement presenting the total assets and liabilities for an agency fund is prepared. An example of a statement for the student activity fund is shown in Figure 11.3. This statement is based on the report shown in Figure 11.2 and simply summarizes the changes in the account totals from the beginning to the end of the fiscal year.

STRATEGIC BUSINESS PLANS FOR PROPRIETARY OPERATIONS

ISLLC

To ensure that the fiscal resources in the proprietary operations are administered responsibly, efficiently, and effectively as proposed by the ISLLC (1996), a strategic business plan is needed. As noted, the elements of this plan are different from the strategic financial plan described for the general and special revenue funds; however, they must have a strategic alignment by being tied to the school district's mission. Further, the school district should have a set of rules and procedures developed for each proprietary fund and possibly even separate operating units (such as food services and athletics) in a fund that provides for the needs and limitations of the service, activity, or program.

The purpose of the business plan for proprietary operations is providing a blueprint for school administrators to follow. First of all, the business plan must be strategically aligned with the district objectives that support the goals and mission of the district. When this occurs, the justification for a business operation is contained in the district's objectives. For example, having a cafeteria would meet an objective of a school district directing that each school provide food services for students.

This alignment prevents the establishment of entrepreneurial enterprises that may require the use of resources intended for academic programs. In addition, it should prohibit the sale of goods and services that have not been approved by the school board (which happens) and that may not be appropriate; for instance, sales or services that are in direct competition with a tax-paying business in the local community (this is illegal in some states) or a service that should be provided via a private for-profit company. In some states, the government may not be permitted to offer goods or services that are not within the realm of its mission, and, if they are offered, the income may be subject to taxes.

Therefore, each authorized business activity in a school district should prepare long-range goals, which should be idealistically in support of the strategic objectives of the school district. Supporting the operational goals, a list of objectives offering definition to the product or service being delivered should be drawn up. For example, one goal for a cafeteria may be to promote positive nutritional habits. One of the objectives may be to offer students a selection of nutritional food (as opposed to junk food) in a clean and pleasant environment, whereas other objectives may focus on operational effectiveness and efficiencies. Further, students in an efficient operation would eat their lunch at a reasonable time within the school day (such as 11:30 a.m. to 1:30 p.m. and not from 9:30 a.m. to 2:30 p.m.).

The remaining basic components that should be included in a business plan are as follows:

1. Identification of the different personnel needed to manage and work in the operation. This section should specify the education, experience, special skills, health, disposition, and energy needed by the individuals for the operation.
2. Creation of a management team with a description of duties where relevant. This team could include the manager of the operation, school principal, business administrator, superintendent, members of a school board committee or representative, and site-team members (stakeholders).
3. Development of an organizational chart. The diagram should ensure that team members are aware of their own position of authority and of those of the other team members in the operational subsystem.
4. Description of the customers who would buy the goods and services offered by the business. This section discusses the customer base in terms of their demographics and a marketing plan to maintain currency. For example, a student customer base for a food services operation may be considerably different from the customers/attendees of athletic events.
5. Description of the ideal facility, furniture, and related equipment. This section should ensure the layout and furnishings are flexible in terms of expansion and change.
6. The financial section. It must provide the budget projections needed to monitor costs and set prices and income projections for a break-even operation, a profit to ensure asset replacement, and a profit to ensure asset replacement plus improvement of services. These income and cost projections should have monthly targets for benchmark reviews.

7. Contingency plans. When a benchmark review indicates a target is not being met, a contingency plan should indicate what action to take (Jensen, 2001; Lasher, 1994).

Once the business plan is developed, the manager of the business operation and the management team should monitor operations in reference to the plan. At the end of the fiscal year, the plan should be reviewed and, if necessary, adjustments should be made.

FINANCIAL PLANS FOR FIDUCIARY TRUSTS

The assumption of a fiduciary trust by a school district must be in accordance with its mission. The intent or conditions of the trust should describe the purpose or objective of the deposit. As a result of the intent, the administration of a trust focuses on a plan for processing receipts and disbursements. Of course, the plans and procedures must allow for differences among schools and site-based units. For instance, the process for handling receipts and authorizing expenditures in a small elementary school would be different from that of a large high school.

With respect to the student activity trust, the oversight of the accounts is typically assigned to the school principal and managed by the classroom teacher or class/club advisor. A general rule is that when teachers/advisors receive money, they should provide a prenumbered receipt from a book with receipt stubs to the person giving them the money. The money received should then be transmitted through the system as described in chapter 8. Procedures should also require the authorization signature of the classroom teacher or advisor and the school principal for all disbursements from an account. In addition, interest earned from money held in the student fund should be distributed proportionately among the fund accounts.

Upon graduation, class members may be required to remove their money from the student activity fund and place it in a special account administered by the elected officers of the class for reunions and other events. In some cases, the graduating class donates the balance in their account to the school district as a class gift. In Figure 11.2, for example, the graduating class of 2001 may remove their balance of $394 from the student activity fund or donate it to the district whereupon it would be transferred to a trust fund.

THE ADMINISTRATION OF NONINSTRUCTIONAL FINANCIAL OPERATIONS

As a legal corporate entity, the business operations of a school district are a local concern, and the board members of the school district have almost total discretion over the use of the resources in these funds. Of course, limitations are placed on the use of money received from the state and federal governments and transferred into a proprietary fund, such as money for free or reduced meals, or any money held under a trust agreement, such as donations for scholarships. The annual financial statements and audits for the noninstructional operations are, therefore, intended more for public review than for state and federal examination. Recognizing this basic difference between government and nongovernmental funds is key to understanding the administrative regulations, practices, and responsibilities with respect to these funds.

Administering Enterprise Operations

Income is recorded in the enterprise funds when it is earned (not when cash is received). For example, if a school district has a food services fund, income is recorded at the time a person buys a meal. If a person pays cash for a meal, then money is placed in the cash account and recorded as income. If a person receives a meal but the money is not received until a government reimburses the district, the sale is also recorded as income when the meal is purchased, rather than when the money is received from the government.

Administrators must monitor the receipt and recording of sales and the balance in the cash account of the enterprise funds. For example, in one school district the receipts from athletic events are kept in a gym locker. Expenditures are made from the money in the locker. Records of receipts and for expenditures do not exist. If anyone suspects improper conduct, the administrators have no defense. Are they breaking the public trust?

As in a private business, the school district's enterprise funds should have enough money in the cash account to pay the district's invoices. Because the cash for all funds is kept in the same bank account, if the cash balance in an enterprise fund is not adequate to pay an invoice, the school district may have to draw on the cash balances in other funds. However, if an enterprise fund is operating with a negative cash flow and money is spent from the cash account in the general fund or money is permanently transferred from the general fund to the enterprise fund, financial stress is created for programs in the general fund.

Even though a budget may not be entered into the accounting records as described for the expenditure accounts in government funds, a proposed budget estimating receipts and expenditures should be created to monitor the noninstructional operations. Using the fund's financial report, such as the one in Figure 11.1, the actual receipts and expenditures should be compared to those estimated for the operation. In addition, the percentage of the differences between the actual and estimated amounts should be calculated as well as the percentages of the total operating and nonoperating expenses, salaries, wages, and food in relation to operating revenue, operating income, and net profit or loss.

The income/cost percentages and other comparisons can provide invaluable insights for the management team. For example, what should be the percentage of the cost of personnel and food compared to operating income and net income? If the monthly report indicates that this percentage is significantly greater or smaller than its projection in the business plan, the management team should make adjustments or possibly break down the sales; for instance, receipts and costs for breakfast and lunch, receipts and costs for different menues, and patterns of receipts on different days of the week.

If the percentage of salaries and wages compared to revenues is excessive, the management team might examine if there are too many cafeteria employees, if the employees are overpaid or putting in more hours than necessary (this could be a problem in the absence of line managers), if there should be an increase in the price charged for meals and snacks (although government reimbursements may limit the amount charged for a full meal, other prices may be adjusted), if too few children are eating in the cafeteria, if the menu needs to be more appealing (school cafeterias must recognize and react to competition—some lunches purchased in a supermarket may be more appealing and less costly than cafeteria food), if all money collected is being deposited, if the charges for reimbursement via state and federal reimbursement programs are being processed (the cafeteria records may not be correct), if debit cards should be used, and so on.

Administering Internal Service Operations

When a school district does not have any special internal service operations, one fund is used to handle all receipts and expenditures. However, a separate fund may be established when a district has a special internal operation, such as a central supply operation or a physical plant operation. Using separate funds offers many advantages, such as a reduction in costs from bulk purchasing, faster delivery service, and reducing the number of purchasing orders. Another benefit is that the site-based unit is the customer, who may be able to exercise some influence on the quality and quantity of work conducted in their facility.

For example, in one school district the employees in the facilities division perform minor repairs and renovations to the buildings, especially over the summer recess, through a physical plant fund. The district budget allocation to facilities acquisition and construction, which is object code number 4000 in Resource E, pays for the repairs and renovations. This operation has saved the district considerable money and is a benefit to the employees (including some teachers) by providing them with summer employment.

As an illustration of the financial process that should be followed by an internal service operation, assume that a district has a central supply. When a site-based unit orders supplies, it processes an internal purchase order to central supply. When the order is filled, a transfer is made from the budget unit's allocation to the supplies budget object number 610 (in Resource E) into the income account number 1970 in (Resource C) in the central supply internal service fund. The central supply operation then uses the money to purchase more supplies and to meet the costs of providing the service.

In some cases, a school district budget may allocate money in the general fund for an internal services operation to pay for all or a portion of the administrative and overhead costs (heat, light, etc.). This would then lower the costs to all site-based units for the goods or services provided. Transfers, however, from the general fund to an internal service fund may not be a means to shift money from the general fund to avoid an excessive surplus. Auditors will detect such a transfer without difficulty.

Obviously, enterprise and internal service operations can be a benefit to school districts and site-based units when they are administered properly. One recommendation is that one fund should not contain too many operations and activities, and separate funds should be used for large operations, such as food services or a central supply store. If one enterprise and one internal service fund are used, receipts should be separated for each operating unit with expenditures entered against the activity or service accounts. Financial reports should then be prepared so that the receipts and disbursements for each can be verified. If operating units are not separated and reports are not provided, control at the site-based level is compromised.

Administering Trust and Agency Funds

The focus for the administration of fiduciary trust and agency money is to ensure that they operate within the limitations of the trust arrangement or the agency assignment. Probably the most active fiduciary operation for school administrators to oversee is the student activity fund. Although the student activity fund typically does not require the direct involvement of school administrators, it is their duty to ensure that the receipts and expenditures made by the students are appropriate. To accomplish this, the school administrators and district business administrator should review and approve the requests of the students.

To ensure student leaders and advisors handle the collection and expenditure of student activity money properly, the school board should review, update, and approve policies for the student activity funds on an annual basis, even if there are no changes to the policy. This policy should require site administrators, teacher/advisors, and student leaders to review their monthly budget reports to confirm the accuracy of the deposits, expenditures, and the return and deposit of unspent withdrawals.

Monitoring Payroll

Although the payroll fund is the responsibility of the school business administrator, site administrators should be familiar with its purpose and procedures. The objective for the payroll fund is to receive transfers of money from other funds for the payment of salaries, wages, taxes, employee benefits, and other deductions.

Monitoring the payroll is not a major task for site administrators; however, the failure to verify payroll charges can create distress for the school board. For example, in one district with a $60 million budget, approximately $48 million was spent on salaries for the year. Because the turnover of personnel was not properly monitored, an overexpenditure in salaries was discovered in early spring and estimated to be between $500,000 and $1 million. Not only did the overexpenditure in salaries become a public issue but also the public awareness of the continued payment of employees after their departure was most embarrassing.

The monitoring of payroll charges was also problematic in another district when the school board recognized that the number of substitute teachers exceeded the number of days the teachers were recorded as absent. The days taken off by the teachers were not being reported by the school principals and in one case the business office was not informed of a teacher's absences until after the end of the year. Because this teacher was not returning, but she had been overpaid, the school district could not recover the money. As a result, some principals were suspected of incompetence or unprofessional conduct as the reason for their failure to report teacher absences. Because of these and other discrepancies, a call for an audit was made to state officials. Although the audit did not uncover any illegal or improper conduct, they did find fault with the general lack of attention given to financial and personnel matters.

Another payroll consideration for site administrators is regarding employees whose assignments are split between teaching and other duties. Assume that in one school the librarian and the school principal spend 20% of their time teaching children. As a result, 20% of their salary should be allocated to the instruction function budget number 1000 (Resource E). If not, the cost of instruction will be understated and the salaries paid for running the library and for administration will be overstated. In a review of the financial statements at the end of the year, the public will gain an improper impression of the financial support for instruction by the school, especially if comparisons are made to the administrative and instructional expenditures per student spent by other site units in the school and other school districts.

Because of payroll issues and problems, such as those noted above, many school districts use the services of a private vendor to prepare their payroll. Even so, site administrators are still the ones who are directly aware of personnel absences, turnover, and assignments. As a consequence, even though these administrators may not have much, if anything, to do with the payroll, they must be sure to process records and then verify the personnel attendance and salary reports.

FINAL THOUGHTS

The supervision of proprietary operations and fiduciary activities are becoming more demanding as school districts grow and become more complex. An old saying in business is that the reason for problems in some shops is that the inmates (workers) are running the asylum (shop). Likewise, the suspicion is that the failure to provide adequate professional supervision of noninstructional operations has led to questionable and even unreasonable practices.

One proposal in response to the need for greater control over noninstructional operations has been to hire private for-profit vendors to run them. These contract arrangements for food services, custodial services, transportation, and physical plant maintenance operations for school districts have created a great debate. A recent proposal in one school district has been to hire a vendor to provide counseling services for the district. Such arrangements are often made by some school districts because the noninstructional operations have become a financial burden and created overloads for administrators and board members. The controversy, however, occurs when the public questions why private vendors can provide effective services for a profit and school administrators cannot.

Another controversy is regarding fiduciary donations made by parents to their public school or to a specific grade within the school. For example, in one wealthy school an auction was held and a parent bid $20,000 for a reserved parking space in front of the school where he could drop off and pick up his child. In other cases parents have hired an additional grade school teacher to lower class size, an art teacher for an elementary school, a language teacher for the high school, and so on (Stark, 2001).

Because of concerns about intradistrict inequities, some school boards are refusing donations to a specific school. At the same time, other districts are accepting all donations regardless. One school district refused the donation for an additional teacher but then ended up taking money from its budget to hire the person. An option taken by another was to permit donations if they benefit the entire district and not only one school. However, interdistrict equity is also a concern. For example, while parents in a wealthy school district raised $240,000, the parents in a low-income district could only raise $44 in a yard sale for their school (Stark, 2001). Thus, the issue with respect to fund-raising activities and donations and intra- and interdistrict educational equity has further complicated the equity problems among school districts discussed in chapter 4.

Taking this situation one step further, however, rather than supporting their public school, some parents have established charter schools. In one school district the students were divided sharply by wealth and race between the public school and a new charter school. The establishment of a charter school reduced the financial resources received by the school district because they had to pay the charter schools 90% of the revenue received per student. As a result, the school district, which lost over 25% of its students and considerable revenue to the charter school, decided to take aggressive actions to win back most, if not all, of these students. Some believe this type of competition will improve education but the danger is that it may hinder efforts to ensure educational equity.

DISCUSSION QUESTIONS

1. What are the differences in the purposes and financial operations between the:
   a. instructional and noninstructional operations;
   b. proprietary and fiduciary operations;
   c. enterprise and internal service operations;
   d. trust and agency operations; and
   e. strategic *financial* plan and strategic *business* plan.

2. One objective of a school district is to offer a summer technical education program for students and adults. The program must be self-supporting and is expected to pay the school district a set dollar amount for each student enrolled. What would be the major considerations for a business plan for the program?

3. The author explained that some school boards were not permitting parents to make donations to benefit the school or classroom their child was attending; for example, paying the salary for an arts teacher or hiring a second teacher for a classroom. Do you agree or disagree with the decision that such donations should not be accepted unless they benefit the entire district? Why or why not?

APPLICATION PROBLEMS

1. As a school principal you are responsible for supervising the food service operation and student activity accounts.
   a. Outline a plan for the supervision and administration of the food services operation.
   b. What rules would you establish for processing the receipts of the food services operation?
   c. What rules would you establish for the expenditure of the money for the food services operation?
   d. What rules would you establish for processing the receipts and disbursements of student activity money?

2. Assume you are a school principal and the school board has assigned to you the responsibility of supervising the food services operation in your school. Because the cafeteria has been operating at a loss, you must determine the financial viability of the service. Using the example in Figure 11.1, identify the ratios and percentages you would compute to conduct an evaluation of the operation. Based on these comparisons, what insights or recommendations could you offer to the board?

3. The Parent Teachers Association wishes to donate money for the acquisition of an elaborate $2,500 playground structure at the Gillman Elementary School. Because the cost exceeds the state threshold of $2,000 for a direct purchase, bids must be requested. The parents are quite upset because the PTA used pictures of the structure to raise the money with the understanding that this equipment would be purchased. What is the solution to the problem? (Answer at the end of the chapter.)

CLINICAL PRACTICUM EXERCISES

In response to the clinical exercises below, the suggested format is to: (a) state the question, (b) answer the question, and (c) discuss your answer in reference to the content presented in the text. If supporting material is discussed and can be made available, it should be referenced in the discussion as an appendix and attached to the end of the report. Note that one of the objectives of part 3 is to show that the material in the book has been read, comprehended, and applied.

   Using the information in this chapter as a reference, report your findings on the following:

1. Name the noninstructional operations and activities (proprietary and fiduciary) in the district, including all extracurricular activities that receive money from the public or another governmental body.
   a. What funds are used for these operations and activities?
   b. Are budget reports prepared for these operations and activities?
   c. Who monitors the financial reports for these operations and activities?

2. Do the proprietary operations have goals, objectives, and financial plans?
   a. Are the operations defined by district objectives?
   b. If financial or business plans are used, how do they correspond to the elements of a business plan presented in this chapter?
3. What are the responsibilities of the site administrators for the proprietary operations?
   a. Are management or site-based teams used?
   b. How do the procedures used by the proprietary operations for processing receipts and expenditures compare to those discussed in this book?
   c. Are the people handling money bonded?
4. What are the fiduciary activities in the school district?
   a. Who administers the fiduciary trusts?
   b. How are the student activity accounts managed at both the school and the district level?

WEB ADDRESSES

Dissent Magazine (by subscription only)
http://www.dissentmagazine.org

REFERENCES

Governmental Accounting Standards Board (2001). *Codification of governmental accounting and financial reporting standards.* Norwalk, CT: Author.

Interstate School Leaders Licensure Consortium (1996). *Standards for school leaders.* Washington, DC: Council of Chief State School Officers.

Jensen, M. (2001). *The everything business planning book.* Holbrook, MA: Adams Media Corporation.

Lasher, W. (1994). *The perfect business plan made simple.* New York: Doubleday.

Stark, A. (2001). What's wrong with private funding for public schools? [Online]. Retrieved January 23, 2001, from http://www.dissentmagazine.org

ANSWERS TO APPLICATION PROBLEMS

3. Have the Parent Teachers Association purchase the equipment and donate it (not the money) to the school.

Chapter 12

Financial Reports, Performance Assessments, and Accountability

In recent years, the calls for educators to be more accountable have come from several sources. Likely, the actions of the federal government in the 1990s, which were discussed in chapter 1, have been the most influential.

In addition to the federal actions, the Interstate School Leaders Licensure Con-

ISLLC

sortium (ISLLC, 1996) and the Governmental Accounting Standards Board (GASB, 2001) propose for reasons of accountability that school districts provide financial and performance reports to the public for appraisal. More specifically, according to the ISLLC's Standards, administrators are expected to fulfill all legal and contractual obligations and to open their schools to public scrutiny. At the same time, the GASB directs all state and local governments to demonstrate to the public that they comply with all legal and contractual provisions. To accomplish this, they state that "every governmental entity should prepare and publish, as a matter of public record, a Comprehensive Annual Financial Report (CAFR) that encompasses all funds . . ." (Cod. Sec. 2200.101). Of course, the public reports will hopefully show that school districts have expended their money properly to generate expected performance outcomes and outputs.

At the same time, the National Policy Board for Educational Administration (NPBEA) and the National Council for Accreditation of Teacher Education (NCATE) also recognize the call for accountability. The NPBEA (2002a) explains that one of the shifts in the knowledge and skills expected of educational leaders is from an allocation of resources to an "accountability for learning processes and results" and that in their reports the leaders must "focus on performances" (p. 3).

Correspondingly, Standard 1 of NCATE (NPBEA, 2002b) stresses the importance both of candidates building district leadership positions and of their ability to conduct data-based research, which has to include performance and financial assessments. To accomplish this, as NCATE proposes, candidates must be able to apply and assess current technologies used for school management, business procedures, and scheduling purposes and to understand school finance structures and models. Of course, to show evidence that they have applied current technologies correctly and allocated resources properly for generating the expected outcomes and outputs, school leaders must have appropriate, valid, and reliable data. To simply declare that a school year has ended and that students have been promoted or graduated is no longer an acceptable report of performance.

Therefore, the purpose of this chapter is to discuss the reports generated by the accounting and budgeting systems and the use of the data generated by these reports for cost assessments. This discussion begins with recognizing the difference between costs and expenditures and goes on to tell how cost data is obtained. The chapter continues with a review of effectiveness and efficiency assessments that may be conducted and the creation of budget blueprints for planning and management purposes. It then concludes with a presentation on data-based research that may be conducted by referencing the accounting and budgeting reports. The Final Thoughts section closes the chapter and the book with the proposal that when effectiveness, efficiency, and cost assessments are totally ignored, the ultimate damage may be that a school district has unknowingly dropped into a state of organizational disintegration and **instructional disengagement** to the degree that a positive relationship between education and the economy is not possible.

WHAT ARE COSTS?

When conducting cost assessments, a clear understanding of the meaning of costs is important. For example, Fowler and Monk (2001) point out the importance of recognizing that expenditures are not the same as costs. The expenditures of a school district or a program are added to formulate its cost. Then the costs, not expenditures, are examined in relation to outcomes and outputs. The different expenditures that make up a total cost may be reviewed for diagnostic purposes. Consequently, the mechanics of a cost analysis and expenditure diagnosis for a school district and site-based units are related but not the same.

A thorough cost analysis that includes programs, services, and activities must reference the site-based budgets. When the expenditures for each object number in a site-based budget report are totaled, the sum represents the operational cost of the unit. When the costs of the site-based units are combined, they create the costs for larger units; for example, a cost report for a high school would combine the costs for all site-based program and support service units in the high school. As the cost information is combined up through the organizational structure of the school district, it continues to be compiled until a cost report for the entire district is created.

THE ANNUAL FINANCIAL REPORTS

As noted in previous chapters, the accounting system is used for generating a school district's monthly and annual reports. Regardless of their names, which may vary from state to state, a set of monthly reports and annual financial statements is prepared for each fund in the school district.

The annual financial report for governments, including school districts, is called the CAFR. The statements in the annual CAFR and the monthly financial reports can be classified into three basic types: (a) reports on real accounts (assets, liabilities, and fund balance), (b) cash flow reports, and (c) reports on nominal accounts (revenues and expenditures). The statements in the CAFR are prepared for the school district and then for each of the funds used by the district; however, they are not prepared for the site-based operating units.

Monthly and annual reports on real accounts are called balance sheets. The account information in balance sheets and cash flow statements is pertinent to the school board members, business officers, accountants, banks, investors, and the treasurer of the school district. The reports on the nominal accounts are popularly referred to as the revenue and expenditure reports but their formal title is The Statement of Revenues, Expenditures, and Changes in Fund Balance (or Net Assets). Because these reports present the financial operating data needed by school administrators and site-based teams for conducting cost assessments and expenditure analyses, they are the statements discussed in this chapter.

REVENUE AND EXPENDITURE REPORTS: GOVERNMENT FUNDS

The annual revenue and expenditure statements for government funds show the sources of the revenues and the expenditures made by the school district. Figure 12.1 presents a typical format for this report in a CAFR for a general fund. The monthly budget report, which was discussed and displayed in chapter 9, follows the same format except the budget account numbers are listed on the left side of the statement. Although the monthly reports may be for the school district and for each site-based unit, the annual report in the CAFR is for the school district, although end-of-year statements may be generated for each operating unit.

An example of a Statement of Revenue, Expenditures, and Fund Balance is exhibited in Resource N, which is nine pages long. This report consolidates the revenue and expenditure accounts used by the school district for the current and previous fiscal year. Although the account balances may be the same as the last monthly budget report, there may be some changes owing to the adjusting and closing entries discussed in chapter 7. When this report appears in the CAFR, this is an indication that it has been audited, is considered the official final report, and is a public document.

**General Fund
Statement of Revenues, Expenditures, and Changes in Fund Balance
for the Fiscal Year Ended June 30, 20x1**

Revenues		
(List of receipts, amount taken from the fund balance surplus, accounting fund transfers, and other receipts listed by revenue number)	xxxxxx	
Total Revenues		xxxxxx
Expenditures		
(List of expenditures according to budget number with subtotals)	xxxxxx	
Total Expenditures		xxxxxx
Excess of Revenues Over (Under) Expenditures	xxxxxx	
Fund Balance: Beginning of Year	xxxxxx	
Fund Balance: End of Year		xxxxxx

**FIGURE 12.1
Format for Revenue, Expenditure, and Fund Balance Statement**

In the report shown in Resource N, the final budget and actual expenditures for the reported year and previous fiscal year are shown along with the balances for each account. This permits the reader of the report to compare the two fiscal years. For example on page 1 of the report, the school district underestimated the amount of tuition to be collected in year 20x1 and overestimated the amount in year 20x0. On page 9, the reader may note that the fund balance at the end of the year was over $100,000 more than the ending fund balance of the previous year.

Problem 12.1: Using Resource N, what was the cost for the regular programs for 20x1? (Answer given at the end of the chapter.)

Problem 12.2: Using Resource N, what was the total instructional cost for year 20x1? (Answer given at the end of the chapter.)

Problem 12.3: Using Resource N, what was the percentage of the total cost of instruction spent for regular instruction? (Answer given at the end of the chapter.)

Problem 12.4: Using Resource N, what was the percentage of the total revenue spent on instruction? (Answer given at the end of the chapter.)

With computer software programs, an analysis of the district costs can be separated by each accounting program number (such as preschool/kindergarten shown as program number 110 in Resource D) and by function (such as instruction, shown as function number 1000 in Resource E, or support services, function number 2000). In addition, a study of total district expenditures can be conducted through the amounts shown in the object numbers (such as general supplies, object number 610 in Resource F). However, school leaders cannot conduct an analysis of the site-based operating units, such as the elementary grades or schools, unless the budget numbers are included in the computer program.

Finally, by using the statement shown in Resource N, another set of analyses might compare the budgeted to the actual receipts and expenditures. Because of the seemingly large increase in the fund balance at the end of the year over the beginning fund balance, the expenditure categories would have to be examined in relation to the amount budgeted. For example, on page 7 of Resource N, the unspent budget allocation in the total for the operations and maintenance of plant services seems large for the current and previous year. Specifically, the amount budgeted for other purchased services was less than anticipated. Why?

Of course, when state law does not permit expenditures to exceed budget allocations in any expenditure category, the budget amounts must be adjusted throughout the year to eliminate deficits. In these cases, the budgeted and actual amounts may equal each other or the budgeted amount may exceed the actual expenditures.

The Combined Statement

Another useful annual statement in the CAFR is a combined statement that presents the revenues, expenditures, and fund balances of all funds used by the school district or in a set of funds. As shown in Figure 12.2, this statement lists account names on the left side of the form and the accounting funds in columns across the top. Note that the title of the statement indicates that it presents the fund balance or equity. This is because the term equity, as opposed to fund balance, may be used for proprietary funds.

Resource O shows an example of a combined statement of the revenues, expenditures, and fund balance for the government funds. The totals for the revenue and major expenditure categories are shown along with their totals across the funds for the end of the reported fiscal year (20x1) and the previous fiscal year (20x0). This report can offer a view of the bigger picture as well as radical changes across both fiscal years. For example, the receipts and expenditures in the special revenue fund are important because they supplement the general fund operations. Further, the report indicates that the debt service fund is active but the capital projects fund is not. Thus, the bonds are still paying off a debt for construction that has been completed. This observation may lead to a review of the debt service fund to determine when the bonds will be paid and the reason for a fund balance at the end of the year.

> **Problem 12.5:** Using Resource O, what was the percentage of the total instructional expenditure for instruction from the special revenue fund? (Answer given at the end of the chapter.)

<table>
<tr><td colspan="6">**Combined Statement of Revenues, Expenditures, and
Changes in Fund Balance/Equity—All Funds
for the Fiscal Year Ended June 30, 20x1**</td></tr>
<tr><td></td><td>**General Fund**</td><td>**Special Revenue Fund**</td><td>**Enterprise Fund**</td><td>**Internal Service Fund**</td><td>**Fiduciary Fund**</td></tr>
<tr><td>Revenues
  (list of accounts)
Total Revenue</td><td></td><td></td><td></td><td></td><td></td></tr>
<tr><td>Expenditures
  (list of accounts)
  Total Expenditures</td><td></td><td></td><td></td><td></td><td></td></tr>
<tr><td>Excess of Revenues
  Over (Under)
  Expenditures</td><td></td><td></td><td></td><td></td><td></td></tr>
<tr><td>Other Financial
  Sources (Uses)</td><td></td><td></td><td></td><td></td><td></td></tr>
<tr><td>Total Other Financial
  Sources</td><td></td><td></td><td></td><td></td><td></td></tr>
<tr><td>Excess of Revenues
  Over (Under)
  Expenditures</td><td></td><td></td><td></td><td></td><td></td></tr>
<tr><td>Fund Balance/
  Equity July 1st</td><td></td><td></td><td></td><td></td><td></td></tr>
<tr><td>Fund Balance/
  Equity June 30th</td><td></td><td></td><td></td><td></td><td></td></tr>
</table>

FIGURE 12.2
Format for Combined Statement

RECEIPT AND EXPENSE/DISBURSEMENT REPORTS: NONGOVERNMENTAL FUNDS

The annual income and expenditure statements for proprietary and fiduciary funds were discussed in chapter 11 and examples of financial reports were shown in Figures 11.1 to 11.3. In Figure 11.1 a financial report for an enterprise fund was shown for a food services operation, and an analysis of the income and expenses was discussed. Another type of report that may be used for proprietary funds that sell goods is shown in Figure 12.3. This report is useful because it contains a section that permits the comparison of sales to the cost of the goods sold plus the calculation of the percentage of the purchases, returns, discounts, gross profit, total operating expenses, net income as well as each expense account to gross sales. For

Enterprise Fund Income Statement—Book Store for the Fiscal Year Ended June 20x1				
Sales				
Gross Sales				$12,000
Less: Sales returns		$ 600		
Sales discounts		750		1,350
Net Sales				$ 10,650
Cost of Goods Sold				
Inventory, July 1, 20x0			$ 5,000	
Purchases		$6,400		
Less: Purchase returns	$100			
Purchase discounts	90	190		
Net Purchases		5,210		
Add: Shipping		350		
Cost of Goods Purchased			5,560	
Cost of Goods Available for Sale			$10,560	
Less: Inventory, June 30, 20x1			4,000	
Cost of Goods Sold				6,560
Gross Profit on Sales				$ 4,090
Operating Expenses				
Wages			$ 2,000	
Supplies			500	
Plant services			1,500	
Total Operating Expenses				$ 4,000
Net Income				$ 90

FIGURE 12.3
Income Statement for Sale of Goods

example, are the total net sales of $10,650 less than, equal to, or greater than the estimated sales in the business plan? Is the percentage of the costs of goods sold ($6,560) to the net sales ($10,650) acceptable? This type of information is important in a review of operations and when making decisions, such as adjusting prices, changing vendors, using discounts, and cutting expenses.

EFFECTIVENESS AND EFFICIENCY ASSESSMENTS

When preparing and discussing performance and financial reports, school leaders must maintain a clear distinction between the terms *effectiveness* and *efficiency*. Over the past 30 years there have been discussions about these terms in numerous articles and books; however, Etzioni (1964) described them, their relationship to each other, and the reasons for their importance quite succinctly.

In his dicussion, Etzioni (1964) explained that society "placed a high moral value on rationality, effectiveness, and efficiency" (p. 1) and that organizations have become powerful features in society through the rational and businesslike use of a combination of resources. To manage the large number of actions they must take, he proposed that these organizations must continually conduct self-evaluations to adjust themselves so that they may achieve their goals. An organization's self-evaluation of its effectiveness, according to Etzioni, "is determined by the degree to which it realizes its goals" and an efficiency self-evaluation "is measured by the amount of resources needed to produce a unit of output" (p. 8). These definitions are the ones referenced in the discussion of outcomes and outputs throughout this book, and they are key to the conduct of cost assessments on performance.

Effectiveness Assessments

To realize their visionary goals, a school district or site-based operational unit's focus in an effectiveness evaluation must be on qualitative outcomes. The qualitative outcomes, as discussed previously, are to meet objectives that lead to the attainment of the visionary goals that are established to achieve the mission of the school district. As a result, periodic effectiveness evaluations should be conducted to compare the proposed outcomes in a strategic plan to the actual outcomes.

A cost-effectiveness evaluation would examine the costs incurred in generating the outcomes, regardless of the program's success in attaining the predetermined targets. The question to be answered in a cost-effectiveness analysis is whether the costs incurred to produce the outcomes were inadequate, reasonable, or excessive.

Outcome measures suggested by the GASB (1990) for elementary and secondary schools include: achievement test scores, percentage of students scoring higher than prespecified scores on self-esteem and specified physical fitness standards, percentage gainfully employed or continuing education after graduation, and ratings of students and parents. In these cases, the periodic benchmark and annual effectiveness evaluations would compare the expectations set forth in the strategic financial plan to the degree of success experienced by the program and then the cost incurred to generate the outcome.

Efficiency Assessments

Efficiency targets are proposed outputs generated by a school district or site-based unit. An efficiency analysis would compare the unit's production of a program in reference to the proposed units of production in a strategic financial plan. The purpose of a cost-efficiency analysis is to determine "the amount of resources needed to produce a unit of output" (Etzioni, 1964, p. 8). The first question is whether the production met expectations. The next question is whether the cost incurred in producing the output was too low (cheap), appropriate, or too great (expensive). The follow-up question will likely have to refer to an effectiveness assessment on student performance for further analysis.

Efficiency output measures suggested by the GASB (1990) for elementary and secondary schools include: number of student-days (thousands), number of students promoted, Carnegie credits earned by students in terms of the percentage of the number required, absenteeism, and dropout rate. They further suggest that schools might calculate the cost per student-day, the cost per graduate, and the cost of an hour of instruction.

One popular measure of school efficiency has been district size under the seemingly logical conclusion that larger districts are more cost efficient. As discussed in the section on cost-effectiveness and efficiency research, this efficiency assumption was examined in reference to effectiveness. In some cases, size reaches a point of efficiency whereby education becomes ineffective.

CONDUCTING COST ASSESSMENTS

Assume the total expenditures for instruction for a social studies program are added up and then divided by the number of students in the program to obtain an average instructional cost per student, which is $950. This information by itself does not reveal much; however, it may offer some insights when related to an effectiveness assessment that reviews student performances on a state test.

For instance, assume the school board sets effectiveness targets for all programs in terms of ranges for the average student scores on state or standardized tests as follows: high proficiency at 90–100%, proficient at 80–89%, and not proficient below 80%. Assume the average program scores earned by students on the social studies test fell below 80%. In response, the program's site administrator must determine the reason(s) for the low score. In the review, in addition to instruction, curriculum, and other teaching/learning influences, the administrator should look at the cost of $950. One cost review would exam the various expenditures that made up the cost measure. Another would compare the average cost to those of previous years, to other programs in the school district, to programs in the county and state, and to programs in similar school districts.

From the results of the cost comparisons, many questions might be asked. For example, are any of the expenditures that made up the cost significantly different from those in the proposed budget plan or from previous years? Are the expenditures significantly different from those of other programs? The observations and conclusions drawn from the cost comparisons and expenditure analyses must be fed back to a review of the strategic plan proposed for the current and following fiscal year so that adjustments may be made.

With respect to an analysis of a cost-efficiency assessment, assume a school district tracks the number of student-days of attendance and determines the cost per student-day of instruction. In cases where absenteeism is excessive, the cost of instruction per student-day of attendance will be excessive. The problem, therefore, is not cost but student attendance.

In another case, assume the average cost per student for a high school site-based operational unit determines that the unit's cost is excessive and a review of the program reveals that it offers three advanced placement courses per year with small enrollments. A comparison of the cost per student for this program to one that offers three elective courses with large classes would not be valid. Likewise, the years of service for the teachers in a unit must be considered in a cost comparison. The average instructional cost for a site-based unit with a teaching staff of less than 20% nontenured teachers cannot be compared to a unit with over 50% nontenured faculty. The effect of the teachers' salaries must be adjusted for an accurate comparison of the costs.

Horizontal and Vertical Cost Assessments

Two standard methods used to conduct cost assessments are horizontal and vertical analyses. In a horizontal analysis, which may also be referred to as a trend analysis, the current program costs, expenditures, outcomes, and outputs are compared to those generated in previous years. In plotting the data, the primary objective of the analysis is usually to prepare a plan, possibly a long-term plan, for forecasting future potentials based on past trends.

A vertical analysis, which may be called a static analysis, compares data from one time period to another within the fiscal year for management purposes. Specifically, the cost, expenditure, outcome, and output data is plotted by month or marking period to gain insights for making necessary adjustments in operations and budget plans. In some cases, graphs are quite useful for exhibiting any affect a change has had from one period to another.

Basic Types of Cost Reviews

Obviously, many means are available to school leaders when reviewing costs. One approach for ensuring that the basic types of reviews are considered is to place them into four categories.

The first category reviews the costs in relation to the scope and quality of the program, service, or activity delivered. The questions to ask in this review are whether the costs are too high or too low, and/or if the outcome and output targets are improperly established (too high, too low). In this review, the important task is to make the right adjustment to the budget and/or the targets.

A second category reviews the costs for the delivery of the program, service, or activity. Such a review considers potential improvements in the delivery methods, facilities, technology, organizational structure, design of the workplace, personnel qualifications, and so on.

The third category, which is too often the first consideration, is an examination of the expenditures for personnel, goods, and services used by the program, service, or activity. If charges for goods and services are believed to be excessive or inadequate, new business arrangements may be in order.

A fourth option is to examine the means of providing the program, service, or activity to improve productivity, as opposed to reducing costs. This may require an intensive review of the assignment of duties, the purchasing of new equipment, offering personnel development programs, and so on.

In some productivity reviews, the findings may suggest that teachers and other personnel have become involved in tasks that are detrimental to their effectiveness and efficiency. When this occurs, a realignment of work activities to the strategic plan may be necessary; however, another concern is whether the plan and budget are constraining the teachers. A set of questions that may assist in this review, according to Jordan (2003), is that asked by the U.S. Department of Defense when conducting a strategic budget analysis. These questions are as follows: "How well are the realizations aligned with the plan? If realizations and plans differ significantly, what can be learned about the source of those differences? Do realizations and plans converge over time?" (p. 45).

BUDGET BLUEPRINTS

One objective for a school district should be to create budget blueprints for both the district and the site-based operational units in the district. The purpose of the blueprints would be to suggest the ideal allocation of money to different expenditure categories. The ideal allocations may be expressed in terms of dollars per student or percentage of dollars allocated to the expenditure accounts in the unit.

Through the use of accounting and budgeting data generated over several fiscal years, the creation of blueprints is quite basic. By plotting the effectiveness and efficiency performances over several previous years and then examining the cost and expenditure data to identify the most effective and efficient units, expenditure profiles can be generated for the district and site-based units. Of course, the district would have to adjust the blueprint as local circumstances dictate; for example, one elementary school in a district may have a larger number of remedial and bilingual classes than the other elementary schools in the district.

One of the advantages of the blueprints is to ease the burden of preparing budget plans by site-based operational teams and to allow them to focus on the more important effectiveness and efficiency performance objectives. For instance, budget blueprints are available for different types of profit businesses that use them to set up business plans. As a co-owner and accountant for a family business, the author had a master blueprint for preparing the business plan and budget for the corporation, for monitoring the income and expense reports on a weekly basis, for conducting monthly and annual cost analyses, and for making operational and financial adjustments as conditions changed. One of the features of the preferred accounting software was the immediate calculation of percentages and ratios when receipts were entered or expenditures made.

The master blueprint used by the corporation came from the data gathered from successful businesses in the same industry by a consulting firm that calculated the average or optimum percentages for each income and expense category. For example, a suggested ideal percentage for advertising ranged from 5 to 8% of gross sales. If the recommended percentages in the budget blueprint were followed, then mathematically a company would show a net profit after taxes within a percentage range (such as 18–22%). After a business has been in operation for a few years, it would establish its own budget blueprint (for example, if a business attains a good reputation, its advertising expenses could be reduced by 2 to 5% and in consequence its net profit increased by 2 to 5%).

In addition to school blueprints, a state-wide blueprint based on the expenditures of successful school districts and programs is possible due to the implementation of the GAAP accounting and budgeting systems. For example, what is the ideal percentage range for teacher salaries, teacher aides salaries, instructional supplies, and so on, in successful school districts and site-based units? Of course, the percentages would have to be adjusted for the regional socioeconomic conditions, or, ideally, separate blueprints would be created for different socioeconomic settings and school district sizes.

AN ILLUSTRATION OF STUDIES ON COST-EFFECTIVENESS AND EFFICIENCY

A set of cost-effectiveness and efficiency investigations were conducted by the author and several doctoral students from the financial data generated by school districts in New Jersey. The districts in New Jersey are required by state law to abide by the standards of the GASB and to use budget numbers that correspond to the schematic set forth by the National Center for Education Statistics (NCES). These research projects were limited to using the school district as the unit of study since site-based budget information was not available. In addition, the studies were tested for statistical significance to determine if the relationships and differences were true at a specified level of probability.

Before an overview of the studies can be presented, the unique situation in New Jersey must be noted. As discussed in chapter 4, in 1985 a series of legal challenges, which are referred to as the Abbott cases, were started on behalf of school children in poor urban school districts, which are known as the Abbott districts. As per the court directives, the Abbott districts, which eventually encompassed 30 districts, were to receive a substantial amount of the state education aid collected through the state income tax.

The aid to the Abbott districts began in the early to mid-1990s while other school districts were receiving transition aid that eventually was reduced or eliminated. Eventually the 30 Abbott districts were receiving the vast majority of the state income tax aid. Therefore, the property taxes and expenditures per child in New Jersey districts changed dramatically. Periodic studies, some of which are noted below, have attempted to examine these changes and related performances. The primary questions behind these studies concerned the relationship between money and student performance (cost-effectiveness) and money and district size (cost-efficiency).

Another important variable in some studies was the socioeconomic index used to classify the New Jersey school districts. The index, which is referred to as District Factor Groupings (DFG), is based on the education, income, and unemployment of the people who live in the district plus the poverty, population, and population density in the district. The index uses alphabetical letters in classifying the districts from the lowest to the highest rated DFG districts as follows: A ($n = 24$ school districts), B ($n = 32$), CD ($n = 35$), DE ($n = 46$), FG ($n = 38$), GH ($n = 34$), I ($n = 49$), and J ($n = 3$). The Abbott districts are in the A and B index class.

New Jersey also administers several statewide achievement tests to all school children. The test scores were used as the effectiveness measures in the studies described below. Further, because of the dramatic actions taken by the courts in New Jersey, the studies included and then excluded the Abbott districts in some comparisons.

Cost-Effectiveness Studies

Crisfield (1999) examined the 1995–1996 and 1996–1997 school district average cost per student in relation to the percentage of students in the district who passed the 8th grade achievement test in 214 school districts and who passed the 11th grade achievement test in 209 school districts. The percentage achieving a passing score (not the average score) on the first attempt were examined in reference to the district's total spending, total cost for classroom instruction, total cost for support services, and total administrative cost.

When examining all of the districts, Crisfield (1999) found a significant relationship ($p < .05$) between the percentage passing and all costs, except in 1995–1996 for the percentage passing the 8th grade test and administrative costs and for the percentage passing the 11th grade test and total spending and total instructional costs. When Crisfield removed the Abbott districts from the database, not only were significant relationships ($p < .05$) found in all comparisons, but the correlation coefficient increased considerably. In other words, when the Abbott districts were removed, the large amounts of state aid were also removed and the relationship between performances and costs were even greater.

In a pilot study on 261 New Jersey school districts, Braun (2002) looked at the 11th grade achievement test scores and a district's average cost per student (the total cost divided by the number of students in the district) for the 1999–2000 school year. The results of this project again showed a significant relationship ($p < .05$) between the percentage of students passing the 11th grade tests and the cost per student. However, when Braun compared the average scores earned by the students in a school district (not percentage of students passing the test) to the average cost per student, the results showed that the two were not significantly related ($p > .05$). In other words, this finding appears to indicate that if one school has a passing rate of 90% and another has a passing rate of 87%, the district with 87% passing might have a higher average score. Obviously more research is needed to examine the spread of scores in selected school districts.

In addition, Braun (2002) examined the school districts in reference to their DFG index. First, the cost per student in 1999–2000 was found to range from a high of $11,541 for the lower socioeconomic type A districts, which included most of the Abbott districts, to $9,932 for the midrange DE districts. The mean test scores (not percentage passing) on the 11th grade test were significantly different among the DFG groups. The average test scores began at 60.47 for the type A districts and increased at each socioeconomic index level up to 99.47 for the J districts.

Finally, Braun (2002) compared the average test scores for the school districts based on their student population as follows: small districts up to 1800 students, medium districts from 1801–3500 students, and large districts with over 3500 students. In the comparison of the average test scores, the large districts' average score (82.01) was found to be significantly lower ($p < .05$) than the scores of the smaller districts (90.72) and the medium-sized districts (89.03).

Taking a somewhat different slant on this research, Savage (2003) also examined the cost-effectiveness of 214 K–12 school districts in New Jersey for the 2000–2001 school year, which was 5 years after Crisfield measured the initial impact of the Abbott decision. For one part of the study, the school districts were divided into two groups based on the passing rate of students on state achievement tests for students in the 4th, 8th, and 11th grades. Districts in which 70% or more of the students scored at the proficient and advanced-proficient level (referred to as the *passing districts*) were compared to those in which 70% or fewer of the students did not (referred to as the *nonpassing districts*). The cost data used for the comparison was the average cost per student of the district, classroom instruction, classroom supplies and textbooks, support services, administrative services, and operation and maintenance of school plant. The results, which included the Abbotts, revealed that in all measures except one (classroom instruction and the 8th grade exam) the passing districts spent less than the nonpassing districts. Ten of the 18 comparisons were significantly ($p < .05$) different, meaning the differences were considered to be true at that level of significance. Likely the removal of the greatest portion of state aide from the non-Abbott districts reduced the average costs in these districts when compared to previous years.

In conclusion, although research findings can offer answers, provide insights, and change opinions, they often raise more questions than they answer. As a consequence of the above findings, a dissection of the districts is needed, and, as conditions change, researchers must be committed to continually dissecting and reviewing the districts.

Cost-Efficiency Studies

In another set of studies, the cost efficiencies of New Jersey school districts were examined. The basis for the initial research was the changing attitudes about the size of formal organizations. The push for larger schools is often attributed to Conant (1959) in his assertion of the advantages offered by larger high schools. Over the years the consolidation of school districts became commonplace and larger school districts were created. More recently, however, scholars and researchers have questioned the benefits of size. Luke, Ventriss, Reed, and Reed (1988) sum up these positions by pointing out that although economies of scale have been associated with larger size, a larger enterprise "no longer automatically means reduced costs" (p. 77). In addition, a study by the U.S. Department of Education (1999) conducted in 1996–1997 found that larger schools have considerably more student behavior problems than smaller schools.

As a result of the above proposal about the benefits of larger districts, Garner (1998) investigated whether or not larger school districts were more cost efficient. This study examined the 1995–1996 total district, instructional, support service, supplies and textbooks, administration, and operation and maintenance costs per student for the K–12 ($n = 209$) school districts in New Jersey. The analysis compared these costs for school districts with enrollments of 0–1800 ($n = 57$), 1801–3500 ($n = 71$), and over 3500 students ($n = 81$). Also compared separately were the average student costs in 14 districts that exceeded 10,000 students.

While the findings by Garner (1998) showed that the average instructional and operations and maintenance costs per student in the medium-size districts were the most cost efficient, the differences were not significant ($p > .05$). All other costs were found to be lowest in the districts with over 3500 students, with the costs for supplies and textbooks and administrative services being significantly less ($p < .05$). In addition, the costs per student in districts with over 10,000 students ($n = 14$) were calculated. These districts, which were in the lower socioeconomic groups, were more cost efficient than the other groups in support services, administration, and total cost per student.

In a replication of Garner's (1998) study of the 1995–1996 districts, Savage (2003) again examined the costs for all K–12 districts ($n = 214$) for fiscal year 2000–2001. When compared to the number of school districts in 1995–1996, the distribution of districts in each group changed to 48 small districts, 70 medium districts, and 96 large districts. In the comparisons, Savage found considerable change had taken place over the 5-year period whereby the smaller districts (up to 1800 students) had the lowest average cost in all categories except administrative services. The lowest cost for administration, however, was again found in the larger districts and again was significant in reference to the smaller districts.

When cost efficiencies for administration are compared to the findings on administrative costs and effectiveness reported above, serious concerns must be raised. For example, what are the outcome and output performances in regard to the ratio of administrators to students in large districts? Is the difference in student behavior problems in large school districts, reported by the U.S. Department of Education (1999), related more to socioeconomic classification than to size? Do smaller districts in lower socioeconomic settings have a high incidence of student behavior problems when compared to large districts in the same setting? Additional research must also be conducted to find the point where cost-effectiveness and efficiency are in equilibrium. One of the objectives of these examinations must be to define and then identify the successful districts in each group and to generate master budget blueprints.

FINAL THOUGHTS

Educational excellence is sought by every state and every public school district. The achievement of excellence by any organization, including school districts, depends on the ability of the leadership to come up with a plan and set of procedures that will enable them to lead their organization to the desired outcomes and output. When this does not occur, school leaders must seek out the reasons. Of course, there are many possibilities for low performances, but the proposal made by Mintzberg (1983) is insightful, especially for larger districts and those that have experienced unusual growth.

According to Mintzberg's (1983) theory, when management is extended beyond its limits, an organization may experience horizontal or vertical decentralization. **Horizontal decentralization** is the "extent to which nonmanagers control decision processes" (p. 99). In other words, decision making may flow outside the hierarchical structure from line to staff personnel. **Vertical decentralization** occurs when there is a "dispersal of formal power" down the line of authority (p. 99). In these cases, decision making has shifted (not been assigned) to lower levels in the hierarchical structure. If a school is experiencing both horizontal and vertical decentralization, the result may lead to organizational disintegration and instructional disengagement.

With respect to the above studies, the larger districts were found to exhibit both significantly lower costs for administrative services and significantly lower scores on the student tests. These findings propose that some of the larger districts may have entered a state of instructional disintegration. Evidence of disengagement is seen when a school district has extended itself beyond the point of efficacy; that is, it is unable to produce intended results.

In the cases of instructional disengagement, a variety of conditions may exist. For example, if personnel with the appropriate credentials and authority do not provide proper leadership to maintain a sound curriculum, visionary goals, exciting and realistic objectives, a relevant strategic financial plan, proper supervision with performance assessments, and a personnel development program, then the administrative practices will likely shift from providing leadership to crisis management. Instructional disengagement would be evident in failures to monitor the curriculum and academic performances through benchmark reviews, to maintain acceptable student–teacher ratios in the classrooms, to keep up-to-date materials in the classroom, to properly supervise expenditures, to amend budget plans, to maintain a hospitable learning environment, to offer quality induction and development opportunities for teachers and specialists, to monitor the use of substitutes or aides standing in for teachers, to track student attendance, and so on.

Because of the research findings in numerous reported studies, several questions arise. The most critical, obviously, is whether the poor performance and improper behavior of students are related to a reduced number of administrators who are unable to provide the leadership needed in the large districts? If so, are the poor performance and behavior problems due to the inability of administrators—regardless of numbers, cost, or personal abilities—to manage the super-sized school districts? Further, in these low-performing districts, has decision making been assumed by staff employees who do not have the authority, responsibility, and possibly the knowledge to carry out their assumed duties (horizontal decentralization)? Have the decision-making duties been assigned by default to personnel in the lower levels of the organizational structure where they are possibly given unacceptable attention and improper priority by individuals with limited experience (vertical decentralization)?

In conclusion, the above discussion hopes to illustrate that cost-effectiveness and efficiency evaluations must be recognized as a means, not an end, to move a school district and the community into the future. The push for cost efficiency cannot be taken to extremes or the end product will be a cheap education that, like cheap clothes or shoes, will not stand the test of time.

However, more money alone will not improve educational effectiveness. Instead, school districts must have valid strategic financial plans with effectiveness performance expectations spelled out and tied to a budget. The results of the assessments and analyses of the plan and budget must be monitored and then fed back into the plans to move the district forward. There is no shortcut to this process. It is a lot of work! The ultimate reward is the creation of a synergistic relationship between education and the economy of a community where one plus one is greater than two.

DISCUSSION QUESTIONS

1. If you are a member of a site-based team (select a grade level, program, or service), what effectiveness and efficiency measures would you suggest for an evaluation?
   a. What expenditures (Resource F) would you select to examine the cost of these measures?
   b. Describe a plan you would propose for a site-based team for conducting an evaluation and cost analysis?
2. As an administrator, how would you respond to an inquiry about the increasing accountability demands on school districts?
3. What are the major elements of a strategic planning process—from the mission of a school district with site-based units to the cost analysis?
4. In reference to the research reported on cost efficiency and effectiveness, the author offers several observations and proposes additional research to be conducted.
   a. Can you arrive at any additional observations from the results reported in the chapter?
   b. What would you suggest for further study?

APPLICATION PROBLEMS

The answers are provided at the end of the chapter.

1. Using the report in Resource N, how much was added to the fund balance at the end of the year?
   a. What was the amount proposed to be added/subtracted from the fund balance in the budget?
2. Using the report in Resource N, what was the total for district expenditures?

3. Assume the school district in Resource N has an enrollment of 1000 students.
   a. What was the average total cost per student (rounded to the nearest dollar)?
   b. What was the average instructional cost per student (rounded to the nearest dollar)?
4. Using Resource N, how much was the difference between the budgeted amount and the expenditures for the operation and maintenance (O&M) of plant services for the current year?
   a. What was the amount for the previous year?
   b. Within the O&M budget, what expenditure category would you examine further?
5. The principal of the high school (Mr. Knupp) and the finance committee for his school are meeting to discuss the budget report and the most recent communication from the business administrator. The finance committee represents the teachers and community members who are on the site-based management teams. The practice is for the finance committee to review the monthly budget reports and prepare a reaction for each team to review, possibly amend, and then report back to the finance committee. The finance committee then reviews the responses from the site teams and prepares a recommendation, if needed, to be sent to the business administrator.

   Mr. Knupp's practice has been to have an open budget that presents all budget account allocations, expenditures, encumbrances, and balances. The finance committee determined to take the budget allocation for its school and further subdivide the allotment into more categories for the site-based teams as well as for administration and health services. Upon review of the March budget report, the finance committee report for the general fund budget allocation is as follows:

	Allocations ($)	Expenditures ($)	Encumbrances ($)	Balance ($)
School Accounts				
Teaching Substitutes	12,000	7,900	1,000	3,100
Teaching Supplies	43,400	27,500	4,750	11,150
Textbooks	18,900	16,500	1,100	1,300
Student Class Travel	15,000	8,750	3,150	3,100
Misc. Expenditures	2,600	1,450	75	1,075
Repair of Equipment	9,900	5,200	1,650	3,050
Professional Development	2,500	1,550	75	875
Library—Books	2,000	350	1,650	0
Library—Periodicals	2,000	2,000		0
Library—Supplies	750	250	25	475
Audiovisual Equipment	5,400	3,900	850	650
Administration Accounts:				
Miscellaneous Supplies	12,000	7,775	1,750	2,475
Supplies/Computer	6,600	3,150	1,700	1,750
Miscellaneous Expenses	2,600	1,650	540	410
Health Services Account:				
Medical Supplies	12,000	8,450	1,825	1,725

The circumstances related to the budget are as follows:

- The amount remaining for teaching substitutes will likely be adequate and a surplus is not expected at the end of the year.
- The amount of the balance in teaching supplies is more than sufficient; however, at least $7,000 will be needed for final exams and end-of-year exercises.
- Some textbooks were not ordered yet but some teachers plan on using them in the coming school year. Their estimated cost is $2,150.
- The last class trip cost more than anticipated. An estimated additional $500 is needed in this account to cover the remaining two trips.
- The equipment account will have to repair the public address system and photocopier (estimated at $1,600) and the finance committee had planned to use $900 along with the balance in the equipment account to purchase audiovisual equipment (a video cad camera) so that teachers could make videos for their classes over the summer. The equipment will cost $1,550.
- The requests by teachers for development travel, programs, and courses will overexpend that account by $400.
- Mr. Knupp does not project a surplus in any of the administration or health services accounts.

Mr. Knupp received a notice from the district business office that the high school's budget has been cut by $6,000 and that none of it can come from the health services allotment. He must inform the business office from what accounts the $6,000 should be taken. The plan may include the transfer of money from one account to another account(s). After the committee agrees on a recommendation, they must present it to the site-based management teams for their reaction. Mr. Knupp has been informed that some teachers, who have not received their invoices in order to submit them for reimbursement for their professional development courses, are quite upset. Further, because one teacher, Ms. Pettigrew, made a downpayment for travel arrangements to make a video on the whale migration, she has filed a union grievance to prevent the cut from eliminating the purchase of the audiovisual equipment. Likewise, some students are quite worried that their class trips may be canceled and have informed their parents. Some of the parents have complained to board members.

Prepare a budget recommendation with a justification for the suggested changes for the finance committee to consider. Again, you must cut $6,000 dollars from the budget and you may not take any of the money from the Health Services Account.

CLINICAL PRACTICUM EXERCISES

In response to the clinical exercises that follow, the suggested format is to: (a) state the question and (b) provide the answer to the question. If supporting material is referenced and a copy of the statement can be made available, it should be noted and an appendix attached to the end of the report. Note that one of the objectives of the exercise is to show that the material in the book has been read, comprehended, and applied.

In the school district you have chosen for your study, obtain a copy of the annual financial statement (CAFR) for the previous fiscal year. In this report locate the statements for revenues and expenditures for the general, special revenue, enterprise (used for food services), and student services funds and determine the following.

1. From the general and special revenue fund reports:
    a. How much revenue was received in each of the funds?
    b. How much is the *total* expenditure for instruction:
        i. in the general fund?
        ii. in the special revenue fund?
    c. When combining the revenues and expenditures for instruction in the two funds, what is the percentage of revenue spent for:
        i. total instruction?
        ii. total instructional salaries?
    d. What is the percentage of revenue spent for instruction:
        i. in the general fund?
        ii. in the special revenue fund?
2. In the general fund, what is the percentage of total revenue spent on:
    a. transportation?
    b. support services?
    c. school administration?
    d. total administration?
    e. extracurricular activities?
3. What is the sum of all of the public revenues (not income earned) received by the district?
4. What is the percentage of the revenue provided to the school district from:
    a. local taxes?
    b. state revenue?
    c. federal revenue?
    d. the unreserved fund balances in the funds?
5. What are the sources and purposes of the revenue placed in the special revenue fund?
    a. What are their percentages in terms of the total revenue in the fund?
6. What is the name of the fund used for food services? In the food services operation, what is the percentage of income and nonoperating revenue spent for:
    a. salaries?
    b. food and supplies?
7. In the enterprise fund, what are the different sources of revenue and income?
    a. What was the profit or loss for each activity in the enterprise fund and for the entire fund for the year?
8. What are the changes in the **fund balance/fund equity** for:
    a. the general fund?
    b. the enterprise fund?
9. In the student services fund, what classes and clubs are served by the fund?

WEB ADDRESSES

National Council for Accreditation of Teacher Education
http://www.ncate.org

National Center for Education Statistics
http://nces.ed.gov

National Policy Board for Educational Administration
http://www.npbea.org

REFERENCES

Braun, E. R. (2002). *Effectiveness in New Jersey school districts containing high schools by district factor group, size, and type.* Unpublished manuscript, Rutgers University, New Brunswick, NJ.

Conant, J. B. (1959). *The American high school today.* New York: McGraw-Hill.

Crisfield, J. A. (1999). *District-level spending and student achievement in New Jersey's public schools.* Unpublished doctoral dissertation, Rutgers University, New Brunswick, NJ.

Etzioni, A. (1964). *Modern organizations.* Upper Saddle River, NJ: Merrill/Prentice Hall.

Fowler, W. J., Jr., & Monk, D. H. (2001). A primer for making cost adjustments in education: An overview. In *Selected Papers in School Finance 2000–01.* (NCES Publication No. 2001-378, pp. 41–54). Washington, DC: U.S. Department of Education.

Garner, C. W. (1998). A cost efficient analysis of school districts: Is larger more efficient? *Public Budgeting, Accounting and Financial Management, 10*(4), 513–526.

Governmental Accounting Standards Board (1990), *Service efforts and accomplishments reporting: Its time has come,* H. P. Hatry, J. R. Fountain, Jr., J. M. Sullivan, & L. Kremer, (Eds.). Norwalk, CT: Author.

Governmental Accounting Standards Board (2001). *Codification of governmental accounting and financial reporting standards.* Norwalk, CT: Author.

Interstate School Leaders Licensure Consortium (1996). *Standards for school leaders.* Washington, DC: Council of Chief State School Officers.

Jordan, L. G. (2003). Strategic budgeting. *Journal of Government Financial Management, 52*(1), 44–52.

Luke, J. S., Ventriss, C., Reed, B. J., & Reed, C. M. (1988). *Managing economic development.* San Francisco: Jossey-Bass.

Mintzberg, H. (1983). *Designing effective organizations: Structure in fives.* Upper Saddle River, NJ: Merrill/Prentice Hall.

National Policy Board for Educational Administration (2002a). *Standards for advanced programs in educational leadership* [Online]. Retrieved February 17, 2003, from http://www.npbea.org

National Policy Board for Educational Administration (2002b). *Standards for advance programs in educational leadership for principals, superintendents, curriculum directors, and supervisors* [Online]. Retrieved February 17, 2003, from http://www.ncate.org

Savage, B. F. (2003). *Examination of school expenditures, student achievement and district size in New Jersey kindergarten through grade twelve school districts.* Unpublished doctoral dissertation, Rutgers University, New Brunswick, NJ.

U.S. Department of Education (1999). *Violence and discipline problems in U.S. public schools: 1996–97.* [Online]. Retrieved March 23, 2002, from http://nces.ed.gov

ANSWERS TO PROBLEMS IN THE TEXT

12.1 $2,801,484

12.2 $3,623,587

12.3 $\dfrac{\$2,801,484}{\$3,623,587} = 77\%$

12.4 $\dfrac{\$3,623,587}{\$7,466,545} = 48.5\%$

12.5 $\dfrac{\$174,759}{\$3,798,346} = 4.6\%$

ANSWERS TO APPLICATION PROBLEMS

1. $113,306
   a. ($151,079)
2. $7,353,239
3. a. $7,353
   b. $3,624
4. $74,155
   a. $50,148
   b. Other purchased services

Chart of Accounts

Current Assets

101   Cash in Bank
102   Cash on Hand
103   Petty Cash
104   Change Cash
105   Cash with Fiscal Agents
111   Investments
112   Unamortized Premiums on Investments
113   Unamortized Discounts on Investments (Credits)
114   Interest Receivable on Investments
115   Accrued Interest on Investments Purchased
121   Taxes Receivable
122   Estimated Uncollectible Taxes
131   Interfund Loans Receivable
132   Interfund Accounts Receivable
141   Intergovernmental Accounts Receivable
151   Loans Receivable
152   Estimated Uncollectible Loans (contra acct.)
153   Other Accounts Receivable
154   Estimated Uncollectible Accounts Receivable (contra acct.)
161   Bonds Proceeds Receivable
171   Inventories for Consumption
172   Inventories for Resale
181   Prepaid Expenses
191   Deposits
199   Other Current Assets

Fixed Assets

211   Sites
221   Site Improvements

222   Accumulated Depreciation on Site Improvements (contra acct.)
231   Buildings and Building Improvements
232   Accumulated Depreciation on Buildings and Building Improvements (contra acct.)
241   Machinery and Equipment
242   Accumulated Depreciation on Machinery and Equipment (contra acct.)
251   Construction in Progress

Budget Accounts and Other Debit Balances
301   Estimated Revenues
302   Revenues
303   Amount Available in Debt Service Funds
304   Amount to be Provided for Retirement of General Long-Term Debt

Current Liabilities
401   Interfund Loans Payable
402   Interfund Accounts Payable
411   Intergovernmental Accounts Payable
421   Accounts Payable
422   Judgements Payable
423   Warrants Payable
431   Contracts Payable
432   Contracts Payable—Retained Percentage
433   Construction Contracts Payable
441   Matured Bonds Payable
442   Bonds Payable
443   Unamortized Premiums on Bonds Sold
451   Loans Payable
455   Interest Payable
461   Accrued Salaries and Benefits
471   Payroll Deductions and Witholdings
481   Deferred Revenues
491   Deposits Payable
492   Due to Fiscal Agent
499   Other Current Liabilities

Long Term Liabilities
511   Bonds Payable
521   Loans Payable
531   Lease Obligations
541   Unfunded Pension Liabilities
590   Other Long-Term Liabilities

Budget Accounts
601   Appropriations
602   Expenditures/Expenses
603   Encumbrances

Fund Equity

711   Investment in General Fixed Assets
721   Contributed Capital
730   Reserved—Retained Earnings
740   Unreserved—Retained Earnings
751   Reserve for Inventories
752   Reserve for Prepaid Expenses
753   Reserve for Encumbrances
760   Reserved Fund Balance
770   Unreserved Fund Balance

Note: The reference for the above chart of accounts was prepared by the National Center for Education Statistics in 1990 and reprinted in 1995. See http://nces.ed.gov, financial accounting for local and state school systems.

Set of Accounting Funds for a School District

Fund Number	Fund Name
10	General Fund
20	Special Revenue Fund
30	Capital Projects Fund
40	Debt Service Fund
45	Permanent Fund
50	Enterprise Fund
55	Internal Service Fund
60	Pension Fund
65	Investment Trust Fund
70	Private Purpose Trust Fund
80	Agency Fund
90	Student Activity Fund

Note: The above funds correspond to the major types of funds proposed in 1990 by the National Center for Education Statistics (http://nces.ed.gov) and the Governmental Accounting Standards Board. The fund numbers are typical numbers assigned to the funds. The student activity fund was added to the suggested list of funds because it is used by school districts.

Revenue Budget Numbers and Sources

Revenue Numbers	Source
1000 Series	Revenues from Local Sources
1100	Taxes levied/assessed by school district
1110	Ad valorem (local tax levy) taxes
1120	Sales and use taxes
1130	Income taxes
1140	Penalties and interest on taxes
1190	Other taxes
1200	Revenue from Local Governmental Units other than School Districts
1210	Ad valorem taxes
1220	Sales and use taxes
1230	Income taxes
1240	Penalties and interest on taxes
1280	Revenue in lieu of taxes
1290	Other taxes
1300	Tuition
1310	Tuition—individuals
1320	Tuition—other districts within the state
1330	Tuition—other districts outside the state
1340	Tuition—other sources
1400	Transportation
1410	Transportation fees—individuals
1420	Transportation fees—other districts within the state
1430	Transportation fees—other districts outside the state
1440	Transportation fees—other sources
1500	Earnings on Investments
1510	Interest on investments
1520	Dividends on investments
1530	Gains (losses) on sale of investments
1540	Earnings on investments in real property

1600	Food Services
1610	Food sales—reimbursable
1611	Food sales—reimbursable school lunch program
1612	Food sales—reimbursable school breakfast program
1613	Food sales—reimbursable milk program
1620	Food sales—nonreimbursable
1630	Food sales—special functions
1700	Student Activities
1710	Admission—school-sponsored activities
1720	Bookstore sales
1730	Student organization membership dues/fees
1740	Fees
1790	Other student activity income
1800	Receipts—community service activities
1900	Other Revenues from Local Sources
1910	Rentals
1920	Contributions and donations
1930	Gains (losses) on sale of fixed assets
1940	Textbook sales—rentals
1941	Textbook sales
1942	Textbook rentals
1950	Services to other districts
1951	Services to other districts within state
1952	Services to other districts outside state
1960	Services to other local governments
1970	Services to other accounting funds
1990	Miscellaneous

2000 Series	Revenues from Intermediate Sources
2100	Unrestricted grants
2200	Restricted grants
2800	Revenue in lieu of taxes
2900	Revenue for/on behalf of the district

3000 Series	Revenues from State Sources
3100	Unrestricted entitlements
3110	Foundation aid
3120	Transportation aid
3130	Special education aid
3140	Bilingual aid
3150	Aid for at risk students
3160	Debt service aid
3170	Transition aid
3200	Restricted entitlements
3220	State school lunch aid
3221	Nonpublic aid (aid provided to nonpublic school students)—textbooks
3222	Nonpublic aid—basic skills/remedial
3223	Nonpublic aid—E.S.L.
3224	Nonpublic aid—home instruction
3225	Nonpublic aid—transportation
3226	Nonpublic handicapped aid—supplemental instruction
3227	Nonpublic handicapped aid—examination and classification
3228	Nonpublic handicapped aid—speech correction

3229	Nonpublic nursing services aid
3230	Emergency aid
3250	School building aid
3260	General vocational education
3270	Adult and continuing education
3280	Evening school for foreign born
3290	Other special state projects
3800	Revenue in lieu of taxes
3900	Revenue for/on behalf of local district
3901	Pension aid
3902	Social security aid

4000 Series	Revenues from Federal Sources
4100	Unrestricted grants direct from the federal government
4200	Unrestricted grants from the federal government through the state
4300	Restricted grants from the federal government
4500	Restricted grants from the federal government through the state
4510	The education consolidation and improvement act (E.S.S.I.A.)
4511	Chapter I—Part A
4512	Chapter I—Handicapped
4513	Chapter I—Carryover
4514	Chapter I—Reallocated
4515	Chapter II—Block grants
4516	Chapter II—Block grants carryover
4517	Migrant
4518	Migrant carryover
4521	I.D.E.A. (Individuals with Disabilities Education Act) Part B Basic
4522	I.D.E.A. Part B Basic carryover
4523	I.D.E.A. Part B Preschool
4524	I.D.E.A. Part B Preschool Bonus
4525	I.D.E.A. Part B Discretionary
4526	I.D.E.A. Part B Deaf Education
4530	P.L. 101-392 Vocational—account numbers by title
4531	Consumer and Homemaking
4532	Secondary
4533	Disadvantaged
4534	Handicapped
4535	Adult
4536	Sub 3
4537	Sub 4—Special Disadvantaged
4538	Other Vocational
4540	P.L. 91-230 Adult Basic Education
4550	P.L. 100-297 Eisenhower Math/Science: account numbers by title
4551	IKE Math/Science—Entitlement
4552	IKE Math/Science—Other
4553	IKE Math/Science—Carryover
4560	Nutrition Reimbursement
4561	School Breakfast Program
4562	National School Lunch Program
4563	Special Milk Program for Children
4564	Other Nutrition Reimbursements
4570	P.L. 99-570 Drug Free Schools and Communities Act—account numbers by title

4571	DFSCA—Entitlement
4572	DFSCA—Other
4573	DFSCA—Carryover
4580	Other special federal projects
4700	Grants via other agencies
4800	Revenue in lieu of taxes
4900	Revenue for/on behalf of the LEA
4910	USDA Commodities

5000 Series   **Other Financing Sources**

5100	Sale of bonds
5110	Bond principal
5120	Bond premium
5130	Accrued interest
5200	Interfund transfers
5300	Sale or compensation—fixed assets
5400	Loans
5500	Capital leases
5600	Lease purchasing proceeds
5700	Proceeds—refunding bonds

Note: The reference used for the above revenue numbers was presented by the National Center for Education Statistics in 1990 and revised in 1995. See http://nces.ed.gov, financial accounting for local and state school systems.

Expenditure Numbers: Program

Program Numbers	Description
100 Series	Regular Programs—Elementary and Secondary
110	Preschool/Kindergarten
120	Grades 1–5
130	Grades 6–8
140	Grades 9–12
190	Undistributed
200 Series	Special Programs
201	Mentally Retarded—Educable
202	Mentally Retarded—Trainable
203	Orthopedically Handicapped
204	Neurologically Impaired
205	Perceptually Impaired
206	Visually Handicapped
207	Auditorily Handicapped
208	Communication Handicapped
209	Emotionally Disturbed
210	Socially Maladjusted
211	Chronically Ill
212	Multiply Handicapped
213	Resource Room
214	Autistic
215	Pre-School Handicapped—Part-time
216	Pre-School Handicapped—Full-time
217	Supplementary Instruction
218	Speech Instruction
219	Home Instruction
220	Extraordinary Services
221	Extended School Year
222	Day Training Eligible
230	Basic Skills/Remedial
231	Basic Skills, Part A
232	Basic Skills—Chapter I—Handicapped, Early Intervention

233	Basic Skills—Reallocated
234	Basic Skills—Part A carryover
235	Basic Skills—Chapter I—Handicapped, Early Intervention, carryover
236	Basic Skills—Chapter I, Migrant
237	Basic Skills—Chapter I, Migrant carryover
240	Bilingual Education
250–259	I.D.E.A. Part B
260	Chapter II, E.S.S.I.A.
261	Chapter II, E.S.S.I.A., carryover
270–279	P.L. 100-297 Eisenhower Math/Science
280–289	P.L. 99-570 Drug Free Schools and Communities Act
290–299	Other Special Programs

300 Series   Vocational Programs

301	Vocational Programs—local
302	Agriculture
303	Distributive Education
304	Health Occupations
305	Home Economics—Occupational
306	Home Economics—Consumer and Homemaking
307	Industrial Arts
308	Office Occupations
309	Technical Education
310	Trade and Industrial Education
311	Other
331	Vocational Programs—state
332	Agriculture
333	Distributive Education
334	Health Occupations
335	Home Economics—Occupational
336	Home Economics—Consumer and Homemaking
337	Industrial Arts
338	Office Occupations
339	Technical Education
340	Trade and Industrial Education
341	Other
361	Vocational Programs—federal
362	Agriculture
363	Distributive Education
364	Health Occupations
365	Home Economics—Occupational
366	Home Economics—Consumer and Homemaking
367	Industrial Arts
368	Office Occupations
369	Technical Education
370	Trade and Industrial Education
371	Other

400 Series   Other Instructional Programs—Elementary/Secondary

410	School-Sponsored Cocurricular Activities
420	School-Sponsored Athletics
430	Summer School
490	Other

500 Series	Nonpublic School Programs

600 Series	Adult/Continuing Education Programs
601	Accredited Evening/Adult High School/ Post-Graduate
602	Adult Education—local
603–618	Adult Education—state
619–628	Adult Education—federal
629	Vocational Evening—local
630	Vocational Evening—state

700 Series	Debt Service
701	Debt Service—Regular

800 Series	Community Services Programs
810	Community Recreation
820	Civic Services
830	Public Library Services
840	Custody and Child Care Services
850	Welfare Activities
890	Other Community Activities

900 Series	Enterprise Programs
910	Food Services
990	Other Enterprise Funds

1000 Series	Undistributed Expenditures

Note: The reference used for the above expenditure numbers was presented by the National Center for Education Statistics in 1990 and revised in 1995. See http://nces.ed.gov, financial accounting for local and state school systems.

Expenditure Numbers: Function

Function Numbers	Description
1000 Series	Instruction
2000 Series	Support Services
2100	Support Services—Students
2110	Attendance and Social Work Services
2111	Supervision of Attendance and Social Work Services
2112	Attendance
2113	Social Work
2114	Student Accounting
2119	Other Attendance and Social Work Services
2120	Guidance
2121	Supervision of Guidance Services
2122	Counseling
2123	Appraisal
2124	Information
2125	Record Maintenance
2126	Placement
2129	Other Guidance
2130	Health Services
2131	Supervision of Health Services
2132	Medical
2133	Dental
2134	Nursing
2139	Other Health Services
2140	Psychological Services
2141	Supervision of Psychological Services
2142	Psychological Testing
2143	Psychological Counseling
2144	Psychotherapy
2149	Other Psychological Services
2150	Speech Pathology and Audiology Services
2151	Supervision of Speech Pathology and Audiology Services
2152	Speech Pathology

2153		Audiology
2159		Other Speech Pathology and Audiology Services
2190		Other Support Services—Student
2200		Support Services—Instructional Staff
2210		Improvement of Instructional Services
2211		Supervision of Improvement of Instructional Services
2212		Instruction and Curriculum Development
2213		Instructional Staff Training
2219		Other
2220		Education Media Services
2221		Supervision of Educational Media Services
2222		School Library
2223		Audiovisual
2224		Educational Television
2225		Computer-Assisted Instruction
2229		Other Educational Media Services
2290		Other Support Services—Instructional Staff
2300		Support Services—General Administration
2310		Board of Education Services
2311		Supervision of Board of Education Services
2312		Board Secretary/Clerk
2313		Board Treasurer
2314		Election
2315		Tax Assessment and Collection
2316		Staff Relations and Negotiation
2319		Other Board of Education Service
2320		Executive Administration Services
2321		Office of the Superintendent
2322		Community Relations
2323		State and Federal Relations
2329		Other Executive Administration Services
2330		Special Area Administration Services
2400		Support Services—School Administration
2410		Office of the Principal Services
2490		Other Support Services—School Administration
2500		Support Services—Business
2510		Fiscal Services
2511		Supervision of Fiscal Services
2512		Budgeting
2513		Receiving and Disbursing Funds
2514		Payroll
2515		Financial Accounting
2516		Internal Auditing
2517		Property Accounting
2519		Other Fiscal Services
2520		Purchasing Services
2530		Warehousing and Distributing Services
2540		Printing, Publishing, and Duplicating Services
2590		Other Support Services—Business
2600		Operation and Maintenance of Plant Services
2610		Operation of Building Services
2620		Care and Upkeep of Grounds Services
2630		Care and Upkeep of Equipment Services
2640		Vehicle Operation and Maintenance Services (other than student transportation)

2650	Security Services
2690	Other Operation/Maintenance Plant Services
2700	Student Transportation Services
2710	Vehicle Operation
2720	Monitoring
2730	Vehicle Servicing and Maintenance
2790	Other Student Transportation Services
2800	Support Services—General
2810	Planning, Research, Development, and Evaluation Services
2820	Information Services
2821	Supervision of Information Services
2822	Internal Information
2823	Public Information
2824	Management Information
2829	Other Information Services
2830	Staff Services
2831	Supervision of Staff Services
2832	Recruitment and Replacement
2833	Staff Accounting
2834	In-service Training (noninstructional staff)
2835	Health
2839	Other Staff Services
2840	Data Processing Services
2841	Supervision of Data Processing Services
2842	System Analysis
2843	Programming
2844	Operations
2849	Other Data Processing Services
2900	Other Support Services

3000 Series	**Operation of Noninstructional Services**
3100	Food Services Operations
3200	Other Enterprise Operations
3300	Community Services Operations

4000 Series	**Facilities Acquisition and Construction Services**
4100	Site Acquisition Services
4200	Site Improvement Services
4300	Architecture and Engineering Services
4400	Educational Specifications Development Services
4500	Building Acquisition and Construction Services
4600	Building Improvement Services
4900	Other Facilities and Acquisition Services

5000 Series	**Other Uses (Government Funds Only)**
5100	Debt Service
5200	Fund Transfer

Note: The reference used for the above expenditure numbers was presented by the National Center for Education Statistics in 1990 and revised in 1995. See http://nces.ed.gov, financial accounting for local and state school systems.

Expenditure Numbers: Object

Object Numbers	Description
100 Series	Personal Services—Salaries
110	Regular Employees
120	Temporary Employees
130	Overtime
140	Sabbatical Leaves
200 Series	Personal Services—Employee Benefits
210	Group Insurance
220	Social Security Contributions
230	Retirement Contributions
240	Tuition Reimbursement
250	Unemployment Compensation
260	Workman's Compensation
290	Other Employee Benefits
300 Series	Purchased Professional and Technical Services
310	Official/Administrative
320	Professional—Educational
330	Technical Services
390	Other Professional Services
400 Series	Purchased Property Services
410	Utility Services
411	Water/Sewer
420	Cleaning
421	Disposal
422	Snow Plowing
423	Custodial
424	Lawn Care
430	Repair and Maintenance Services
440	Rentals
441	Rental of Land and Buildings
442	Rental of Equipment and Vehicles
450	Construction Services
490	Other Purchased Property Services

500 Series	Other Purchased Services
510	Student Transportation Services
511	Student Transportation Purchased from Another LEA Within the State
512	Student Transportation Purchased from Another LEA Outside the State
519	Student Transportation Purchased from Other Sources
520	Insurance, Other than Employee Benefits
530	Communications/Telephone
540	Advertising
550	Printing and Binding
560	Tuition
561	Tuition to Other LEAs Within the State
562	Tuition to Other LEAs Outside the State
563	Tuition to Private Schools
569	Other
570	Food Services Management
580	Travel
590	Miscellaneous Purchased Services
591	Services Purchased Locally
592	Services Purchased from Another LEA Within the State
593	Services Purchased from Another LEA Outside the State

600 Series	Supplies and Materials
610	General Supplies
620	Energy (use only with function 260)
621	Natural Gas
622	Electricity
623	Bottled Gas
624	Oil
625	Coal
626	Gasoline
629	Other
630	Food
640	Books and Periodicals

700 Series	Property
710	Land and Improvements (government funds only)
720	Buildings (government funds only)
730	Equipment (government funds only)
731	Machinery
732	Vehicles
733	Furniture and Fixtures
739	Other Equipment
740	Depreciation

800 Series	Other Objects
810	Dues and Fees
820	Judgments Against the School District
830	Interest
840	Contingency (for budgeting purposes only)
890	Miscellaneous Expenditures

900 Series	Other Uses of Funds (Government Funds Only)
910	Redemption of Principal
920	Housing Authority Obligations
930	Fund Transfers

Note: The reference used for the above expenditure numbers was presented by the National Center for Education Statistics in 1990 and revised in 1995. See http://nces.ed.gov, financial accounting for local and state school systems.

Revenue Numbers: General Fund

Revenue Numbers	Source
1000 Series	Revenues from Local Sources

1100	Taxes levied/assessed by school district
1110	Ad valorem (local tax levy) taxes
1120	Sales and use taxes
1130	Income taxes
1140	Penalties and interest on taxes
1190	Other taxes
1200	Revenue from local governmental units other than school districts
1210	Ad valorem taxes
1220	Sales and use taxes
1230	Income taxes
1240	Penalties and interest on taxes
1280	Revenue in lieu of taxes
1290	Other taxes
1300	Tuition
1310	Tuition—Individuals
1320	Tuition—Other districts within the state
1330	Tuition—Other districts outside the state
1340	Tuition—Other sources
1400	Transportation
1410	Transportation fees—Individuals
1420	Transportation fees—Other districts within the state
1430	Transportation fees—Other districts outside the state
1440	Transportation fees—Other sources
1500	Earnings on investments
1510	Interest on investments
1520	Dividends on investments
1530	Gains (losses) on sale of investments
1540	Earnings on investments in real property
1700	Student activities
1710	Admission—School-sponsored activities
1740	Fees
1790	Other student activity income

1800		Receipts—Community service activities
1900		Other revenues from local sources
	1910	Rentals
	1920	Contributions and donations
	1940	Textbook sales—Rentals
	1941	Textbook sales
	1942	Textbook rentals
	1950	Services to other districts
	1951	Services to other districts within the state
	1952	Services to other districts outside the state
1960	Services to other local governments	
1990	Miscellaneous	

2000 Series   Revenues from Intermediate Sources

2100	Unrestricted grants
2800	Revenue in lieu of taxes
2900	Revenue for/on behalf of the district

3000 Series   Revenues from State Sources

3100		Unrestricted entitlements
	3110	Foundation aid
	3120	Transportation aid
	3130	Special education aid
	3140	Bilingual aid
	3150	Aid for at risk students
	3160	Debt service aid
	3170	Transition aid
	3230	Emergency aid
3800		Revenue in lieu of taxes
3900		Revenue for/on behalf of local district
	3901	Pension aid
	3902	Social security aid

4000 Series   Revenues from Federal Sources

4100		Unrestricted grants direct from the federal government
4200		Unrestricted grants from the federal government through the state
4500		Restricted grants from the federal government through the state
	4560	Nutrition Reimbursement
	4561	School Breakfast Program
	4562	National School Lunch Program
	4563	Special Milk Program for Children
	4564	Other Nutrition Reimbursements
4700		Grants via other agencies
4800		Revenue in lieu of taxes
4900		Revenue for/on behalf of the LEA
	4910	USDA Commodities

5000 Series   Other Financing Sources

5200	Interfund transfers
5300	Sale or compensation—Fixed assets
5400	Loans
5500	Capital leases
5600	Lease purchasing proceeds

Note: The above revenue numbers selected from the list of numbers presented in Resource C were expanded to exhibit greater detail.

Revenue Numbers: Special Revenue Fund

Revenue Numbers	Source
1000 Series	Revenues from Local Sources
1100	Taxes levied/assessed by school district
1110	Ad valorem (local tax levy) taxes
1140	Penalties and interest on taxes
1190	Other taxes
1200	Revenue from local governmental units other than school districts
1210	Ad valorem taxes
1240	Penalties and interest on taxes
1280	Revenue in lieu of taxes
1290	Other taxes
1500	Earnings on investments
1510	Interest on investments
1530	Gains (losses) on sale of investments
1540	Earnings on investments in real property
1990	Miscellaneous
2000 Series	Revenues from Intermediate Sources
2200	Restricted grants
3000 Series	Revenues from State Sources
3200	Restricted entitlements
3220	State school lunch aid
3221	Nonpublic aid (aid provided to nonpublic school students)—Textbooks
3222	Nonpublic aid—Basic skills/remedial
3223	Nonpublic aid—E.S.L.
3224	Nonpublic aid—Home instruction
3225	Nonpublic aid—Transportation
3226	Nonpublic handicapped aid—supplemental instruction
3227	Nonpublic handicapped aid—examination and classification

3228	Nonpublic handicapped aid—speech correction
3229	Nonpublic nursing services aid
3260	General vocational education
3270	Adult and continuing education
3280	Evening school for foreign born
3290	Other special state projects

4000 Series	Revenues from Federal Sources
4300	Restricted grants from the federal government
4500	Restricted grants from the federal government through the state
4510	The education consolidation and improvement act (E.S.S.I.A.)
4511	Chapter I—Part A
4512	Chapter I—Handicapped
4513	Chapter I—Carryover
4514	Chapter I—Reallocated
4515	Chapter II—Block grants
4516	Chapter II—Block grants carryover
4517	Migrant
4518	Migrant carryover
4521	I.D.E.A. (Individuals with Disabilities Education Act) Part B Basic
4522	I.D.E.A. Part B Basic carryover
4523	I.D.E.A. Part B Preschool
4524	I.D.E.A. Part B Preschool Bonus
4525	I.D.E.A. Part B Discretionary
4526	I.D.E.A. Part B Deaf Education
4530	P.L. 101-392 Vocational Education
4531	Consumer and Homemaking
4532	Secondary
4533	Disadvantaged
4534	Handicapped
4535	Adult
4536	Sub 3
4537	Sub 4—Special Disadvantaged
4538	Other Vocational
4540	P.L. 91-230 Adult Basic Education
4550	P.L. 100-297 Eisenhower Math/Science
4551	IKE Math/Science—Entitlment
4552	IKE Math/Science—Other
4553	IKE Math/Science—Carryover
4570	P.L. 99-570 Drug Free Schools and Communities Act—account numbers by title
4571	DFSCA—Entitlement
4572	DFSCA—Other
4573	DFSCA—Carryover
4580	Other special federal projects

5000 Series	Other Financing Sources
5200	Interfund transfers
5300	Sale or compensation—Fixed assets

Note: The above revenue numbers were selected from Resource C and expanded to exhibit greater detail.

Revenue Numbers: Capital Projects Fund

Revenue Numbers	Source
1000 Series	Revenues from Local Sources
1100	Taxes levied/assessed by school district
1110	Ad valorem (local tax levy) taxes
1500	Earnings on investments
1510	Interest on investments
1530	Gains (losses) on sale of investments
1990	Miscellaneous
2000 Series	Revenues from Intermediate Sources
2800	Revenue in lieu of taxes
3000 Series	Revenues from State Sources
3250	School-building aid
3800	Revenue in lieu of taxes
4000 Series	Revenues from Federal Sources
4300	Restricted grants from the federal government
5000 Series	Other Financing Sources
5100	Sale of bonds
5110	Bond principal
5120	Bond premium
5130	Accrued interest
5200	Interfund transfers
5300	Sale or compensation—Fixed assets
5400	Loans

Note: The above revenue numbers were selected from Resource C.

Revenue Numbers: Debt Service Fund

Revenue Numbers	Source
1000 Series	Revenues from Local Sources
1100	Taxes levied/assessed by school district
1110	Ad valorem (local tax levy) taxes
1140	Penalties and interest on taxes
1190	Other taxes
1200	Revenue from local governmental units other than school districts
1210	Ad valorem taxes
1240	Penalties and interest on taxes
1280	Revenue in lieu of taxes
1290	Other taxes
1500	Earnings on investments
1510	Interest on investments
1530	Gains (losses) on sale of investments
1990	Miscellaneous
2000 Series	Revenues from Intermediate Sources
2100	Unrestricted grants
2200	Restricted grants
3000 Series	Revenues from State Sources
3200	Restricted entitlements
3250	School-building aid
3800	Revenue in lieu of taxes
4000 Series	Revenues from Federal Sources
4300	Restricted grants from the federal government

5000 Series	Other Financing Sources
5100	Sale of bonds
5110	Bond principal
5120	Bond premium
5130	Accrued interest
5200	Interfund transfers
5300	Sale or compensation—Fixed assets
5400	Loans
5700	Proceeds—Refunding bonds

Note: The above revenue numbers were selected from Resource C.

Revenue Numbers: Enterprise Funds

Revenue Numbers	Source
1000 Series	Revenues from Local Sources
1500	Earnings on investments
1510	Interest on investments
1520	Dividends on investments
1530	Gains (losses) on sale of investments
1600	Food services
1610	Food sales—Reimbursable
1611	Food sales—Reimbursable school lunch program
1612	Food sales—Reimbursable school breakfast program
1613	Food sales—Reimbursable milk program
1620	Food sales—Nonreimbursable
1630	Food sales—Special functions
1700	Student activities
1710	Admission—School-sponsored activities
1720	Bookstore sales
1730	Student organization membership dues/fees
1740	Fees
1790	Other student activity income
1800	Receipts—Community service activities
1900	Other Revenues from local sources
1910	Rentals
1930	Gains (losses) on sale of fixed assets
1940	Textbook sales—Rentals
1941	Textbook sales
1942	Textbook rentals
1950	Services to other districts
1951	Services to other districts within the state
1952	Services to other districts outside the state
1960	Services to other local governments

1970	Services to other accounting funds
1990	Miscellaneous

2000 Series	**Revenues from Intermediate Sources**

2200	Restricted grants

3000 Series	**Revenues from State Sources**

3200	Restricted entitlements
3220	State school lunch aid

4000 Series	**Revenues from Federal Sources**

4300	Restricted grants from the federal government
4500	Restricted grants from the federal government through the state
4560	Nutrition Reimbursement
4561	School Breakfast Program
4562	National School Lunch Program
4563	Special Milk Program for Children
4564	Other Nutrition Reimbursements
4900	Revenue for/on behalf of the LEA
4910	USDA Commodities

5000 Series	**Other Financing Sources**

5100	Sale of bonds
5110	Bond principal
5120	Bond premium
5130	Accrued interest
5200	Interfund transfers
5300	Sale or compensation—Fixed assets
5400	Loans
5500	Capital leases
5600	Lease purchasing proceeds
5700	Proceeds—Refunding bonds

Note: The above revenue numbers were selected from Resource C.

Revenue Numbers:
Internal Service Funds

Revenue Numbers	Source
1000 Series	Revenues from Local Sources
1500	Earnings on investments
1510	Interest on investments
1530	Gains (losses) on sale of investments
1540	Earnings on investments in real property
1900	Other Revenues from local sources
1910	Rentals
1920	Contributions and donations
1930	Gains (losses) on sale of fixed assets
1950	Services to other districts
1951	Services to other districts within the state
1952	Services to other districts outside the state
1960	Services to other local governments
1970	Services to other accounting funds
1990	Miscellaneous
5000 Series	Other Financing Sources
5100	Sale of bonds
5110	Bond principal
5120	Bond premium
5130	Accrued interest
5200	Interfund transfers
5300	Sale or compensation—Fixed assets
5400	Loans
5500	Capital leases
5600	Lease purchasing proceeds
5700	Proceeds—Refunding bonds

Note: The above revenue numbers were selected from Resource C.

Revenue Numbers: Fiduciary Funds

Revenue Numbers	Source
1510	Interest on investments
1520	Dividends on investments
1530	Gains (losses) on sale of investments
1540	Earnings on investments in real property
1730	Student organization membership dues/fees
1740	Fees
1790	Other student activity income
1910	Rentals
1920	Contributions and donations
5200	Interfund transfers
5300	Sale or compensation—Fixed assets

Note: The above revenue numbers were selected from Resource C.

General Fund: Statement of Revenues, Expenditures and Changes in Fund Balance

General Fund: Statement of Revenues, Expenditures and Changes in Fund Balance—
Budget and Actual for the Fiscal Years Ended June 30, 20x1 and 20x0

	20x1			20x0		
	Final Budget ($)	Actual ($)	Variance Favorable (Unfavorable) ($)	Final Budget ($)	Actual ($)	Variance Favorable (Unfavorable) ($)
Revenue						
Local Sources						
Local Tax Levy	5,737,570	5,737,570		5,370,663	5,370,663	
Tuition	1,064,593	1,113,800	49,207	1,144,465	1,120,443	(24,022)
Miscellaneous	36,000	78,436	42,436	81,500	119,204	37,704
Total Local Sources	6,838,163	6,929,806	91,643	6,596,628	6,610,310	13,682
State Sources						
Transportation Aid	27,571	27,571		27,571	27,571	
Special Education Aid	399,062	399,062		399,062	399,062	
Bilingual Aid	7,811	7,811		7,811	7,811	
Aid for at Risk Pupils	95,896	95,896		95,896	95,896	
Transition Aid	6,399	6,399		52,501	52,501	
Total State Sources	536,739	536,739		582,841	582,841	
Total Revenue	7,374,902	7,466,545	91,643	7,179,469	7,193,151	13,682
Expenditures						
Regular Program—Instruction:						
Preschool/Kindergarten						
Salaries of Teachers	96,663	96,663		114,490	114,159	331
Grades 1–5 Salaries of Teachers	886,480	886,479	1	815,691	815,691	
Grades 6–8 Salaries of Teachers	472,280	472,239	41	431,832	431,832	
Grades 9–12 Salaries of Teachers	1,185,516	1,185,515	1	1,144,667	1,144,667	
Regular Program—						
Undistributed Instruction:						
Other Salaries for Instruction	60,148	60,147	1	50,800	48,316	2,484
General Supplies	79,196	76,875	2,321	81,412	80,320	1,092
Textbooks	26,348	23,566	2,782	25,680	25,184	496
Total Regular Programs	2,806,631	2,801,484	5,147	2,664,572	2,660,169	4,401
Special Education						
Neurologically Impaired						
Salaries of Teachers	129,597	129,597		122,384	120,874	1,510
Other Salaries for Instruction				25,771	25,771	
General Supplies	2,000	1,998	2	750	726	24
Other Objects	29,247	28,060	1,187			
Total Neurologically Impaired	160,844	159,655	1,189	148,905	147,371	1,534

General Fund: Statement of Revenues, Expenditures and Changes in Fund Balance— Budget and Actual for the Fiscal Years Ended June 30, 20x1 and 20x0

	20x1			20x0		
	Final Budget ($)	Actual ($)	Variance Favorable (Unfavorable) ($)	Final Budget ($)	Actual ($)	Variance Favorable (Unfavorable) ($)
Emotionally Disturbed						
Salaries of Teachers	42,080	42,079	1	41,810	41,807	3
General Supplies	3,000	2,885	115	826	798	28
Total Emotionally Disturbed	45,080	44,964	116	42,636	42,605	31
Resource Room						
Salaries of Teachers	184,927	184,927		163,309	163,309	
Other Purchased Services	1,505	1,501	4	844	844	
Total Resource Room	186,432	186,428	4	164,153	164,153	
Preschool Handicapped						
Salaries of Teachers	40,897	40,897		38,422	38,422	
Other Purchased Services	819	818	1	200	200	
Total Preschool Handicapped	41,716	41,715	1	38,622	38,622	
Speech Instruction						
Salaries of Teachers	41,629	41,628	1	38,408	38,408	
Other Purchased Services	1,100	1,100		540	531	9
Total Speech Instruction						
Special Education	42,729	42,728	1	38,948	38,939	9
Home Instruction						
Salaries of Teachers	3,000	1,879	1,121	2,000	910	1,090
Total Home Instruction	3,000	1,879	1,121	2,000	910	1,090
Total Special Education	479,801	477,369	2,432	435,264	432,600	2,664
Basic Skills/Remedial						
Salaries of Teachers	24,000	24,000		19,932	19,241	691
Other Salaries for Instruction	45,000	45,000		45,000	45,000	
Other Purchased Services	3,896	2,340	1,556	3,896	1,692	2,204
General Supplies	16,959	16,831	128	6,200	5,701	499
Textbooks	2,207	2,207		500	418	82
Other Objects	1,984	1,966	18			
Total Basic Skills/Remedial	94,046	92,344	1,702	75,528	72,052	3,476

(continued)

General Fund: Statement of Revenues, Expenditures and Changes in Fund Balance— Budget and Actual for the Fiscal Years Ended June 30, 20x1 and 20x0

	20x1			20x0		
	Final Budget ($)	Actual ($)	Variance Favorable (Unfavorable) ($)	Final Budget ($)	Actual ($)	Variance Favorable (Unfavorable) ($)
Bilingual Education						
Purchased Professional/ Educational Services	7,000	5,687	1,313	9,325	9,325	
General Supplies	811	787	24	586	574	12
Total Bilingual Education	7,811	6,474	1,337	9,911	9,899	12
School Sponsored Cocurricular Activities						
Salaries	175,630	175,530	100	176,430	175,251	1,179
Supplies and Materials	45,776	44,391	1,385	46,050	43,868	2,182
Other Objects	13,072	8,995	4,077	10,870	9,779	1,091
Transfer to Cover Deficit	17,000	17,000		19,824	19,824	
Total School Sponsored Cocurricular Activities	251,478	245,916	5,562	253,174	248,722	4,452
Total Instruction	3,639,767	3,623,587	16,180	3,438,449	3,423,442	15,007
Undistributed Expenditures						
Instruction						
Tuition Private School						
Tuition Handicapped Within State	301,560	292,093	9,467	408,379	408,379	
Tuition State Facility				10,792	10,792	
Tuition Other	2,181	2,181				
Total Tuition	303,741	294,274	9,467	419,171	419,171	
Attendance and Social Work Services	14,196	14,196		13,543	13,543	
Health Services						
Salaries	98,796	97,998	798	94,259	93,498	761
Other Purchased Services	9,982	9,981	1	12,540	12,261	279
Supplies and Materials	4,485	2,938	1,547	4,380	3,811	569
Total Health Services	113,263	110,917	2,346	111,179	109,570	1,609
Other Support Services— Students Regular:						
Salaries of Other Professional Staff	100,797	100,705	92	97,798	96,784	1,014
Other Purchased Services	11,620	11,377	243	6,705	6,201	498

General Fund: Statement of Revenues, Expenditures and Changes in Fund Balance—Budget and Actual for the Fiscal Years Ended June 30, 20x1 and 20x0

	20x1			20x0		
	Final Budget ($)	Actual ($)	Variance Favorable (Unfavorable) ($)	Final Budget ($)	Actual ($)	Variance Favorable (Unfavorable) ($)
Total Other Support Services Students Regular	112,417	112,082	335	104,503	102,991	1,512
Other Support Services—Students Special Services						
Salaries of Other Professional Staff	147,739	147,739		109,045	108,973	72
Salaries of Secretarial and Clerical Assistants	106,301	106,301		98,063	97,946	117
Supplies and Materials	5,900	5,880	20	2,017	1,994	23
Other Objects	1,676	1,676		430	416	14
Total Other Support Services Students—Special Services	261,616	261,596	20	209,555	209,329	226
Improvement of Instruction Services/Other Support Services—Instructional						
Salaries of Supervisor of Instruction	156,466	156,466		148,561	148,556	5
Salaries of Other Professional Staff						
Total Improvement of Instruction Services/Other Support	156,466	156,466		148,561	148,556	5
Educational Media Services/School Library						
Salaries	101,728	98,703	3,025	97,103	97,103	
Supplies and Materials	35,887	30,988	4,899	19,313	18,110	1,203
Total Educational Media Services/School Library	137,615	129,691	7,924	116,416	115,213	1,203
Support Services—General Administration						
Salaries	306,364	305,457	907	301,063	300,167	896
Legal Services	5,000	325	4,675	109	109	
Other Purchased Professional Services	24,200	16,636	7,564	23,909	22,957	952

(continued)

General Fund: Statement of Revenues, Expenditures and Changes in Fund Balance—Budget and Actual for the Fiscal Years Ended June 30, 20x1 and 20x0

	20x1			20x0		
	Final Budget ($)	Actual ($)	Variance Favorable (Unfavorable) ($)	Final Budget ($)	Actual ($)	Variance Favorable (Unfavorable) ($)
Communications/Telephone	25,500	24,902	598	26,000	23,794	2,206
Supplies and Materials	16,916	16,915	1	15,000	14,218	782
Miscellaneous Expenditures	52,986	52,741	245	46,300	42,789	3,511
Total Support Services—General Administration	430,966	416,976	11,990	412,381	404,034	8,347
Support Services—School Administration						
Salaries of Principals/Assistant Principals	209,277	209,277		180,761	179,721	1,040
Salaries Secretarial and Clerical Assistants	105,946	105,945	1	97,834	96,203	1,631
Supplies and Materials	68,089	65,583	2,506	38,499	37,939	560
Other Objects	22,004	20,725	1,279	13,386	11,120	2,266
Total Support Services—School Administration	405,316	401,530	3,786	330,480	324,983	5,497
Operation and Maintenance of Plant Services						
Salaries	322,992	309,581	13,411	329,421	329,381	40
Cleaning, Repair and Maintenance Services	215,819	168,019	47,800	216,380	176,936	39,444
Other Purchased Property Services	1,500	1,080	420	1,170	1,080	90
Insurance	45,702	42,008	3,694	74,998	74,998	
General Supplies	107,461	99,608	7,853	82,635	77,027	5,608
Energy (Heat and Electricity)	171,400	170,442	958	170,502	168,522	1,980
Other Objects	10,179	10,160	19	11,145	8,159	2,986
Total Operations and Maintenance of Plant Services	875,053	800,898	74,155	886,251	836,103	50,148
Student Transportation Services Contracted Services (Between Home and School) Vendors	78,191	77,367	824	115,323	111,409	3,914
Contracted Services (Other than						

General Fund: Statement of Revenues, Expenditures and Changes in Fund Balance—
Budget and Actual for the Fiscal Years Ended June 30, 20x1 and 20x0

	20x1			20x0		
	Final Budget ($)	Actual ($)	Variance Favorable (Unfavorable) ($)	Final Budget ($)	Actual ($)	Variance Favorable (Unfavorable) ($)
Home and School) Vendors	66,515	65,718	797	52,408	52,408	
Supplies and Materials				651	651	
Total Student Transportation Services	144,706	143,085	1,621	168,382	164,468	3,914
Business and Other Support Services						
Social Security	99,531	93,781	5,750	90,131	90,131	
Other Retirement						
Contributions Regular	7,837	7,807	30	33,869	32,339	1,530
Other Employee Benefits	664,731	646,401	18,330	709,565	705,833	3,732
Purchased Professional Services	10,000	600	9,400	9,600	9,000	600
Total Business and Other Support Services	782,099	748,589	33,510	843,165	837,303	5,862
Food Service						
Transfer to Cover Deficit	7,699		7,699	10,000		10,000
Total Undistributed Expenditures	3,745,153	3,590,300	154,853	3,773,587	3,685,264	88,323
Total Expenditures—Current Expense	7,384,920	7,213,887	171,033	7,212,036	7,108,706	103,330
Capital Outlay						
Regular Program–Instruction Grades 9–12	2,760	2,760		51,950	51,039	911
Undistributed Expenditures						
Support Services—Instructional Staff	59,778	59,180	598	2,095	2,013	82
School Administration				6,425	5,850	575
Operation and Maintenance of Plant Services	75,523	77,412	(1,889)	52,828	52,628	200
Special Schools (All Programs)	3,000		3,000	25,722	100	25,622
Total Capital Outlay Expenditures	141,061	139,352	1,709	139,020	111,630	27,390

(continued)

General Fund: Statement of Revenues, Expenditures and Changes in Fund Balance—
Budget and Actual for the Fiscal Years Ended June 30, 20x1 and 20x0

	20x1			20x0		
	Final Budget ($)	Actual ($)	Variance Favorable (Unfavorable) ($)	Final Budget ($)	Actual ($)	Variance Favorable (Unfavorable) ($)
Total Expenditures	7,525,981	7,353,239	172,742	7,351,056	7,220,336	130,720
Excess (Deficiency) of Revenue over (Under) Expenditures	(151,079)	113,306	264,385	(171,587)	(27,185)	144,402
Other Financing Sources (Users) Transfer to Capital Projects					(435)	(435)
Excess (Deficiency) of Revenues and Other Financing Sources (Users)	(151,079)	113,306	264,385	(171,587)	(27,620)	143,967
Fund Balance July 1st	355,788	355,788		383,408	383,408	
Fund Balance June 30th	204,709	469,094	264,385	211,821	355,788	143,967

Combined Statement of Revenues, Expenditures, and Changes in Fund Balance

Combined Statement of Revenues Expenditures, and Changes in Fund Balance— All Governmental Fund Types for the Fiscal Year Ended June 30, 20x1 (with Comparative Totals for June 30, 20x0)

	General ($)	Special Revenue Fund ($)	Capital Projects Fund ($)	Debt Service Fund ($)	Totals ($) (Memorandum Only) 20x1	20x0
Revenue						
Local Sources						
Local Tax Levy	5,737,570				6,044,728	5,688,571
Tuition	1,113,800				1,113,800	1,120,443
Miscellaneous	78,436				78,436	119,204
Total Revenue and Local Sources	6,929,806				7,236,964	6,928,218
State Sources	536,739	76,902			613,641	727,525
Federal Sources		113,615			113,615	123,836
Total Revenue	7,466,545	190,517	0	307,158	7,964,220	7,779,579
Expenditures						
Current Expense						
Instruction	3,623,587	174,759			3,798,346	3,585,520
Undistributed Expenditures	3,590,300	15,758			3,606,058	3,758,706
Capital Outlay	139,352				139,352	144,630
Debt Service				307,405	307,405	316,735
Total Expenditures	7,353,239	190,517	0	307,405	7,851,161	7,805,591
Excess (Deficiency) of Revenue over (Under) Expenditures	113,306			(247)	113,059	(26,012)
Other Financing Sources (Uses)						
Operating Transfers in						435
Operating Transfers out						(435)
Excess (Deficiency) of Revenue Other Financing Sources over (Under) Expenditures Financing Uses and Other	113,306			(247)	113,059	(26,012)
Fund Balance July 1st	355,788			1,173	356,961	382,973
Fund Balance June 30th	$469,094			926	470,020	356,961

Glossary

Accounting   a process that records, classifies, and summarizes business transactions and provides a history of the business activities of the school district.

Accounting Fund   an independent operating unit with an accounting and budgeting system and a set of financial reports.

Accrual Accounting   records revenue or income when earned and expenses or expenditures when services are received or goods are used.

Agency Fund   to account for the receipt of money or assets held for custodial purposes.

Appropriation   money authorized for specific expenditure by an elected body or the public.

Arbitrage   when the interest earned by a school district from the investment of borrowed money is greater than the interest being paid on the loan.

Assets   accounts that exhibit what a school district owns, is owed, and has retained for future economic benefit.

Bond   a certificate of debt issued by a school district in exchange for an agreed on sum of cash.

Bond Anticipatory Notes (BAN)   a short-term loan made by a school district to be paid from revenue received from a bond sale.

Bond Discount   the amount that a bond sells below the face value or asking price.

Bond Premium   the amount that a bond sells above the face value or asking price.

Bond Rating   an assessment of a borrower's potential to make payments on the debt incurred through a bond sale.

Bond Recall   when a school district redeems a bond issue prior to maturity at the face value or a predetermined amount, usually to reissue the bonds.

Book Entry Bond   when the name of the buyer of a bond is recorded in the books of the seller or seller's representative.

Budgeting   the allocation of scarce resources.

Capital Assets   buildings, land, and equipment whose purchase price or value exceeds a predetermined amount.

Capital Projects Fund   to account for revenues received for the acquisition or construction of major capital projects.

Cash Accounting   records revenue or income when cash is received and expenses or expenditures when cash is paid.

Charter School   a privately operated school that has been given permission to operate and receive public financial support by a governmental body.

Contra Accounts   accounts that reduce the balance of an asset account.

Costs   compilation of expenditures incurred in the delivery of a program, service, or activity.

Cost-Effectiveness   the cost incurred to generate program, service, and/or activity outcomes.

Cost-Efficiency   the cost incurred to generate program, service, and/or activity outputs.

Debt Service Fund   to account for the accumulation of receipts for the payment of general long-term debt and related interest incurred through the capital projects fund.

Depreciation   the allocation of the cost of a capital asset over the life of the asset.

Double Entry Accounting   a method of accounting that uses an algebraic formula to maintain the balances of all accounts.

Economics   a study of the use of scarce resources to satisfy unlimited wants for goods and services.

Effectiveness   characterized by qualitative outcomes.

Efficiency   characterized by quantitative outputs.

Elasticity   the proportional change in tax yield in relation to economic growth.

Encumbrance   a nominal account used to set aside money when a purchase order is processed or contract awarded.

Enterprise Fund   to account for income received from the sale of goods or services to the public.

Equalized Property Value   a calculation of comparable property wealth of school districts.

Excise Tax   a federal sales tax on goods, such as cigarettes.

Federal Reserve Board Discount Rate   the interest rate banks pay on loans from a Federal Reserve Bank.

Federal Reserve Board Reserve Requirement   the amount of money a bank must set aside in its vault or with a Federal Reserve Bank.

Fidelity Bond   an insurance policy for embezzlement on employees who handle money.

Fiduciary   a person or organization that holds money in trust for another person or organization.

Fiduciary Fund   to account for money received as a donation or to be held in trust.

Financial Accounting Standards Board (FASB) sets national accounting principles for entities other than state and local governments.

Fiscal Neutrality the proposal that the quality of a child's education should be based on the wealth of the state and not on the wealth of the child's school district.

Function Budget Numbers define the activity or purpose of program budget allocations.

Fund Balance/Fund Equity accounts that exhibit how much a school district would have if the assets were liquidated and used to pay the liabilities.

Fund Balance Surplus the balance when revenues exceed expenditures.

General Fund to account for all financial resources of the school district except those accounted for in another fund.

Generally Accepted Accounting Principles (GAAP) "uniform minimum standards of and guidelines to financial accounting and reporting" (GASB 2001, Cod. Sec. 1200.101).

Goals statements expressing visionary and idealistic ends to be attained.

Governmental Accounting Standards Board (GASB) sets national accounting principles for state and local governmental bodies.

Gross Domestic Product (GDP) a measure of the market value of all goods and services produced for consumption by workers and capital in the country regardless of ownership excluding income generated by U.S. citizens from foreign investments and possessions.

Gross National Product (GNP) a measure of the market value of goods and services produced by workers and capital in the country excluding domestic earnings by foreign investors and including income earned by U.S. citizens from foreign investments.

Gross State Product (GSP) a measure of the goods and services produced by workers and capital in a state regardless of ownership.

Horizontal Decentralization the "extent to which non-managers control decision processes" (Mintzberg, 1983, p. 99).

Human Capital Theory proposes a relationship between the investment of time and resources in education and production or individual earnings.

Income money received from the sale of goods and/or services.

Income Tax a tax based on earned and possibly unearned income received by a person, organization, or business.

Instructional Disengagement when a school district is extended beyond the point of efficacy; meaning it is unable to produce intended results.

Intermediate Government a county or regional governmental body as opposed to a local or state government.

Internal Rate of Return a human capital measure that compares lifetime earnings of individuals at various levels of education to the cost of providing the education up to and including that level.

Internal Service Fund   to account for income received from the sale of goods or services to a site-based unit in the school district or another government.

Investment Trust Fund   for investment pools used by the school district.

Lease-Purchase Agreement   an agreement whereby a school district makes payments on a capital asset (such as a building or major piece of equipment) over a period of time at the end of which they attain ownership of the asset.

Liabilities   accounts that represent what a school district owes.

Line-Item Budgeting   estimated expenditures listed by budget category.

Magnet School   a public school limited to the offering of a particular curriculum or program; such as science or art.

Marginal Propensity to Consume (MPC)   the proportion of extra income spent when additional money is placed in the economy.

Marginal Propensity to Save (MPS)   the proportion of extra income placed in savings when additional money is placed in the economy.

Mission Statement   the reason or purpose for a school district's existence.

Multiplier   an economic measure that represents the relationship between an increase in income and investment and spending.

Nominal Accounts   accounts that are closed to a zero balance at the end of the fiscal year.

Nonoperating Expenses   indirect expenses incurred to provide for the delivery of a program, service, activity, and/or goods or the production of goods to be sold.

Object Budget Numbers   classification of program and function budget allocations to specific expenditure accounts.

Objectives   statements that indicate what will be accomplished.

Open Market Operations   the purchasing and selling of securities, such as Treasury securities and bonds, in the marketplace.

Open Systems Theory   proposes that organizations interact with their environment and therefore shift their focus from structure to process.

Operating Expenses   expenses incurred to present a program, service, or activity; to offer goods for sale; or for the production of goods to be sold.

Outcomes   qualitative measures of accomplishments.

Outputs   quantitative measures of production.

Par Value   the principal amount of a bond that will be paid when it matures.

Payroll Fund   to account for money held for payroll checks and withholdings for taxes and benefit payments.

Pension Trust Fund   to account for money held in trust for pensions and other employee benefit plans.

Performance Budgeting presents a list or description of proposed accomplishments, preferably in measurable terms, with estimated expenditures listed by budget category.

Permanent Fund for donations from which only the earnings and not the principal can be spent for "purposes that support the [school district's] programs—that is for the benefit of the [school district] or its citizenry" (GASB 2001, Cod. Sec. 1300.108).

Planning, Programming Budgeting System (PPBS) presents program objectives, a plan, and a schedule for systematic reviews with estimated expenditures listed by budget category.

Present Value a calculation involving the effect of time on the value of money.

Private Purpose Trust Fund for expendable trust donations from which the principal and/or interest earned may be used to benefit the school district as well as schools, individuals, programs, and other organizations in the district.

Privatization occurs when a school district hires a vendor to manage a school district or a program, service, or activity within the district; such as food services or transportation.

Privilege Tax fees charged by a government for licenses, inspections, failure to obey the law, copies of records, plus many other services.

Program Budgeting presents program objectives with estimated expenditures listed by budget category.

Program Budget Numbers classify budget allocations for expenditure according to type of program, grade level, and student classification.

Progressive Tax represents a tax that collects more tax money from individuals as their income increases.

Proportional Tax represents a tax that collects the same percentage of taxes from people regardless of income and wealth.

Proprietary Funds a group of funds (enterprise and internal service funds) that account for income received from the sale of goods and services.

Purchase Order presents a proposed business transaction from the school district to a vendor.

Real Accounts accounts whose balances are carried over from one fiscal year to the next.

Registered Bond when the name of the buyer of a bond is printed in the records of the issuer.

Regressive Tax a tax levy that takes a decreasing amount of tax as a person's income or wealth increases.

Revenue money received directly or indirectly from a governmental tax levy.

Revenue Anticipatory Notes (RAN) a short-term loan made by a school district to be paid from a future revenue award.

Revenue Budget Numbers identify the source of money received by a school district.

Sales Tax a tax assessment based on the price of a good or service purchased.

Securities and Exchange Commission (SEC)   an independent federal agency established to oversee the accounting and financial reporting standards for all businesses, non-profit agencies, and governments.

Serial Bond   a bond issue in which the bonds mature over a period of years.

Single Entry Accounting   uses the cash method of accounting in which the records of receipts and expenditures are limited to the fiscal year in which the money was received and spent.

Special Revenue Fund   accounts for revenue legally restricted for specified purposes.

Strategic Budgeting   presents goals, objectives, and measurable outcomes and outputs with estimated expenditures listed by budget category.

Student Activity Fund   a special agency fund to account for resources owned, operated, and managed by the student body under the supervision of the school district.

Tax Anticipatory Notes (TAN)   a short-term loan made by a school district to be paid from revenue received from the collection of taxes.

Term Bond   a bond issue in which all of the bonds mature on the same date.

Unemployment Trust Fund   holds money in reserve for unemployment compensation claims.

Value-Added Benefit   when the cost of a purchase includes something extra at no additional charge to the customer.

Vertical Decentralization   the "dispersal of formal power" down the line of authority (Mintzberg, 1983, p. 99)

Voucher   form used to process a request when a hard copy of the request is needed.

Wealth Tax   a tax based on the value of property.

Yield to Maturity   the rate of return an investor realizes over the life of a bond.

Zero-Based Budgeting (ZBB)   budget requests that begin with a zero balance and all estimated expenditures must be accompanied with a proposal to justify the financial request.

REFERENCES

Governmental Accounting Standards Board (2001). *Codification of governmental accounting and financial reporting standards.* Norwalk, CT: Author.

Mintzberg, H. (1983). *Designing effective organizations: Structure in fives.* Upper Saddle River, NJ: Merrill/Prentice Hall.

Name Index

Subject Index